DON'T TELL THE PRESIDENT

ALSO BY JEAN BECKER

The Man I Knew
Character Matters

DON'T TELL THE PRESIDENT

THE BEST, WORST, AND MOSTLY UNTOLD
STORIES FROM PRESIDENTIAL ADVANCE

JEAN BECKER AND
TOM COLLAMORE

HARPER

An Imprint of HarperCollins*Publishers*

HarperCollins books may be purchased for educational, business, or sales promotional use. For information, please email the Special Markets Department at SPsales@harpercollins.com.

hc.com

FIRST EDITION

Designed by Michele Cameron

Library of Congress Cataloging-in-Publication Data has been applied for.

ISBN 978-0-06-344677-9

Printed in the United States of America

25 26 27 28 29 LBC 5 4 3 2 1

We dedicate this book to the advance professionals who work tirelessly behind the scenes not just on behalf of our presidents, but on behalf of all Americans.

You often are the ones who make good things happen.

From Jean:

To my sisters, Millie and JoAnn, and my brother, Eddie, and to all my wonderful friends (you know who you are).

I appreciate your putting up with me disappearing down my writing rabbit hole and being there for me when I peeked out.

From Tom:

To my wife, Jake, who makes me better in every way and is the center of our life filled with love, faith, and adventure.

To our children, Tommy, Pauline, Sallie, and Katherine, whose resilience, character, and sense of purpose inspire me.

And to my parents, Bacon and Betty Collamore—I think of them every day and am grateful beyond measure for all they did to show me the way.

CONTENTS

AUTHOR'S NOTE

It all appears so seamless.

From the minute Air Force One descends from the sky to touch down somewhere in America or across the ocean, to that moment when the President and First Lady—having just climbed the stairs of Air Force One—turn for one final wave goodbye, it's almost as if we have just watched a well-scripted documentary.

Everyone and everything were on time. Everyone stood and did what they were supposed to do. The airplane steps worked. The lights worked. The sound worked. The motorcade was in place. The press was in place. The band was in place.

Lights, camera, action.

This book is not about any of that.

Because the truth of what happens *behind* the scenes of presidential visits is so much more fun.

Sure, you are aware of a mishap or two. One moment that comes to mind is Queen Elizabeth's state visit in 1991. After the six-foot-two-inch President George H. W. Bush welcomed the Queen to the White House, an advance man forgot to pull out the step stool for the five-foot-three-inch queen to stand on while she gave her remarks. It became known as the "talking purple hat" speech, since all anyone could see was—well, her hat.

These mishaps make big news because they hardly ever happen. So what's the big deal?

What readers will find so surprising—and definitely entertaining—is how many times a presidential, or vice presidential, visit teeters on the precipice of chaos, and sometimes even disaster.

And then there are the stories that are humbling and even scary: a behind-the-scenes look at everything President George W. Bush dealt with on 9/11; the day Sara Jane Moore tried to assassinate President Gerald Ford; the secret meeting between Vice President George H. W. Bush and Polish resistance leader Lech Walesa.

We invited advance men and women for all the presidents going as far back as President Lyndon B. Johnson to share their stories of the last-minute problems they had to troubleshoot: the infighting behind the scenes; the miscommunication on the ground that once led to the motorcade going to the wrong place; and in the case of a former president, a secret burial in a backyard.

We also invited the Presidents' and First Ladies' former aides and White House staffers to share some never-before-heard stories about what sometimes happens—or doesn't happen—right before a president walks out onstage. Or sometimes what happens right in the Oval Office. Technically, they are not advance stories, but they provide some wonderful behind-the-scenes color.

We decided it would be best not to seek stories about either President Donald Trump or President Joe Biden. "Behind-the-scenes" stories are best told when the presidents' times on center stage have long come and gone.

The purpose of this book is not to tell tales out of school, but to give the reader a peek behind the curtain at the effort it takes to support our leaders so they can focus on governing and not, as they say, sweat the small stuff. And by doing so, you likely will have greater appreciation for those men and women who travel in advance of presidents, First Ladies, and vice presidents; who are out of sight but ever present; and whose main job is to actually sweat the small stuff.

Historian Theodore White quoted in one of his books a longtime senior Democratic operative who said: "One good advance man is worth two Secretaries of State."

President Ronald Reagan once said: "I think of my advance team like an American Express card: I'd never leave home without them."

We hope you will enjoy reading about their adventures—and yes, a misadventure now and then.

—Jean Becker and Tom Collamore

FOREWORD

A ndrew Card thought everything was in place. In the run-up to the 1980 presidential campaign, George H. W. Bush—former Texas congressman, UN ambassador, GOP chair, envoy to China, and CIA director—had asked Card, then a young Republican representative in the Massachusetts state legislature, to set up an afternoon fundraising tea in Springfield. Card made the half-hour drive to pick the candidate up in Hartford, Connecticut, and then the two of them arrived at the venue.

The sign in the living room read: WELCOME GEORGE BUSCH.

"Looks like I need to work on the name recognition thing," Bush said, plunging forward, grabbing every hand.

History teaches us that such are the perils of advance work: One tries to make everything perfect, but nothing ever truly is. And in that aspect, advance is rather like America itself: a thrilling but forever flawed undertaking.

Where did "advance work" begin? In the broadest sense, the first advance man in Western culture was probably John the Baptist—a fitting point of historical embarkation given that so many politicians think of themselves in messianic terms. But the more proximate point of origin for the term as we understand it lies not in the worlds of religion or of politics but in show business.

In the nineteenth century, an "advance agent" was a theatrical promoter, a vital player in the successful staging of live events. "The advance agent," P. T. Barnum was quoted as saying in 1894, "is the mainstay of all shows, whether they be circuses, dramas, operas, or lectures, and the office is an exclusively American one."

In the same year, *The Washington Post* published a piece headlined "HERALDS OF THE STAGE: The Modern Advance Man and His Usual Methods," writing: "Now *The Post* has always been friendly to the advance man. We love him for his genial smile, his pleasant assurance, and above all the breezy style with which he invades a newspaper office, appropriates a corner of our desk, and proceeds to boom his show in the busiest hour of the day."

By 1917, the term also applied to the evangelist Billy Sunday's team of ministers who would prepare the ground for his crusades by preaching in the weeks before Sunday himself arrived.

The political use of "advance man" seems a post–World War II phenomenon. On Monday, April 19, 1948, amid the Republican primary campaign for the nomination to challenge President Harry S. Truman, *The New York Times* gave its readers the inside dope: "Advance men for both Gov. Thomas E. Dewey of New York and Harold E. Stassen of Minnesota are already in Oregon, and the likelihood today is that the two candidates will be close behind them to get in early and hard licks for the Presidential primary on May 21."

Dewey would prevail, of course, but then go on to lose to Truman in the fall. It would take another four years, and Dwight D. Eisenhower, to break the twenty-year Democratic hold on the White House—and Eisenhower, as a military man, believed strongly in preparing the ground for attack.

The "I Like Ike" advance team was sophisticated in the context of the times. *The Washington Post* wrote that, with "vast quantities of confetti, barrels of Ike buttons and thousands of copies of a campaign song about Ike and also copies of 'Mamie—What a Wonderful Name for a First Lady of the Land,'" Eisenhower's World War II mess sergeant, Marty Snyder, traveled with an old Army jeep inside a truck "almost as large as a railroad boxcar." The confetti was perhaps the greatest draw. "It's like a wedding," Snyder said. "People like to throw rice at a wedding. It makes them think, 'I helped to marry 'em.' That's the way it is about throwing confetti. It makes people think they're having a real part in a presidential campaign." It worked: Eisenhower dominated the decade.

And then came John F. Kennedy. With the New Frontier's genius for communications, the Kennedy world brought us Jerry Bruno's *Advance Man*, a memoir (cowritten with the journalist Jeff Greenfield) that popularized the term in the political sphere.

"Advance men were the unsung heroes of the campaign," the Kennedy counsel and speechwriter Ted Sorensen recalled of 1960. "Arriving several days before the candidate, they worked with local party leaders to plan the schedule, determine the motorcade route, decide on platform sites and seating, turn out the crowds, work with the police and the local press, and distribute flags, press kits, and buttons."

Sorensen loved it when the advance team produced "'spontaneous' hand-lettered signs, usually hoisted by the children of local party workers and volunteers, which impressed the press with such messages as 'Baptists for Kennedy.'"

Then there were the inadvertently memorable ones: "Some, of course—such as 'Let's Put a New John in the White House'—actually were spontaneous."

That wouldn't have surprised Andy Card and the future forty-first president of the United States. You can't advance perfection. And that's what makes it all so much fun.

—Jon Meacham
Historian and Pulitzer Prize–winning author

PREFACE

How Our Stories Began

TOM COLLAMORE

While still in college in 1979 and 1980, I worked for the George Bush for President campaign in Connecticut, where I became a planner for Mr. Bush's many visits to the state. We had an early primary, and Connecticut was one of his several "home" states and therefore considered a must-win for Bush in his competitive race against Ronald Reagan. For a week ahead of the primary in March 1980, we planned an endless series of events, traveling the state as if running a race for governor. I drove the Winnebago we had rented for him to travel in, with the Secret Service riding shotgun—they had never driven one and wanted no part of it. The little secret I can tell now is I'd never driven one either, but I wasn't going to tell them that! Pulling the RV out on the highway for the first time, I can still hear the lead agent quietly say into his microphone for all the protective detail to hear: "So far, so good." Well, I navigated the Winnebago around the state for a week without incident and George Bush won the Connecticut primary, but he ultimately lost the nomination to Reagan.

Our little delegation, led by future Commerce Secretary Mac

Baldrige, was on the floor of the convention in Detroit when Reagan announced he was choosing Bush as his running mate.

Fast-forward to the spring of 1985 when I was asked to leave my job on Secretary Baldrige's small staff to join Vice President Bush's team at the White House. I held the post of staff secretary and later head of operations. That meant I coordinated Bush's in and out box, including working with the writers on final speech preparation, briefing documents for meetings and events, and binders for every trip that contained detailed schedules and background material. I traveled on most trips and worked closely with the advance staff, Secret Service, and other support folks to ensure Mr. Bush was well briefed and had everything he needed.

As things heated up in the race for the 1988 nomination, we were on the road six to seven days a week, and when my boss stayed in Washington, I was often the traveling chief of staff. Cell phones, texting, and email were nonexistent. Land lines and fax machines were our life-support system. If the Vice President made changes to a speech on the plane there wasn't always time to retype it (yes, that's right, type!). I remember one event in New Hampshire where the Vice President was speaking and I was behind a curtain dictating changes to the teleprompter operator, struggling to stay a few pages ahead of his delivery.

These situations were slightly stressful but not unusual. One thing always made the difference and was the key to success: the dedicated and hard-working advance staff who made sure every event went smoothly. Much like the duck on a pond who seems to be gliding effortlessly across the water, we hope this book will tell you about the often-frenetic struggle below the surface to stay afloat.

Here are just two of my examples:

On September 19, 1987, Vice President and Mrs. Bush flew to Detroit to bid farewell to Pope John Paul II as he ended his historic visit to the United States. The plan was for the Bushes to meet with His Holiness at the Detroit airport to thank him on behalf of President Reagan and the American people for coming to America, and then to participate in a farewell ceremony on the airport tarmac.

Pretty basic stuff.

Until it wasn't.

Air Force Two arrived early, and the Bushes had some scheduled down time in a nearby hotel before the Pope's arrival. When we arrived in the suite, the advance team, as was protocol, had the television turned to the local news, which was reporting live from the airport about the upcoming departure. The first thing the Bushes heard was a reporter talking about the controversy between the Vice President's and the Pope's advance teams regarding a disagreement over what backdrop to use for the departure ceremony. The reporter went on to say how the VP team had rejected the papal white and yellow backdrop and were insisting on using a presidential blue curtain instead. George and Barbara Bush turned in unison to me with looks that required no words. I simply said, "I'll take care of it," turned, and left.

Needless to say, a misunderstanding between the planning teams had escalated, putting the Bushes in an embarrassing light. Simply put: An advance man who will remain nameless had decided the Vice President trumped the Pope.

My job was to fix the problem quickly. Luckily, we had our seasoned and savvy deputy director of advance on the trip, my colleague Judd Swift. I huddled with Judd, explained the problem, and told him what had just been reported on television. We gathered our advance team and press staff, who then went and found their Vatican counterparts and worked to ensure ruffled feathers were calmed and that the Pope's backdrop was prominently positioned for the departure ceremony.

While no one on the advance team intended to insult anyone or create a news or diplomatic flap, lessons were clearly learned that day. A basic rule you learned right away when working with the

Bushes: "Don't be a big shot." Always polite and gracious, the Bushes had a remarkable radar for anyone crossing the line or overstepping. Throwing your weight around with the Vatican on their behalf was as bad as I'd seen, that's for sure. (Stay tuned for many more Vatican stories to come.)

Just a year later, at the conclusion of the 1988 Republican National Convention in New Orleans, the newly minted ticket of George Bush and Dan Quayle flew to Indiana for a series of rallies in Quayle's home state. This is a fairly traditional way to launch the fall general election campaign, and the two candidates would soon separate until Election Day, crisscrossing the country seeking support.

James A. Baker, III, chairman of the Bush-Quayle campaign, was on the trip to assess the traveling operation. At one stop a local politician was being pretty long-winded in his introduction of George Bush, and Mr. Baker was not pleased. John Keller was the director of advance and highly respected, but Mr. Baker wanted to set a tone for the advance team and used this as a teachable moment. A former marine, the future Secretary of State got in Keller's face and made it clear that his number one job was to protect George Bush from the kind of B***S*** that was happening on stage at that very moment.

I'm quite certain no introducer said anything more than "Ladies and Gentlemen, the next president of the United States" from that day forward! It was a short but most memorable moment.

JEAN BECKER

One night in January 1989 I went to bed as a political reporter for *USA Today* and the next morning I woke up as a deputy press secretary to the First Lady of the United States.

I had been a reporter my entire adult life. I knew how to be a reporter. I didn't know how to do anything else.

It didn't help that by taking this new job, I was both literally and figuratively "crossing the river."

When I told *USA Today* I was jumping ship, the paper's chief editor, Peter Prichard, screamed at me for an hour, high atop the paper's skyscraper headquarters on the Virginia side of the Potomac River. "If you cross that river, you'll never come back," he said, looking at me in disbelief and pointing across the Potomac to the nation's capital. "You are making a big mistake." (He was right and wrong: I never came back; it was not a mistake.)

Figuratively, I went from being a working member of the press to a job that included handling the press. I really had no idea how to handle people like me.

As it turns out, my new job was even more complicated than I realized. I thought I would mostly be taking questions from the press about the First Lady's schedule; confirming the names and ages of all the Bush grandkids; and giving out copies of her favorite chocolate chip cookie recipe.

As it turns out, the main part of my job was none of that. I was one of several people assigned to travel ahead of the First Lady and make the necessary arrangements for whatever she was going to do in whatever city she was going to visit. My specific job was to organize the press coverage, but under that responsibility came the broader and more nuanced assignment to make sure the trip went off without a hitch. In other words, don't give the press anything to write about except the message of the day.

In one fell swoop, I became an advance person. I had never heard the term.

My first trip was February 9, 1989, to New York City, to arrange for the new First Lady to visit the Bronx Educational Services to highlight their adult literacy education program, which in turn would give Barbara Bush a chance to remind the country that her passion was literacy.

After our first meeting with the host organization, I fled back to my hotel room to try to figure out what I should do next. What I really wanted to do was crawl under the bedcovers. Before long there came a soft knock on the door. There stood my Secret Service counterpart, Skip Lacy, who looked at me with both sympathy and concern: "You have no idea what you are doing, do you?"

And that's how my four years of doing advance for the First Lady of the United States began.

Thanks to the patience and advice of a host of experienced advance people, and always the Secret Service, I eventually figured it out.

It was always hard work. It often was complicated if not downright nerve-racking. But it also was always an adventure.

I did everything from drinking moonshine in Appalachia with the proud owner of an illegal still to working with the Vatican on Mrs. Bush's visit to the Sistine Chapel.

I once assured Princess Diana it was okay for her sons William and Harry to visit Air Force One. Even then, I knew it was a memorable moment.

Yet, it might have been the very next week when I had to explain to Barbara Bush how I managed to have all the cows standing with their backs to the TV cameras during her visit to the Florida State Fair. This was only a big deal because the cows kept raising their tails during her speech and . . . well, pooping. Enough said. The press was amused; the First Lady was not.

Oddly, when someone asks me to tell one of my favorite advance stories, the one that comes to mind is the time I was in Hawai'i advancing Mrs. Bush's upcoming trip. I felt quite smug with this assignment as I had never been to the great state of Hawai'i and suddenly, here I was in paradise.

It was a Sunday afternoon in 1990 and I needed to report back to Mrs. Bush's chief of staff, Susan Porter Rose, as soon as my meetings concluded. I got on the road from the meeting site, but because of the six-hour time difference between the islands and Washington, DC, I quickly realized I did not have time to get back to my hotel to make the call. So I stopped at a gas station with a phone booth.

We had just started our conversation when a motorcycle gang roared into the parking lot, racing their motors just outside my phone booth. I finally asked Susan to hold for just a minute while I went outside and very politely told the boys that I was on an important work call and could they go rev their motors on the other side of the street?

Off they went, so I went back to my call with my boss. But a few minutes later I became aware of a strange sound, a strange smell, and a strange . . . well, feeling. I turned around and discovered several of the gang members peeing into the phone booth and, yes, onto me.

Ah, yes, the glamour of doing advance work for the President and First Lady of the United States.

Let the stories begin.

CHAPTER ONE

WHEN AIR FORCE ONE COMES TO YOUR HOMETOWN

*A*s you have already seen from our random tales from the road, there are big stories and small ones to be told about the life of an advance person. Often when their day begins, they have no idea how it will end and where their story will belong in history.

And yes, more than once, their day ended in a bar, telling a captive audience: You won't believe what I pulled off today.

We will start with some stories from the early days of advance.

LARRY TEMPLE,
close friend of President Johnson:

I can't tell you when or where it happened or who the advance man was, but this story became legend in LBJ world.

As part of a long trip the President was taking, there was a planned stop at a military base for Air Force One to refuel, during which LBJ would review the troops. The advance man suggested to the base commander that as part of the welcoming ceremony, there should be a flyover—a group of jets flying in formation to salute the President. The commander was reluctant.

When the advance man met with the commander a second time, he had a bell in his pocket—one that might be found on a bicycle, and he had a telephone receiver, which was attached to nothing, in his briefcase. Keep in mind that this was years before there was such a thing as a cell phone. At some point in his conversation with the commander, the advance man reached in his pocket and rang the bell. Then he reacted as if the ring was on the telephone receiver in his briefcase. He opened the briefcase and put the receiver to his ear and said "Hello," followed by, "Yes, I can wait." He told the commander that the White House was calling. After a little wait, the conversation went something like this:

"Yes, sir, Mr. President. I am here at (whatever camp) and Commander (whatever his name was) is being very helpful and is looking forward to hosting you." Pause.

"Yes, sir, I told him that you are looking forward to reviewing his troops, and plans are in place for a good ceremony. We have discussed the possibility of having a flyover while you are here." Pause.

"Yes, sir, I thought that would be your view, and I will tell the commander you would love to have a flyover, and I know he will be prepared to recognize your visit with a great reception." Pause.

"Yes, sir, everything will be ready here when you arrive."

Then the advance man put the phone back in his briefcase as if ending the conversation.

When the President arrived and reviewed the troops, there was a flyover of multiple jets in formation to salute the President.

The term "advance man" might have been popularized during President Kennedy's 1960 presidential campaign, but it was President Richard Nixon who made it official. He asked his friend and staffer, Ron Walker, to establish a White House Office of Advance. This essay was written by

Ron's wife, Anne, herself an advance person (and the writer of the two), who sadly passed away in January 2025.

ANNE WALKER:

Ron was a volunteer advance man during the 1968 presidential campaign and then wound up on the payroll of the Department of Commerce after the election.

But his job was not *in* the Department of Commerce; he was an advance man for the President of the United States. That's how it was done in those days. The function of making travel arrangements for the President was hidden away in the bowels of government departments.

President Nixon and Ron Walker would come to legitimize the function of making advance decisions for presidential travel and make it an integral part of the White House. The President felt that the role of the advance man was critical to the day-to-day operation of the White House. It was time to establish the first White House advance office, and Ron was asked to be the first director.

One of the first things he needed to do was start training new people, so he spent five months writing a 397-page advance manual that laid out every job and scenario of how advance teams would prepare for a presidential trip. It's still being used today.

In fact, the manual became quite famous and was often talked about. Once, when Ron was introduced to James Carville, one of President Bill Clinton's top advisors, Carville said, "Ron Walker! I know you. We stole your effing campaign manual,[1] and we did it better than you!" This, of course, was a reference to then Governor Clinton beating President George H. W. Bush in the campaign of 1992.

---

1 *Effing* was not the word Carville used.

Soon after Ron started training the first group of advance people, he came upon a great opportunity for teaching a lesson in advance.

President Nixon declared that July 4, 1970, would be "Honor America Day." He wanted it to be the biggest happening ever on the Fourth of July in Washington, DC.

Ron put every one of the guys on it and turned them loose. They jumped into crowd-raising, handbills, leaflets, and telephone boiler-room operations. They had more than four hundred thousand people turn out on the National Mall.

Everybody took notice and everybody gave the advance men the credit. The Nixon advance office was off and running.

In 1982, at a ten-year reunion of the 1972 election, President Nixon told the story of his first advance man, Ace Anderson. Ace had a convertible and drove the young Richard Nixon to campaign rallies around Orange County, California, during his 1950 Senate campaign. Ace had a wind-up victrola and a loudspeaker in his convertible. He would crank up the sound to attract the crowds, but the only record that Ace owned was, "If I knew you were coming, I'd have baked a cake." President Nixon laughed as he told the story, and at the fact that somehow it all worked.

JIM DAHLEM,
advancing President Reagan:

I had the great fortune of working at the presidential advance office as an intern. This was the final year in President Reagan's second term, and he was helping Vice President Bush win his election to become the next president. Consequently, the more seasoned members of the advance office were deployed around the country for the campaign. So we interns were used for events in and around Washington, DC.

I was sent to assist with an event at a local high school. When I arrived, the secure area had been swept by the dogs and was locked down so that only White House staff and the Secret Service were allowed in this part of the building. We did a walk around to make sure everything was in place, and then we had a meeting with the Secret Service to share any last-minute information.

The Secret Service told us that the photography teacher at the school absolutely loathed the President. He actually required every student who entered his classroom to step on a picture of President Reagan on the floor as they came through the door. This was rather disconcerting since this man was attending the event to take pictures for the school.

It was decided that I would be his escort throughout the event.

He was not particularly talkative or friendly. As usual, the press pool was just off of the stage so they could get the best angles for still photos and video of the President during his speech.[2] The photographer and I had the understanding he would be part of the press pool, and as President Reagan was being introduced, we made our move to get there.

When we arrived at the pool site, the nearest Secret Service agent pointed at the photographer and told him he did not have the proper credentials to be in the pool and instructed him to leave immediately. It was at that point I realized what was going on. I wasn't an "escort"; I was the "mark" for the Secret Service, and the agents must have

---

2 The White House press pool was created during President Eisenhower's term to solve a practical problem: When there is not enough room for the hundreds of media representatives who cover the president, who gets in and who doesn't? The answer was the creation of a small group of journalists who would be the eyes and ears of their colleagues and who would share their photos, footage, and notes. The composition of the pool occasionally changes but typically includes three wire service reporters, two print or online reporters, a radio reporter, four photographers, and a television crew.

been instructed when they saw me to keep us away from the stage and probably keep a close eye on wherever I was located.

The photographer vehemently protested, but I prevailed on him that we had no choice but to leave the pool. We proceeded to the back of the room where his camera equipment bag was located and where the rest of the press was covering the event. He was really angry, but I didn't care. I thought it was a brilliant plan, and I was more than happy to bear the brunt of the anger of this guy!

KIM FULLER,
advancing President Bush 41:[3]

With less than a year under my belt as an advance representative for the administration, my advance team created a firestorm with the locals in Mashpee, Massachusetts.

In our defense: Many assumptions are made by local host committees about what they control and what they don't. As a result, they often jump the gun and make commitments the White House advance team has to undo when they arrive. This time that included delivering the news that the school band would *not* be playing the national anthem or "Hail to the Chief" for the President's visit to Kenneth C. Coombs Middle School.

I didn't think much about it at the time because the Department of Defense (DOD) directive gives guidance on the use of ruffles and flourishes as well as "Hail to the Chief." For the year I had been

---

3 For the sake of expediency, we sometimes will use 41 to refer to President George H. W. Bush and 43 to refer to President George W. Bush. It was complicated after George W. Bush became president to know to whom a speaker was referring when they said "President Bush." The solution: George H. W. Bush was the forty-first president of the United States; President George W. Bush was the forty-third president. Thus, they often were called 41 and 43, and 41 loved the nickname.

doing presidential advance, I knew that the US Marine Corps band, or a college, high school, or similar band, would play the two musical selections that often accompanied a president's visit. If those options weren't available, then the White House Communications Agency (WHCA) would provide an audio version to be used while the president was introduced.[4]

I guess DOD did not think elementary or middle school bands were up to the task as they were not in the "guidance" provided to advance teams.

Everyone in this close-knit Cape Cod town quickly learned that, because there is a presidential "standard," the Mashpee middle school band would not be playing for the President's visit.

So while we were trying to build an enthusiastic crowd there was a growing crisis with local Mashpee band parents. They and the political apparatus of Massachusetts got to work to make sure everyone knew that the White House advance team said their children's band was not up to par to play for the President. They got on the airwaves of every possible television station in Providence, Rhode Island, and Boston and complained big-time. (Keep in mind this was before social media, thank heavens.)

And they made sure that word got to the two Massachusetts natives on the President's senior staff: Deputy White House Chief of Staff Andy Card and Deputy Assistant to the President for Political Affairs, Ron Kaufman.

Fast-forward to the President's visit on November 1, 1990.

Did the middle school band play?

Of course.

For five days the band members ferociously rehearsed the ten bars

---

4 White House Communications Agency staffers are part of the advance team setting up the equipment necessary to make sure the president is in full communication with the world when he travels, even if it's just across town. You will see the acronym WHCA often in this book.

of ruffles and flourishes and the twelve bars of "Hail to the Chief" with WHCA and our staff to perfect what is considered the personal anthem of the President of the United States.

When the President got up on stage, his first words were, "Music to my ears," and he thanked the band.

All's well that ends well.

TOPPER RAY,
advancing President Bush 41:

On September 2, 1992, the President headed to Carswell Air Force Base in Fort Worth, Texas, to showcase the new F-16 fighter jets built by General Dynamics and to announce the sale of 150 jets to Taiwan, which would help safeguard one of our allies while also preserving thousands of jobs.

Two gleaming F-16s served as a stunning backdrop for the arrival of Air Force One. The weather was perfect, and the site was ready with hundreds of General Dynamics employees there to cheer the arrival of President Bush.

As the lead press advance man, my duties that day were clear: Make sure the traveling press got off the press plane and onto the press platform to get the shot of the day—the President with the F-16s. This image would be critical to help illustrate the significance of the $6 billion deal being announced along with 41's commitment to a strong national defense. For President Bush, who was one of the most notable aviators in our nation's history, the event would also help underscore the importance of the $6 billion deal for the campaign. (The event was held on the forty-eighth anniversary of President Bush being shot down while on a bombing run during World War II.)

Did I forget to mention that this event was one of the kickoff events of the fall election campaign season against Bill Clinton? No pressure.

As the press plane began its final approach—as usual, landing ahead of Air Force One—my radio crackled to life, and I began directing the motorcade out onto the tarmac. As the plane landed and began taxiing, I coolly waved to a couple of my good friends from the White House press office who were on board with the traveling media.

Maybe too coolly.

For some reason I decided that I would also help direct the press plane into position on the tarmac, which was 100 percent not my job. Raising my right hand into the air, I gestured decisively toward the cockpit that it was time to turn the plane to the right. With equal decisiveness, the pilot of the plane ignored me and turned the plane to the left.

I was immediately caught in the blast of the jet wash from the engines and blown twenty yards down the tarmac. I did a couple of cartwheels before luckily snagging myself in the stairs to the press plane that was standing by to be moved into position.

I can vividly recall the sound and force of the jet wash, clanging into the stairs, the tear of my suit pants, and holding on for dear life. The whole episode lasted a matter of seconds. Once it was clear that I was generally okay, my first thought was: "Please let no one have seen that!" My friends aboard the press plane, with a clear view of the entire scene, quickly shot down that notion. They were laughing so hard they were crying.

It's possibly the most famous teleprompter mistake in presidential history: the night President Clinton addressed a joint session of Congress with the wrong speech on the teleprompter. How did that happen, you might ask? Well, now you will know.

ANDREW FRIENDLY,
aide to President Clinton:

It was considered the most important speech of his still young presidency: In September 1993, President Clinton was to address Congress, presenting his proposal to reform the health care system.

He had addressed a joint session of Congress earlier that year and had used a teleprompter for that speech. But he very rarely used teleprompters, preferring to speak from notes on index cards.

The WHCA teleprompter operator that night had not worked with President Clinton. So he was green, and so were we.

Before I go much further, it's important to know President Clinton's process. For most of his speeches, the speechwriters would send a draft to the President. He would review it, mark it up, and then usually take the main points and write notes on index cards that he would use for the actual speech. It was very rare for President Clinton to read directly from a prepared speech. He also liked to make edits right up to walking to the podium.

It made the staff's life more challenging, but the President was a real pro—even if he often spoke too long.

In true form, President Clinton was editing his speech with his top advisors in the Oval Office, even as we prepared to leave in the motorcade. At the same time, we tried to update the digital version of the speech with all his edits on a computer down the hall. Then, during the limo ride to the Capitol with Mrs. Clinton, presidential advisor George Stephanopoulos was enlisted as a note taker to continue the editing process.

When we arrived at the Capitol, George and I sprinted to deliver the disk to the teleprompter operator, who was set up in the Speaker's Lobby behind the floor of the House of Representatives, to upload all the last-minute edits. We nailed it with only minutes to spare. Or so we thought.

I took the paper copy with the President's most recent edits and put it on the podium, but we didn't have enough time to give copies to the Vice President or the Speaker of the House, as is customary.

As President Clinton arrived at the podium, he looked at the teleprompter screen, turned to Vice President Al Gore, and mouthed: "Al, it's the wrong speech on the teleprompter." He could tell because the title was from his February address to the Joint Session of Congress.

The teleprompter operator had used this old script as a test to ensure the system worked. Although we had loaded the new speech from the disk I had delivered, in the final frantic minutes as the President walked into the House chamber, the operator mistakenly had switched the screen back to the old speech.

Vice President Gore came down from the podium to George and me and said, "Guys, it's the wrong speech in the teleprompter." Dumbfounded, we ran backstage to the WHCA teleprompter operator.

As we were trying to determine what happened and load the right speech, President Clinton dove right in and started to deliver his remarks—mostly from memory.

It took us six or seven minutes to load the speech and a few more to catch up with where he was in his delivery. As we were fiddling with the teleprompter, President Clinton was looking at the screen with words flying across it. Can you imagine how distracting that would be?

Once we were back on track, about ten minutes had passed. But the President had spoken as if the speech had been in front of him the whole time. The speech was very well received, and nobody in the audience—those in the chamber and those watching on TV—knew what had happened.

Although George and I probably aged twenty years that day, we were incredibly fortunate that President Clinton could, and still can, ad lib.

As for the President: He was worried that the WHCA technician probably thought he was about to be fired, so he called him to personally thank him for his calm under fire.

RANDY BUMGARDNER,
State Department protocol officer, accompanying President Clinton:

In December 1994, President Clinton hosted in Miami the first Summit of the Americas. The main social event was a dinner that President and Mrs. Clinton hosted on Fisher Island for thirty-three presidents and prime ministers and their spouses. The guests were transported to dinner on board the 200-foot yacht *The Virginian*.

I was on a second yacht, accompanying the foreign chiefs of protocol and staff members of the foreign leaders. We could clearly see the leaders engaged in lively conversation on the yacht directly in front of us. When that yacht didn't depart on time, several protocol chiefs came to me asking if there was a problem. I had just learned that the yacht was stuck on a sand bar. (The captain hadn't calculated the effects of low tide.)

My reply: "Isn't it wonderful to see them enjoying the evening? Would you care for a drink?" They took drinks from a passing waiter and that was that. No one noticed the two tugboats approaching the yacht, attaching ropes, and gently pulling the yacht off the sand bar. The magical evening continued as planned.

BRIAN JONES,
advancing President Bush 43:

Advancing off-the-record (OTR) events was always a lot of fun. The work was spontaneous and easy because it didn't require a lot of, well, advance.

Early on October 20, 2006, I was told that the President wanted to stop by a CVS store near the White House to give some off-the-cuff remarks about prescription drugs and Medicare. I was ordered to head over ASAP as the President would arrive in two hours.

I walked into the CVS closest to the White House, and my first challenge was identifying an appropriate spot for the President to speak, one large enough for the press pool to capture the moment. OTRs don't allow the time to build out a stage or a backdrop, so you have to do your best with what is already there to convey the appropriate messaging. Once I homed in on a speech site, I then found the store manager and explained what was coming his way. After a long string of incredulous stares, he basically just told me to "do whatever you need to do."

So I did. I worked my way through the aisles as quickly as possible. The store was a bit of a mess, and that meant there was lots of organization to be done. Snacks, magazines, and boxes of cold medicine were repositioned. Brown inventory boxes were removed. Trash cans were emptied (that was fun). I worked my way through the aisles quickly and with a singular purpose—to make it all look nice. The looks I received from the workers and patrons were beyond hilarious. They asked, "Why is this guy in a suit cleaning the store?" If they only knew.

My eyes caught the attention of a family standing a few feet away—a mom, dad, and two not-quite-teenage children. Dressed in T-shirts and shorts, they clearly were on some type of fall break vacation in our nation's capital. At this moment, however, they weren't basking in the majesty of the Lincoln Memorial or the US Capitol. They were standing in the middle of a CVS in downtown Washington, looking miserable, cranky, and just annoyed to be in each other's company.

Thinking back now, I realize how weird, even creepy, the experience of me approaching them must've been. But I did, interrupting their argument, and asked if they were on vacation, which the mother confirmed. I then said, "This is going to sound strange, and I can't give you any more details, but if you can hang out here in this CVS for a bit, I promise that this will be the highlight of your trip."

After a stunned silence that seemed to last an eternity, Mom was intrigued; Dad was not. But they stayed.

As I got word that the motorcade was approaching, I positioned the family near the spot where the President would greet CVS employees and then speak. As the entourage walked through the door, I turned to the mother and said, "Your patience and faith are about to be rewarded." The expression on their faces as the President walked in was priceless.

KIM PALMESE,
advancing President Bush 43:

How hard can it be? When I first started my life as an advance person, I was told when taking the lead on a presidential trip, the key points to remember are: Don't be in the camera shot; don't make the president look bad; don't babble when asked a question.

There are a lot of points I would add, but for the sake of this story, I'll just mention one: Always listen to the local folks.

In 2008 I was asked to do a trip to Memphis, Tennessee, for President George W. Bush. I was the site person for an outdoor fundraiser at a supporter's residence.

During our initial walk-through we decided on the tent's location and installation plan and looked at the weather for the upcoming event: No rain in the forecast. So no need to add, or pay for, gutters on the tent. I learned from one of the best advance men, Gordon James, that staying within budget was a good thing, and spending money "just because" was not.

The day the tent was being put up I once again looked at the weather and still no rain in the forecast. So "no gutters" was my final call. The tent team and several host committee members did not approve. They informed me that during the summer in the south, rain usually comes every day. This northerner was amazed by their rain stories; they swore rain came even when it wasn't predicted.

You know where this is going.

I was at the residence early that day to ensure things were ready for the President's arrival. It was a very hot, humid, and sunny afternoon—perfect conditions for a severe summer afternoon storm.

An hour before the President's arrival, the black clouds arrived and the clouds opened up with not only heavy rain but strong winds.

The main group of guests made it into the tent, and everyone was standing in the center to avoid the rain that was pouring down from all sides of the tent. The guests were also nervous about the large pools of water gathering on the roof of the tent.

The rain finally started to let up as the President arrived. He started in the house, doing pre-event photos with the larger donors. As people left the photo op and moved outside, I noticed there was no longer any room in the center of the tent. Something had to be done to allow guests to spread out. With the help of one of the WHCA staffers, we decided to get the water off the roof by using broom handles. This truly was not one of my smarter moves as the water that had accumulated now came pouring over the side, all of it on me.

As I stood there soaked through, I finally realized what gutters on the tent would have done—or prevented.

At that moment I was summoned to come inside the house and brief the President about the outside event. I looked like a drowned rat. Mascara was running down my cheeks, my hair was flat, and I squeaked when I walked.

Bottom line: Trust the locals. And if you put up a tent, pay for the gutters, no matter what the forecast is.

CHAPTER TWO

STORIES FROM THE CAMPAIGN TRAIL

*B*efore sharing more presidential advance stories, we thought it might make sense to talk about the "Road to the White House." The campaign trail is, after all, where most advance people learn the trade. And if they do their job, and their candidate wins, well, then you are off to the big show.

Among the surprises in this chapter—you just never know who among us got their start in life by being an advance man or woman. That would include former Ohio Senator Rob Portman and TV and radio personality Michael Smerconish.

But we'll start with Tyler Abell and his advance of Senator Lyndon B. Johnson in 1960.

TYLER ABELL:

A day or two after Labor Day 1960, then Senator Johnson flew to Boston to give a speech. This was his first trip since becoming Kennedy's running mate. He was a senator from Texas and the majority leader of the Senate, but he needed to convince Bostonians he belonged on the ticket.

I was a twenty-eight-year-old lawyer who had gone to law school on the GI Bill, graduating in 1959. I had a wife and two sons—the younger, born that year, was named Lyndon—and had never done advance before.

But James Rowe, a good friend and political advisor of Senator Johnson, seemed to think I would be good at it. He was smart to send seasoned advance man Vince Gaughan to help. (Almost every trip I ever did used two advance men. On one trip I took my wife, Bess, thus producing I think the first ever advance woman. She went on to become the Johnsons' White House social secretary.)

There was no Secret Service in those days for anyone but the president and his family, and as far as the Senate Majority Leader was concerned, we didn't even think about security in 1960.

First, there were some logistic issues to figure out. We needed to work with the airport authority on where to park the plane (a two-engine Convair), where the baggage could be unloaded onto a baggage truck, where a motorcade of cars borrowed from local dealerships could drive up, and where the Majority Leader of the House of Representatives, John McCormack, would greet the Majority Leader of the Senate.

Then came one of the more important jobs of an advance man: getting a big crowd. The appearance of a big crowd makes the candidate look better and feel better.

One of my most important jobs was to fill the venue. I arranged for fixed loudspeakers on the sidewalk so passersby would stop and listen or maybe even be drawn inside.

I ran an advertisement in *The Boston Globe,* which wanted $1,500 paid in advance. The Sheriff of Middlesex County, who was working with us, volunteered to pay it with his Diners Club card since none of us could come up with $1,500 in cash.

Jim Rowe had carefully explained that Senator Johnson was very particular about certain things. I needed to supply Cutty Sark Scotch and small bottles of Clicquot Club Soda, mix the drink very light with lots of club soda and then throw out any soda left in the bottle, and always open a fresh bottle with each drink. I set up a bar in LBJ's suite at the hotel, which was all put on the hotel bill. (I had no idea who would pay or when.)

I preregistered everyone on the passenger list and had schedules printed for the traveling party, which I handed out planeside along with luggage tags so the bellhops could put the luggage in the right room.

At the airport Bill Moyers ran up to tell me that the Senator's luggage had to go in his car.[1] I tried to argue that my plan would put the luggage in the room before the Senator arrived. "No," said Bill, "the Senator's luggage must be with him."

As the motorcade made its way slowly through the streets of Boston, people came running out of buildings to wave, and LBJ got out of his car waving back, shaking hands, and handing out passes to the Senate visitors' gallery. Johnson must have had hundreds of these signed cards in his pocket.

At the hotel I was helping bellhops find bags and hand out guest keys when Moyers arrived, again wanting to know what had happened to LBJ's luggage. I went to the Sheriff's car, where LBJ had ridden, to find it locked in front of the hotel with no driver and no keys. Thankfully, the Sheriff's driver was found in the hotel bar. I got the keys, opened the trunk, and carried the luggage to LBJ's room.

The rest of the trip went without incident. The auditorium was

---

1   Bill was then a top aide to LBJ. He was press secretary to President Johnson from 1965 to 1967. He went on to become a renowned journalist and died in June 2025.

full. There were listeners outside on the sidewalk to hear the first of many speeches given by the Democratic vice-presidential nominee.

"It's a long way from Austin to Boston" were his opening words, which preceded commentary about how Senator Kennedy and Senator Johnson had worked together in the Senate. The speech was credited as one of many things that helped the Kennedy-Johnson ticket win in 1960.

SENATOR ROB PORTMAN,
advancing Vice President Rockefeller:

In the fall of 1976, while my college peers were busy attending lectures and worrying about midterms, I found myself immersed in an entirely different kind of education—one that would help shape the course of my career.

I had taken a semester off to work on the reelection campaign of my local congressman in Cincinnati, Bill Gradison.

Back then, Ohio was the quintessential swing state, and presidential candidates and their surrogates came regularly for events. So it was not surprising that one afternoon the phone rang at campaign headquarters regarding a presidential campaign visit. The voice on the other end belonged to Ernie Minor, a seasoned political operative who had served in the Nixon administration.

I was surprised when Ernie asked me—a college kid working on a local grassroots campaign—if I would be interested in being a member of the advance team for an upcoming visit by Vice President Nelson Rockefeller. Although Rockefeller had been replaced by Senator Bob Dole at the Republican Convention earlier that summer, he continued to campaign vigorously for the Ford-Dole ticket.

Ernie also asked my buddy and high school classmate, Joe Hagin, to help out. Joe had taken time off from college to work on Senator Bob Taft's campaign for reelection. Ernie said something like, "You have to be sharp, know how to think on your feet, and be ready for anything. Are you up for it?"

Without hesitation, I said yes.

It was decided that the event I was organizing would be in a ballroom in the Cincinnati Club, located on a wide boulevard downtown with plenty of room for people to gather outside. I worked hard on trying to get everything right. And everything was all set until a couple of days before the event when Nelson Rockefeller famously responded to a group of antiabortion protesters in Binghamton, New York, by giving them the middle finger.

The photograph of his finger raised and a defiant smile on his face must've been on every front page in America and around the world. This was before the internet or twenty-four-hour cable news, but, trust me, word got around that the Vice President of the United States had flipped the bird to the Right to Life movement.

And his next stop wasn't just any American city—he was coming to Cincinnati, the birthplace of the Right to Life movement and the home of its founder and president, Dr. John Willke.

Suddenly, what was going to be a routine stop had the potential to turn into a massive protest on a hot-button issue.

At twenty years old, with no experience in advance work, I was already in over my head. Now I was imagining the happy warrior, Nelson Rockefeller, giving the finger again to what was sure to be a huge crowd of already angry antiabortion protesters, causing a minor riot on the streets of Cincinnati. At my event!

Honestly, I can't remember all of what happened next because it was mostly a blur. I remember working with local law enforcement and the Cincinnati Club to find additional stanchions and ropes and other temporary fencing to try to keep the crowd from blocking the Vice President from entering the club upon his arrival. In retrospect, I don't know why we didn't bring him in a back entrance, but knowing Vice President Rockefeller, it was probably because he insisted on not sneaking in.

Apparently, the White House and the Ford presidential campaign had made it clear that there would be no more obscene gestures toward unfriendly crowds by the Vice President, so that wasn't an issue. We tightened security and ticketing for the speech to reduce the possibility he would be interrupted, and we called on more volunteers to help coordinate the event.

There was a large crowd on hand to protest the Vice President, but my recollection is that the demonstration was peaceful and Rockefeller restrained himself. It all went okay although I am sure the White House and the Ford campaign weren't happy with the coverage of the demonstrations.

That first experience in advance taught me more than any college semester ever could. It was about more than just logistics. It was about adaptability, expecting the unexpected, working with people and often having to persuade them, anticipating problems before they arose, attention to detail, and creative problem-solving.

Thanks to that call from Ernie Minor, my short but enjoyable adventures in advance had begun—with a bang.

MICHAEL SMERCONISH,
advancing Vice President Bush:

Before I became "that guy on the radio and TV," I was a very proud advance man for Vice President George H. W. Bush. And to think, it was all because of a college kegger that was a bust.

I caught the political bug in 1980, my senior year in high school, when my father ran for the Pennsylvania State Legislature. Although he lost the Republican primary, the experience was life-changing for me. I accompanied him to every campaign event and have vivid memories of standing for hours outside an Acme supermarket handing out rulers with our family name on them.

At the end of August, I packed my bags and headed for Lehigh University in Bethlehem, excited not only about college but also the upcoming 1980 general election. By that time, the Republican ticket was Ronald Reagan and George Bush.

Soon after my arrival, I realized not many students shared my enthusiasm, so I formed a club that I called "Lehigh University Youth for Reagan-Bush." It was tough sledding getting anyone interested. Then came my epiphany moment. Lehigh then had a strong Greek culture and active social life. So I decided that, as a means of recruitment, I would throw a keg party for all supporters on campus for Ronald Reagan and George Bush. Yeah, that'll be the ticket! Little did I know that the night I selected for the affair would coincide with a World Series game between the Philadelphia Phillies and Kansas City Royals. Consequently, nobody, and I mean nobody, came to the kegger.

But my luck was about to change.

I was then living with 150 other freshman guys in a dorm known as Taylor. It was a great place to live but it was a dump. (It has since been renovated and is now a showpiece.) Of course, this was before cell phones and no one had a computer. There was one telephone for an entire hall, and the guys were brutal in taking messages.

That's why it had to be divine intervention that I received Dan Sullivan's call.

About two weeks before the general election, someone yelled down the hall and told me I had a call on the hall phone. When I picked it up, the voice at the other end said, "Is this Michael Smerkonavitch?" badly mispronouncing my name, which I was used to. When I said yes, he asked, "Are you the one who has a club called Lehigh University Youth for Reagan-Bush?" I thought of the keg party disaster and figured I was getting pranked. But then he introduced himself as Dan Sullivan, the head of advance for Ambassador Bush, which was how George H. W. Bush was referred to then. He explained that advance work was the term given to planning the logistics of a visit by a major candidate and that George Bush was coming to Bethlehem to tour the Bethlehem Steel plant during an early morning shift change. More importantly, he said that he desperately needed student volunteers to pull off the visit. Specifically, he needed motorcade drivers, press escorts, luggage handlers, and lots more. He needed my club! If only he knew.

I hung up the telephone and ran down the hall recruiting my hall mates—Republicans, Democrats, Communists, and Independents—with the promise that they could shake the hand of the future Vice President of the United States.

The visit was an unbelievable experience. I missed a few days of class working with Sullivan and the rest of the advance staff. They were staying at the Sheraton hotel in nearby Allentown where Bush would spend a night. When the future Vice President and President arrived, I was able to accompany him during part of his visit when he greeted steel workers. It was quite a high. The only downside was that the elevators at the Sheraton gave out and we had to carry his luggage up the eight flights of stairs. When the visit ended, we all lined up on the tarmac next to the airplane and shook hands with Ambassador Bush. Sullivan thanked me for my efforts, gave me a black-and-white photograph that the future Veep signed for me, and he was off to another city. I went back to class.

Two years later, I was in Washington, DC, to begin the "Washington Semester" at American University, a wonderful program that was one part classroom instruction and one part internship. Mine was to be spent with my congressman, James Coyne. Within days of my arrival, I walked over to the Capitol Hill Club just to look at the facade. I was curious to see this place where Republican fat cats would dine and plot strategy. As I approached the doorway, a few men were exiting. I looked at one and he at me. There was an air of recognition, at least on my part. I'm sure I remembered Dan Sullivan far better than he recalled me. He was now the head of advance for Vice President George Bush, responsible for planning the logistics of all travel that the Vice President would undertake. Little did I know it, but George Bush was on his way to becoming the most traveled vice president ever.

Sullivan handed me his business card and said, "You should do advance for us."

"But I am still in college, and here to intern," I responded. "Call me," he said, and he was off. Well, I not only traded up internships (Congressman Coyne was terrific about that) but also began doing advance work for Vice President George Bush.

DAVID BATES,
personal aide to George H. W. Bush:

I had the privilege of serving as George H. W. Bush's personal aide during the 1980 Bush for President and Reagan-Bush campaigns. By virtue of winning the second-most delegates and a number of primaries and caucuses, he was a scheduled speaker on the next-to-last night of the 1980 Republican National Convention in Detroit. After his speech, Governor Reagan surprised everyone and called to ask Ambassador Bush to be the vice-presidential nominee.[2]

The following night, after Reagan was declared the presidential nominee, he appeared at the podium to deliver his acceptance speech. A couple of minutes after his speech ended and he was acknowledging

---

2 In 1980, we referred to Reagan as Governor Reagan, as he was the former governor of California, and to 41 as Ambassador Bush, as he was the former ambassador to the United Nations.

the crowd's cheers, he was joined on the podium by his running mate. As is customary, they put their arms around each other's shoulders and raised and waved their free arms at the cheering convention attendees. However, my boss kept letting his free arm drop.

Joe Canzeri of the Reagan campaign staff and I were slightly behind and to the side of the podium. Joe, whom I had just met that evening, looked at me and said, "You need to crawl out there and get him"—pointing to my guy—"to raise his arm up." I responded with a slight chuckle as I thought he was joking, but he then emphatically repeated himself.

I was, therefore, confronted with a dilemma. I knew from experience that 41 was never keen to receive sartorial or style advice.

There was a solid, waist-high barrier in front of the podium so, at least, I would be undetected if I decided to follow the high-risk path. So I did, crawling out onto the stage, tugging on his pants cuff, and gesturing to him to raise his free arm. When I did, he glanced down and gave me a look that I had never seen from him before—a mixture of dismay and horror. Nevertheless, he turned, raised his arm and kept it raised.

I was certain that my days as his personal aide were over. But, to my everlasting relief, he never said a further word about it.

PAUL COSTELLO,
assistant press secretary to First Lady Rosalynn Carter:

The 1980 campaign was grueling and, well, depressing. President Carter announced he would not campaign until the US Embassy hostages were released from Iran. That meant the principal surrogates, First Lady Rosalynn Carter and Vice President and Mrs. Mondale, would all be on the road campaigning.

Mrs. Carter was a champion campaigner. Throughout the

Carter presidency, she saw herself as the political eyes and ears for the President. Mrs. Carter actually liked campaigning, getting out of the White House, moving around the nation, and finding out what Americans were thinking. Often, on campaign stops, a local Democratic official would be given an honored gift—a ride with the First Lady in the Secret Service limo. During that time, Mrs. Carter would get a political temperature reading and report back to the political team and the President what she had heard.

As we were climbing to 35,000 feet early one evening headed to another campaign stop in another city, Mrs. Carter told the three staffers traveling with her that she had spoken to the President before we departed. She told him that she had had a very tough day. From her conversations with Democratic officials throughout the day, there had been anger, frustration, and despair about where the campaign was headed. "I've had a tough day, too," the President told her, and didn't want to hear anymore.

She told us she had hung up on him. Him! The President of the United States, albeit her husband.

The pressures of a campaign in good times are horrendously stressful. You can imagine what it's like in tough times. These are human beings, people with real feelings, and that's often lost in the media, in the hype, and in the authority and mystery surrounding the White House.

BRUCE ZANCA,
advancing Vice President Bush:

In October 1987, Vice President Bush was preparing to announce his presidential candidacy. *Newsweek* magazine published a cover photo of Mr. Bush at the helm of his boat with the headline, "Fighting the

'Wimp Factor.'" At the time, I was a twenty-seven-year-old press aide to the Vice President. Really, I was a press-wrangler. My job was to take care of the press pool, which traveled with the Vice President on Air Force Two.

Vice President and Mrs. Bush, their family, and their staff were all upset about the *Newsweek* cover and article. Margaret Warner wrote the piece. We all thought the article and the cover treatment was an uncalled-for cheap shot.

Shortly after the article was published, we made an overnight campaign stop in suburban Detroit, Michigan, with some downtime before the evening event.

The assembly time for the motorcade was 5:30 p.m. in the hotel parking lot for a 5:45 p.m. motorcade departure. Margaret Warner did not show up on time. When advance director John Keller called me on the walkie-talkie and asked me if I was all set for departure, I told him I was missing a reporter, but we should still depart. I said I would arrange for a car to bring her to the next event. I wasn't about to make the Vice President and Mrs. Bush wait for the reporter who penned the offending article. I also admit that I was angry about the story and thought a little retribution was appropriate.

When we got to the event site, word got around to the staff that I had left Margaret Warner behind. Almost instantly, I was summoned to the holding room where Vice President and Mrs. Bush were wait-ing for the event. I went to the holding room and the miffed Vice President said: "Zanca, did you just maroon Margaret Warner?"

I said, "She didn't report on time. She knows the rules. So yes, I left her. I got her a ride, and she's on her way; she won't miss anything."

Said the Vice President: "We are not vindictive, Bruce. That is not how we roll."

As I was leaving the room, Mrs. Bush said to me with a wink, "Good job Bruce; I would've left her, too."

If ever there was a story about why advance is so important, the following might be it.

MIKE LAKE,
advancing Senator Dole:

I had the opportunity to join the Dole for President 1988 presidential campaign as the director of advance and was charged with elevating their advance operation to be consistent with a national campaign.

I was coming from the Reagan White House as a full-time advance man, and it was a tremendous opportunity—and simultaneously, an enormous challenge.

No event reflected this dichotomy more than when our motorcade arrived for an event promoted as an economic success story with huge job creation potential, only to see Woody Woodpecker, Frankenstein, Charlie Chaplin, and Mae West standing ready to greet Senator Dole.

The campaign was scheduled to do a morning event at a local restaurant in Orlando, Florida, and then go to Jacksonville. The afternoon before, I was notified on the campaign plane that a Florida campaign leader suggested we visit Universal Studios' new movie production facility, which was an economic boost to the area and would create hundreds of good-paying jobs. It was still under construction. Senator Dole agreed we should go.

My reaction was, we don't have an advance man on the ground for the event, we have never seen the site, we have no idea what resources are available to support an add-on visit, and we have had no contact with the host.

We were advised that Universal would handle everything; we just needed to show up.

Our anxiety was justified. We pulled into a large dirt field with construction equipment and a couple of buildings. We could have explained that to our busload of traveling press, except for the fact that as we got close to our arrival point, we could see our greeting party of Frankenstein, Woody Woodpecker, Mae West, and Charlie Chaplin.

The first reaction was let's just turn the car around and drive away. But that wasn't an option. Our goal now was to get in and out as soon as possible.

Senator Dole fortunately had a sharp wit and sense of humor. As we moved toward the movie characters, surrounded by the media, he made comments along the lines of, "Let's go meet my new cabinet," and when standing next to a voluptuous Mae West, "Well, things are starting to look up."

Unfortunately, this isn't the end of the story. The campaign was facing internal battles between the leadership team of Chairman Bill Brock and two conservative political activists, David Keene and Don Devine. At the morning breakfast, Brock notified Keene and Devine that they were fired from the campaign. The following day we saw headlines saying, "Top Consultants Fired from Dole Campaign," accompanied by pictures of Senator Dole with Woody Woodpecker, Frankenstein, Mae West, and Charlie Chaplin.

The perils of politics . . .

GORDON JAMES,
advancing Vice President Bush:

One of my less memorable Iowa events took place in Davenport, Iowa, in May 1988.

The venue was very rural. Someone on the host committee

thought it would be fun to hand the Vice President a piglet at the end
of his remarks.

Iowa, for goodness sakes, is the leading producer of hogs, cattle,
corn, and soybeans. It would be a great photo. Good idea. Here, hold
my beer. What could go wrong?

We also thought that not letting the Vice President know what
we had planned would make it even cooler.

So we asked a local farmer to supply a piglet. At the end of the
Vice President's remarks, the farmer handed the piglet up onto the
stage. Vice President Bush had no choice but to take it in his arms
where it proceeded to pee like a racehorse. I mean rivers.

Someone handed the Vice President a hand towel, and he held
the piglet up for the money shot.

Of course, this was the photo of the day. Embarrassed as I was,
I was thankful to be working with someone who could roll with the
punches and knew how to take advantage of a potential disaster.

His thank you note to me said, "Thanks for all the great events."

I don't know if he was serious or not.

*By the time the primary season was over in 1988, the two left standing were
Vice President George H. W. Bush for the Republicans and Massachusetts
Governor Michael Dukakis for the Democrats.*

*We'll begin the general election stories with one the Democrats would
like to forget: One of the more infamous campaign gaffes of all time came on
September 13, 1988, when Governor Dukakis donned a helmet and rode
around in an army tank. It did not go well.*

*Dukakis campaign staffer Josh King wrote an article about the unfor-
tunate incident for* Politico *magazine in 2013, the twenty-fifth anniversary of the Governor's tank ride. He later expanded the story in his book*
Off Script: An Advance Man's Guide to White House Stagecraft,
Campaign Spectacle, and Political Suicide. *This essay is adapted from
the* Politico *piece.*

JOSH KING:

Matt Bennett can still hear the reporters laughing, all ninety of them. He can still picture Sam Donaldson doubled over, guffawing, on a riser that looked out over a dusty field in suburban Detroit.

Bennett was a twenty-three-year-old political rookie in 1988 when he was sent to a General Dynamics facility in Sterling Heights, Michigan, to organize a campaign stop for Democratic presidential nominee Michael Dukakis: a ride in a sixty-eight-ton M1A1 Abrams Main Battle Tank. The visit, meant to bolster the candidate's credibility as a future commander in chief, would go down as one of the worst campaign backfires in history.

Following the event, after the reporters' laughter subsided and Dukakis's entourage was preparing to leave, one of the candidate's traveling aides approached Bennett. "Nice event, Matt," he deadpanned. "It may have cost us the election. But beside that, it was great."

Twenty-five years after the notorious disaster, I set out to discover what had set the infamous tank ride in motion and why no one had put a stop to it.

The truth is, many of Dukakis's advisors did try to forestall the tank ride even while others were convinced the photo op was essential. They argued with each other over it, sent warnings back to headquarters, huddled in anxious meetings, and even dispatched an expert fixer, all to no avail.

Bennett arrived in Sterling Heights, in the center of Michigan's Macomb County—a Detroit suburb rich in Reagan Democrats that Dukakis needed to court—on Thursday, September 8. He had received his marching orders from Katie Whelan, his scheduler at headquarters: orchestrate a tank ride for the Governor, to be followed by a speech. At the time, the directive seemed logical enough.

The campaign staff knew they had a steep hill to climb on national defense. Dukakis had served in the army for two years after college, but his terms as a state representative and then governor left him with a thinner résumé on national security than his opponent, who was a World War II aviator, congressman, ambassador, director of Central Intelligence, and two-term vice president.

The campaign's Michigan director, John Eades, wanted his candidate in Macomb County, but he was wary of Dukakis's ability to pull off the event. "All of a sudden," he recalled, "the campaign wanted to turn him into a hawk who loves the military and wants to hug a tank."

Bennet knew this would be no ordinary visual. The tank stood eight feet high, with Dukakis's torso sticking up another three feet from his planned perch in the turret. A press riser would have to be built higher than normal to keep the cameras and the candidate at the same level, a hard-and-fast rule from the campaign advance manual. Bennett also grappled with the tricky choreography of getting Dukakis aboard the tank while avoiding unflattering imagery of a five-foot-eight-inch man climbing up an eight-foot-high tank. That problem was solved by arranging for Dukakis to board the tank behind closed doors.

But then there was the matter of the helmet, which General Dynamics officials insisted was necessary both for safety, if the tank ran at its full speed of more than forty miles per hour, and for radio communications among the riders.

Joyce Carrier, the campaign's director of advance, recalls that the Dukakis campaign up to that point had been particularly hat averse. "Beside the fact that he didn't look good in them," she told me, "you could just never imagine him with a hat on."

All of which made Bennett nervous. "This is going to be a freaking disaster," he recalled telling at least one boss.

Eventually, trip director Jack Weeks, who had been traveling with Dukakis, was sent ahead to Michigan to adjudicate last-minute issues of choreography.

Weeks saw few good options on the helmet question. Scuttling the tank ride would have brought a host of questions from the press corps. Simply kicking the tank's treads would have seemed like a cop-out. And taking a slow crawl around the test track without the helmet would have invited its own chorus of ridicule.

Weeks met with Bennett and the rest of the advance team early on the morning of game day. Weeks recalls Paul Holtzman, the lead advance man, modeling the gray General Dynamics coveralls and the olive-green helmet that Dukakis would wear. When he saw Holtzman in the helmet, he said, "Go look in the mirror. . . . You look like a goofy fuck. No helmet."

Advance people consider themselves more practical and logistics-minded than headquarters staff, but how they—who were actually responsible for guiding Dukakis through the General Dynamics facility—addressed the issue remains a matter of dispute. Bennett wrote in his 1988 diary that they developed a compromise, then crossed their fingers: Dukakis would emerge from the garage with the helmet on and make a full-speed demo run. He would then take off his helmet while the tank made a slower pass by the cameras.

"I told Weeks the brutal facts: Dukakis would look like a goof if he wore the helmet, but he wouldn't be able to hear, and he would feel genuinely unsafe without it," Bennett wrote in his diary. "Jack ruled that he would wear the helmet for the fast passes, and doff his headgear for a slow, picture-taking pass."

Two things were clear: Bennett was mistaken on the order of the passes. Photos show Dukakis emerging from the garage without a helmet, and Weeks maintains there was no compromise plan, that he stuck to his initial instincts. "There was supposed to be no helmet," he told me.

Bennett, meanwhile, is just as adamant that Dukakis was fully briefed on the slow pass/fast pass choreography. "I remember it like it was yesterday," he said. "And I wrote it down."

Upon arrival, Dukakis met with representatives from General Dynamics while the press assembled on the elevated reviewing stand. The candidate then pulled on his protective coveralls emblazoned with his name and made his way to the awaiting tank. He then climbed aboard the tank behind closed doors. The General Dynamics crew gave him the helmet, explaining he had to wear it to hear the audio instructions.

The tank cruised slowly to the far end of the test track as the photographers and cameramen tracked its moves with their long lenses. It then paused for a long time before turning back toward the onlookers.

"My reaction is, 'Holy shit, the tank ran out of gas,'" Weeks told me. "The headline running through my head is, 'Dukakis campaign runs out of gas.' All of a sudden, it kicks up into speed, it comes running by, and he's got the helmet on."

Weeks said he was surprised to see the helmet, and he regrets that, as the campaign's top advance person, he wasn't aboard the tank during the ride to keep it off his boss's head. "If anyone asks me what the screw-up was, it was not having an advance person with him to protect him."

On the final pass in front of the press riser, the tank approached the cameras head-on, veering away at the last second, the tank's barrel swerving so close that reporters remember having to duck to avoid decapitation. Had the tank kept its distance, the iconic image of Dukakis never would have been captured.

Instead, the close-up shot, capturing a smiling Dukakis—pointing a finger and wearing a helmet with his name stenciled across the brow like a summer-camp name tag—would grace the next day's front pages.

Joe Lockhart, the deputy press secretary, recalled someone on the campaign plane later that afternoon asking Dukakis why he wore the helmet. Dukakis said he wanted to hear the narration. "This is quintessential Mike Dukakis," Lockhart told me. "For everybody else, this was a photo op. Dukakis wanted to understand how the tank worked."

Lockhart and the others on the ground knew it wasn't "the best thing we ever did," Lockhart told me. "I wasn't sure it was the worst thing."

Back in Boston, though, the headquarters staff had a clearer assessment. "The second we saw that picture on the six o'clock news, we had pains in our stomach," recalled scheduling director Mindy Lubber. "Regardless of anything that came out of the Governor's mouth, we saw the picture, which was Mike Dukakis with his head sticking up in that goofy hat."

By Tuesday, one poll found that Dukakis had lost significant ground, with 25 percent saying they were less likely to vote for him because of the tank ride.

Making matters worse was a thirty-second campaign spot called "Tank Ride," created by Bush-Quayle adman Sig Rogich, that premiered during the third game of the World Series between the Los Angeles Dodgers and the Oakland A's. Just a few seconds of the unfortunate video, supplemented by graphics and artificial sound effects, aired before millions of viewers on the national telecast.

Matt Bennett still preserves the tank suit Dukakis wore that day in his closet. For years he wore it on Halloween.

And he never forgot the lessons of Sterling Heights. He applied them when he became Vice President Al Gore's trip director—the role Jack Weeks had played in the Dukakis race. As he told me: "If an advance person said to me, 'This is going to be bad,' I spent serious time thinking about that because I've been that guy."

Brad Blakeman could argue he was almost "that guy."

BRAD BLAKEMAN,
advancing Vice President Bush:

The George Bush for President campaign of 1988 sent me, a Jewish lawyer from New York, to arrange a Texas barbecue in McAllen, Texas. Makes sense, right?

When I arrived in McAllen, a border town directly south of San Antonio, I was greeted by a member of the Mayor's entourage who escorted me to city hall for a meeting with "Boss Hogg," the memorable protagonist from television's *Dukes of Hazzard*. The Mayor certainly looked the part with his polyester suit, cowboy boots, and a big silver belt buckle that could've been used to serve turkey at Thanksgiving. He was large and in charge. He gave orders and did not take a second to listen. He was that guy.

As we discussed the BBQ, I found him to be utterly dismissive of the Vice President's needs in terms of protocols, security, and the like. I usually get along with just about everyone, but when it came to the Mayor, not so much.

For example, he insisted that the Vice President ride in his police cruiser from the airport to the BBQ. When I told the Mayor that the Secret Service would require the use of armored cars, specifically flown in for the Vice President, he balked, suggesting that this was the way it had always been done with past visits by presidents and vice presidents.

I tried to joke with him and asked, "Who was the last president or VP who visited? Lincoln?" He didn't find that amusing. Nor did he think it was funny when I told him that the Secret Service was ordering the Food and Drug Administration to do an inspection of the caterer and the meal processing. In fact, he flipped out.

He barked at me, "There is not going to be a damned inspection of the caterer, and if you insist, you can just cancel the whole damn thing!" I tried to calm him down and told him that it was standard operating procedure and that it had to occur if the Vice President was to attend. He then told me where to "stick" that procedure. I reported back to the White House and the campaign that the Mayor wasn't acting cooperatively. I recommended that the event be canceled, and they agreed.

I telephoned the Mayor to deliver the news. He responded with some wonderfully amusing and creative insults and then hung up the phone. I then told my advance staff and our support agencies that we would be canceling the visit and leaving McAllen the next day.

I then put my head on the pillow and fell asleep. I was awakened by loud banging on my hotel room door. I jumped out of bed, got dressed, and looked out the peephole where I saw the Mayor and his posse. I told them to wait while I telephoned the lead Secret Service agent who was also staying at the hotel. I asked him to immediately come to my room, preferably armed.

With that, I opened the door and they all piled in my room. The Mayor raised his voice and said, "You can have your damned FDA inspection and all the other nonsense, but you are never welcome in Texas again!" He was so abusive to me that the agent told him to leave my room and not return.

The next day, cooler heads prevailed, and since the Mayor had conceded to all our requests, I put the visit back on the schedule. The BBQ ended up being a success. The Vice President was greeted by the Mayor at the airport, and the two rode in a Secret Service limousine to the event. The FDA inspection was completed with no issues, and it looked like everyone was having a great time.

But then I noticed something. The Mayor was talking to the Vice President and motioning toward me across the room. I thought to myself, This can't be good. When I caught up with the Vice President backstage, he put his arm around me and said, "It looks like you and the Mayor did not get along." I replied, "Yes, sir, he is crazy." We both laughed and the Vice President said, "I know. Don't worry about it."

I stayed behind and left the next day. As I was leaving for the airport, I ran into the Mayor who told me, "You're shit-canned. I talked to the Vice President and you are done." I told him that I was only doing what was expected of me and that I was sorry we did not get along better.

I thought, or maybe hoped, that I would never see the Mayor again, but I wasn't so lucky.

After the election, I was given the responsibility of managing numerous Inaugural events in and around Washington, including Texas's "Black Tie & Boots" ball. Not surprisingly, I spied the Mayor of McAllen in the crowd. I went up to him and asked him, "Hello, Mayor, do you remember me?"

He turned ghost white and looked like he was about to have a heart attack. Before he could answer, I said, "Thank you for speaking to the Vice President about my future. Clearly you had a real impression on him since he made me a managing director of the Inaugural." With that, I turned around and left him with his mouth hanging open.

TOM SCULLY,
working for Vice President Bush:

In the spring of 1988, I took time out from my law practice to serve as communications/press director for the Republican Convention in New Orleans. The day after the convention ended, I was planning to go back to being a lawyer.

But as we packed up, the Democratic nominee for president, Governor Michael Dukakis, started offering all his events by a satellite link (very new tech then) along with daily interviews to local news stations.

Our campaign folks flipped out, and communications director Dave Demarest asked: "Who knows how to do that with a satellite?"

I was a satellite lawyer, I had worked at COMSAT for two years,[3] and I knew how that all worked. So Dave sucked me into staying for the rest of the campaign to do the TV work. We offered a lot of local stations interviews with the Vice President, along with a satellite link to live events when he was in a big venue. We also did all the post-debate responses from our surrogates—people like Barbara Bush and Dan Quayle—along with interviews with them from the campaign trail.

The last two weeks I was sent on the road to go ahead of the Vice President to find and set up a satellite truck in each town and broad-cast his speech live, and then do six separate five-minute TV spots with him for top local news stations.

It was a complete "wing it" operation. It was just me, whatever TV truck I could rent that day, a phone line, and the Vice President. We broadcast from grade school libraries, the Notre Dame gym (with legendary coach Digger Phelps), a city hall, and every other space I could find that I could get a TV cable into. This went on for twelve days.

Then came the last day, November 2, Grand Rapids, Michigan. The Vice President was giving a noon speech in the outdoor Monroe Amphitheater in the middle of Grand Rapids with President Jerry Ford.

The only satellite truck I could find to rent was a crappy old one from Traverse City, Michigan, which is a few hours away. It arrived at 7:00 a.m. The truck had only fifty feet of cable for the camera. It was very tough to get the camera close enough to broadcast the speech and then find a place to do six postspeech interviews—again, all within fifty feet of the truck.

The only option turned out to be the small storeroom basement of the WDOG hot dog stand, located below the local AM radio station

---

3 COMSAT is short for Communications Satellite Corporation.

and accessed only from an outside beaten-up staircase. The basement storeroom was maybe 6 by 12 feet and filled with junk. I cleaned out all the paper plates, cups, etc., and rented some blue pipe and drape and created a very small space for me, the cameraman, and a chair for the Vice President.

It was freezing cold and windy. The Secret Service and WHCA were not happy with the arrangement and yelled at me all morning as I set it up and crammed TV cables down the small basement stairs. They kept threatening to cancel the Vice President from showing up for the interviews postspeech because the setup was such a rat hole! But I had the top stations in New York City, Detroit, Chicago, Los Angeles, Dallas, and Boston scheduled. I pleaded to go ahead.

When the Vice President finished his speech—which we successfully beamed off the satellite—I grabbed the camera guy and ran back to the WDOG basement storeroom to set up for the interview. A very tired George Bush eventually came down the very crumbly, cement basement stairs, looked in the cramped little tunnel we had created, and rolled his eyes a bit as he sat down to mic up. I closed the door for the fortieth time that day over all the cables—and the door fell off its hinges! The WHCA guys screamed: "That's it—we have to get him out of here." It was still really windy and cold, and the Vice President said something like, "Hey, I can't do this, let's go."

I said, "Please sir, we have the top six TV markets in the country. We can't cancel—PLEASE!"

So he hung in there, freezing, with no door in the basement of a hot dog stand and did thirty minutes of perfect interviews with each of the local anchors. I can't say he was happy, but he was very cool (while the WHCA and Secret Service were not).

I went home to bed with a 104-degree temperature on Election Day.

Despite all of this, I got hired to be part of the White House staff, reporting to Dick Darman in the Office of Management and Budget.

The first time I went to a meeting with the President in his office—yes, that would be the Oval Office—along with some members of his senior staff, he looked at me and said, incredibly nicely, "Hey, you work here? I thought you were a TV guy!"

STEPHEN M. STUDDERT,
assistant to President Bush 41:

Two days after the 1988 Republican National Convention, where then Vice President Bush formally accepted the party's nomination, I received a telephone call from the newly appointed campaign chairman, James A. Baker, who asked me to "get on George's campaign airplane for the duration and oversee all the on-the-road stuff."

After a short conversation, and a quick check with my wife, I accepted this assignment and the very next day joined his Air Force Two team. Never once in the ensuing two months did the Vice President fire me, but at a couple of events he questioned my judgment. Yet he was always a good sport about my ideas.

The day after he won the election, on the flight back from Houston to Washington, now President-Elect Bush asked me to direct his Inaugural. That was a giant assignment and one I had not anticipated. But I accepted his generous invitation and committed my best to him and Mrs. Bush.

He pretty much gave us free rein and empowered us to do our best to represent him, the new First Lady, the Bush family, and their values and principles. But over the sixty days of preparation, he telephoned me several times with very specific instructions, seven of which were:

1. My mother wouldn't be pleased if this is all about me. Nor would I. Make it about America.

2. Make sure my mother doesn't have to stand in any rain or the cold.

3. Take good care of my friend Jesse Jackson. And here's his phone number.

4. Make the Inaugural activities as accessible to the greater American public as possible.

5. Barbara and I want to walk part of the Inaugural Parade route. Please figure out the best and safest place.

6. Please include my favorite country and western entertainers and jazz great Bo Diddley in the festivities.

7. I want to communicate to all Americans my love of this country.

We honored every one of those requests fully.

BEN AUSTIN,
advancing Governor Clinton:

I was on Governor Clinton's advance staff for the 1992 campaign, my primary duty being motorcades. As campaign jobs go, that does not fall in the "top strategist" category.

The sardonic Hollywood producer, Mort Engelberg, was our head of advance and was also good friends with the Governor. One day, almost in passing, Mort suggested that I color coordinate the motorcade for an upcoming trip to Milwaukee.

As an overly eager young staffer, I took on Mort's clarion call with gusto.

We had to a find a fleet of midnight-blue mini vans, which was the color I had chosen. When the exasperated car rental staffers would ask if "sky blue" or "light green" or "maybe a neutral color" would do for just a few of the cars, maybe at the end of the motorcade, I would smile and politely ask if they were joking. When they said they would need to truck vehicles in from other states at great and unnecessary expense, I replied, "OK."

On game day, I watched as all my work paid off. The newly assembled fleet lined up with such beautiful precision, it was like watching a military maneuver.

When the campaign plane finally taxied to a stop, the motorcade proceeded to the stairs of the plane to assemble the Governor along with dozens of staff and press. When Governor Clinton finally walked down the stairs to his armored limousine, Mort pulled me over to introduce me.

"Governor," Mort called to him. "I want you to meet Ben Austin. He's the staffer who pulled off this midnight-blue motorcade."

I stood proudly as the Governor peered back at my work of art, quizzically cocked his head, then whispered to Mort, "It kind of looks like a funeral."

That's when I learned the important lesson that motorcade advance was not my path to political stardom.

Probably neither was this incident.

Governor Clinton and Senator Gore embarked on a traditional campaign bus tour. We were in Corsicana, Texas, and I remember being stressed because it was not only one of my first trips, it was also one of my first jobs as a recent college graduate. It would be an understatement to say that my colleague and I, two kids from California, didn't fit into the culture of this small Texas town.

We parked and quickly exited the car for a last-minute errand before our rally. Just as we shut the doors, we realized we had locked our keys in the car.

We both quickly began to lose our cool in a way that belied our youth, until we looked up and realized that we had literally locked our keys in the car right in front of a locksmith.

"What luck!" we proclaimed as we high-fived and ran into the locksmith store to meet a man slowly rocking in a chair, wearing a hat with a sexist message about his wife, and who introduced himself only as "Brown."

We introduced ourselves as staffers for Governor Clinton—likely our first fatal mistake (after all, we were in President Bush's home state)—then proceeded to tell him about our conundrum.

After we finished speaking, Brown kept rocking, took a beat to consider our situation, then said: "I'd like to help you boys, but I stopped doing outside work in 1987."

Outside work?

We were genuinely confused, so I interjected to clarify, "I don't think you understand, our car is literally right in front of your store." I pointed out the door and he craned his head to see it, then nodded at me.

"I'd like to help you," Brown said, then repeated that he'd stopped doing "outside work" in 1987. Then I posited to Brown the hypothetical: "If our car was twenty feet over, and technically inside the boundaries of your store, could you open it?"

"Sure I could," he proudly replied. "It would take less than one minute!"

"But if you step onto your store's porch and jump, you could probably touch our car, so can we just pretend that our car is 'inside' for the sake of this analysis?"

"I stopped doing outside work in 1987."

We then thanked Brown for his time and threw a brick through the car window.

BRAD BLAKEMAN,
advancing Governor Bush:

In 1999, in the heat (no pun intended) of the New Hampshire primary, I was busy organizing Texas Governor George W. Bush's appearance at one of the first primary events where all Republicans and Democrats running for president would appear, at a Fourth of July parade in Merrimack.

The one thing about the New Hampshire primary is that there are rules and traditions for everything. The campaign representatives met in the local fire station to pick a parade position out of a fire hat. Every candidate was encouraged to walk the parade route, and in addition to the candidate, every campaign could have two parade entries, like a marching band, car, or cheerleaders. If you had animals, you had to provide people who would clean up after them.

I met with our team and decided that we would have a high school marching band in front of Governor Bush, who would be riding in a horse-driven buckboard filled with kids holding "Bush for President" signs and red, white, and blue pom-poms.

Most of the campaigns saw this for what it was: a parade, not a debate. No one was really trying to find a competitive edge to exploit or to be disagreeable.

Some, however, were very mysterious and vague about their parade component to the point of obnoxiousness. Such was the case with the campaign of former Cabinet Secretary Elizabeth Dole. We ended up getting positioned in between Family Research Council President Gary Bauer and Mrs. Dole in the parade.

On the day of the parade, the Dole campaign people were being difficult, so I thought I would have a little fun. I moved the kids, who had originally been assigned to pick up after the horses, into the buckboard, leaving us without poop picker-uppers. I told the horse handlers that I hoped the horses were well fed.

No sooner had we started the parade than the horses began to poop. I probably took a little too much enjoyment watching Mrs. Dole navigating her way through the orchard of horse apples that littered her path. Needless to say, her staff was livid with me, especially since they were forced to use her campaign signs to push away the poop from her path.

I did feel bad about my trick, but only because the city had to clean up the mess. So I made sure we paid Merrimack a clean-up fee.

PETER NEWELL,
advancing Senator Obama:

It was a drizzly morning in Greenwood, South Carolina, in 2007, and I, as the site guy, was feeling the full weight of impending disaster.

We had hastily squeezed in a 10:00 a.m. "coffee with the candidate" for then Senator Barack Obama at the local civic center, which was a last-minute addition to a packed schedule. The local state senator had promised fifty attendees, but as the motorcade pulled up, a mere twenty-five people, plus a handful of campaign staff and a box of Dunkin' Donuts munchkins, dotted the cavernous room.

Senator Obama entered, his face betraying a tired frown, clearly already briefed on the dismal turnout and likely frustrated he wasn't back working on the major Father's Day speech he was to deliver the next day. I held the door, avoiding eye contact, and slipped into a corner, ready for a quick, awkward forty-five-minute meet and greet. Feeling like there were more staff than guests, I stepped into the hall to commiserate with others, rolling my eyes at the unfolding catastrophe.

Then, a shout cut through the quiet, a woman's voice: "Fire!" My mind was racing on where to find extinguishers. But then it grew louder, clearer. Others joined in, a grumbling chorus rising to a chant: "Fired Up! Ready to Go!"

This jumbled room of twenty-five people suddenly found its voice, rallying with an electrifying energy. From my vantage point,

I saw the Senator's profile, his head (and ears!) beginning to nod in rhythm with the chant. The chanting built, cheers erupted, and the room was transformed.

What I didn't know then was that this small, seemingly disastrous event would become a cornerstone of both the 2008 and 2012 campaigns. Senator Obama would later recount this very exchange as a metaphor for how one voice can change a room, and ultimately, the world. I was just the lucky guy who got to witness history being forged in a nearly empty civic center, a moment that proved the future president's incredible ability to connect, be present, and inspire, even when the odds—and the turnout—were stacked against him.

MICHAEL RUEMMLER,
advancing Senator Obama:

It was late March 2007. Several friends and former colleagues had thrown my résumé into the pile at the nascent Obama campaign because I was from Illinois. I got a voicemail from Liz Reiter, deputy director of advance, who said there was a trip going to Iowa the next week and wondered if I was able to join.

I called back and, as calmly as I could, said, yes, I thought I could make that work for my schedule.

Eight months later, December 8 to be exact, I stood at the loading dock of Hy-Vee Hall in Des Moines, which had become a second home for the Obama advance staff. Word had trickled down to us that Oprah was going to be doing a campaign swing and the first leg was a stop in Des Moines.

I had been assigned as the site lead for Oprah's first rally!

We had a live band for the preshow and a large open hall that accommodated 18,000 Iowans with bleachers at the back that would hopefully show off a cascade of people—all under a truss that held twelve letters cut out from particle board with Christmas lights on the borders: IOWA FOR OBAMA.

This was not the Oprah studio production team in Chicago. The sign was hardly caliber for a high school play and probably cost less than $100.

It snowed, iced, hailed, and blew sideways every single day between late November and Caucus Day, and this day was no different. The high was about twenty degrees, snowy and blustery. There was *one* dressing room and, at least for this day, Barack Obama was not the biggest star of the show. It would be reserved for our special guest.

We had gone to great lengths to make sure the backstage area was warm, adding as many heaters as we could find. The Secret Service team members were truly wonderful to work with and we all considered them colleagues, but they often have a way of throwing off your best-laid plans. When the motorcade was five minutes out, the site agent pushed a button that quickly raised the rollup doors to the loading dock.

By the time the cars pulled in, it was ice cold. Oprah and her friend Gayle King went to the dressing room. The Obamas shivered with the rest of us waiting for Oprah to be ready. She's Oprah, she can do whatever she wants.

When she was ready, Oprah and Michelle Obama stood on each side of me with Senator Obama looking over my shoulder as I showed them a diagram of the event site. I described to them where they should walk, where cameras were positioned, and where the ladies should sit after they spoke. At least I think that's what happened because even that day, that moment was a blur. I don't recall any questions; we cued the music, and off they went one by one. Only later did I think to ask, as I had briefed three of the most famous people *on the planet* simultaneously, if anyone had gotten a picture. They had not.

Fast-forward to the general election campaign.

I became close enough with our team at HQ that I would some-times get a preview of my next stop a little sooner than before. Dave Cusack, our deputy director of advance, told me that I was going back to Sunrise, Florida, for a rally the following Wednesday. I had done a rally there just before Memorial Day, so I knew the venue and even the staff there. Easy, right?

Then I read that the campaign—flush with enthusiastic cash—was going to be spending millions on an infomercial. It was to air on the major networks, plus a few cable networks, in prime time. Pretty cool! And it was going to be on Wednesday night.

"That's odd," I said to Dave. "It seems like you'd want people to be home watching that instead of at a rally, especially in Florida. But what do I know? I just do what I'm told."

"No, your rally is going to be part of the infomercial."

"The rally is going to be an infomercial?"

"No. It's going to be *part* of the infomercial."

That made no more sense to me, but it was made more plain to me that the campaign had produced a twenty-seven-ish-minute in-fomercial, and the denouement would be in the final three minutes, where they cut to our rally happening live. Furthermore, the rally would need to be timed to conclude along with those three minutes.

"Wait . . . what? Can you explain that again?"

I decided I would put my head down and go about my job for a bit and let people much smarter than I figure out what all this meant, but here are some of the things that needed to happen.

Both Senators Obama and Biden would be there and both would be speaking, with Senator Biden introducing Senator Obama. For Senator Obama to hit his closing at 8:27 p.m., we would have to know for exactly how long he would speak, and how long Biden would speak.

I thought, How are we supposed to know that? What about

applause lines? What if the microphone cuts out? What if the mags are backed up and the crowd isn't in?[4] What if the rally ends before it's supposed to? And a hundred other what-ifs.

Speechwriters for both principals timed their bosses' "closing arguments" and gave us an average. That meant Biden would be announced to stage at a precise time and Obama needed to be announced to stage by Biden at a precise time. The night before, during our daily trip call, fifty people or more reviewed the timing for one final go. The cell service inside the arena was awful, but I heard Alyssa Mastromonaco authoritatively break through the clutter of tired conversations and squabbling as only she could: "Guys, this is Alyssa. Why don't we ask Ruemmler how long it will take to walk from the offstage announcement area to the lectern?"

Tired, frustrated, stressed, half-listening, and now put on the spot, I was standing on the stage and, using my background as a golfer, quickly estimated the paces required, and then completely made it up. "I say forty-five seconds." Case closed. It was built into the timeline.

Ricky Kirshner produces live events on TV—the Tonys, the Super Bowl halftime show, and every Democratic convention since 1992. He and his team were brought in to film the rally and push it out live to the networks. They had camera positions that were unusual for us, plus a jib (a camera on an arm that gets moving shots and does what a drone would likely do now) and a flat-screen TV that functioned as a teleprompter just below the main head-on camera.

Kirshner's team was eager to see a final lighting set, which took far too long, and I had asked our stagehands to hang and light a thirty-foot American flag directly above the stage. It was only a few minutes until the doors were to open when they finally got their one

---

4 Short for magnetometers, which are used to check for weapons.

and only final preview. There are a few things that look better than a well-lit American flag, but not many. It glowed and its scale was perfect for the cavernous arena.

I carefully looked at the angles from the Kirshner cameras and realized that one was shooting through Obama and would have a vomitorium—the nickname for the tunnel-like entrance into a stadium that looked like a gaping hole—in the background. I grabbed bunting and taped it to the railing to help cover it up.

Everything was as set as it was going to be.

The senators were at a nearby hotel and were en route. Marvin Nicholson, the trip director who traveled everywhere with Senator Obama, called to check in. "Any overflow?" I told him there were several hundred people outside. At any other event, the candidates would make an unannounced stop to greet those people and make them feel good for having come but not gotten in.

"Biden wants to stop at overflow." Of course he did! Biden was the ultimate retail politician who truly loved shaking hands and talking to people. So much so that his schedule was padded for it.

Advance is a can-do job. There is an old saying that if an advance person is asked to find a donkey for the candidate's room, you're supposed to ask what color eyes it should have. Against character and typical protocol, I pushed back. "Marvin, please do not do that. Not tonight. We *cannot* miss the start time." Ultimately, they relented and drove directly to the loading dock.

One last look at the site. No! The bunting on that rail was about to fall! I ran into the seats and explained firmly and quickly to the gentleman seated behind it that the camera over there needs to have this piece of bunting behind Obama's head and that it was up to him to keep that bunting in place, that people across the country would see him on TV, and that if it fell we would probably lose the election. It was all I could do at that point. Months later, when I finally got to see the finished product, I could see that man's hand firmly holding the bunting in place.

Senator Biden was introduced to stage, began his remarks, and it wasn't long before we realized he was far behind. Rick Siger, Biden's trip director and our advance lead from Iowa days, stood over the teleprompter operator backstage with a copy of the remarks. Biden would hit an applause line, and you could see words flying down the flat-screen TV. Ultimately, they guided the prepared remarks to a perfect landing and Biden brought Obama onto the stage.

At around 8:26, a countdown to live air began. At 8:27 and a few seconds, Obama hit an applause line. The rally was now live to over thirty million viewers across the country, and most importantly, to my bosses back in Chicago. A camera high in the rafters welcomed America into the rally. The crowd was cheering, Old Glory glowed, and the red light of the head-on camera went on.

"So to all of you, and to all those who have joined us across the country. . . . In six days, if you'll knock on doors for me, if you'll make calls for me, if you tell your friends and family to vote for me, then we won't just win an election, but together we will change the world!"

Infomercial music played, the crowd roared, Biden and Obama stepped out in front of the lectern to join hands and wave. In my ear, Ricky Kirshner said, "Aaand, we're out." Stevie Wonder's "Signed, Sealed, Delivered" blared and I breathed for the first time in two days.

The poor cell service had eaten my BlackBerry battery, so I quickly ran backstage and saw Jim Margolis, one of the campaign ad makers. "Did we nail it?"

"We nailed it!"

I had been living in hotels across the country for about eighteen months. I worked on events in thirty-four states and even Jerusalem. The experience in its entirety—the sheer luck of finding my way onto the staff, their willingness to keep putting me into the game, a history nerd helping create actual American history working for any candidate, let alone a Black American, rising to win the presidency—is still hard to fathom, even seventeen years later.

We will end this chapter with the sad story of two presidential candidates— President Gerald Ford in 1976 and Senator John Kerry in 2004—who possibly single-handedly ruined their chances of winning the election by . . . eating.

DAVID BATES:

Being offered an unfamiliar, regional food dish on the campaign trail is a political minefield for the candidate and staff.

In April 1976, President Gerald Ford was visiting the Alamo in San Antonio, Texas. There, a member of the Daughters of the Republic of Texas offered him a plate of tamales. He took one and bit into it without removing the husk. The lady who had offered him the tamale stopped him after the first bite to tell him to remove the husk, which he did before finishing the tamale.

Too late. Photos of the gaffe were front-page news across the country.

Everybody knows you remove the husk, right?

The San Antonio Mayor at the time, Lila Cockrell, later told the *Houston Chronicle* that "it was obvious he didn't get a briefing on the eating of tamales."

Fast-forward to August 2003, when presidential candidate John Kerry was in Philadelphia and ordered a Philadelphia cheesesteak with . . . Swiss cheese. He then proceeded to eat the tainted sandwich with "dainty bites," reported the local media.

The problem: Philadelphia cheesesteaks are made mostly with Cheez Whiz, and sometimes American or Provolone cheese. Never, ever Swiss cheese.

The media was merciless. On the twentieth anniversary of the "incident," one social media writer said it was the day Senator Kerry's aspirations "melted like a dollop of Cheez Whiz in the sun." (He did win the Democratic primary but lost the general election to George W. Bush.)

Note to future campaign advance men and women: Make sure you are familiar with the do's and don'ts of the local food culture and then make sure the candidate knows them, too.

CHAPTER THREE

ADVANCING HISTORY

*M*ost of the stories in this chapter you already know. You either lived them or studied them in a history class.

What you likely have not heard are the stories of the men and women on the ground and behind the scenes of these historic events, many of which changed their lives forever.

The first stories are about the assassination attempts on President Gerald Ford and President Ronald Reagan.

And the last story is an advance man's memory of 9/11.

In between are some stories of triumph where there were more smiles than tears—and maybe a few sighs of relief.

BOB GOODWIN,
advancing President Ford:

At 3:30 p.m. on the afternoon of September 22, 1975, President Gerald Ford walked out the front door of the St. Francis Hotel in San Francisco and was about to get in his motorcade for a routine forty-minute drive to Air Force One.

Seconds after the President stepped onto the sidewalk, Sara Jane Moore fired one shot at him. It was off target. She was using a gun that she had hastily purchased just that morning. Realizing she had missed, she fired again. The second shot missed as well. Both bullets flew about six inches over the President's head and over the rest of us who were with the President at that moment. The bullets slammed into the hotel's stone facade.[1]

I was the lead advance for this trip by the President, who had been in the Bay Area for two days. On the day of the shooting, he spoke at a luncheon of the World Affairs Council of Northern California at the St. Francis Hotel.

Later that afternoon I was directly behind the President when he walked out the front door of the hotel. A large and supportive crowd of about 3,000 people lined the opposite side of Powell Street, directly across from the entrance of the hotel.

There could have been more serious consequences for the President had it not been for a last-minute change in plans.

Thirty minutes prior to the President's departure, the lead Secret Service agent sought me out and said, "There's something about this crowd that we don't like. I can't put my finger on it. Would you ask the President to go directly to the limo when he comes out of the hotel." I went upstairs to the President's suite and conveyed the message.

The usual practice for President Ford in similar situations was to walk to the front of his limo and wave to a crowd and then move to the rear of the limo and wave again before getting in the car. If he had done that on this day he would have been in the direct line of sight of the shooter as she aimed her .38-caliber revolver from not more than forty feet away.

---

1 The bullet holes from that day were clearly visible in the side of the hotel and they remained that way for several decades. That made the front of the St. Francis Hotel a tourist attraction of sorts. I have always believed that they remained unrepaired on purpose.

The second bullet fired by Sara Jane Moore flew over the President's head by six inches but only because at the last second her arm was knocked upward by Oliver Sipple, a former marine, who was standing next to her in the crowd. However, the bullet ricocheted and hit a forty-two-year-old taxi driver who was standing in a nearby crowd. He survived.

Eerily, this was not new to President Ford. Just a few weeks earlier on September 5, 1975, Squeaky Fromme, a Charles Manson follower, had tried to shoot President Ford while he was shaking hands along a rope line in Sacramento, California. She had a Colt .45 caliber semiautomatic pistol and was thwarted by Larry Buendorf, the President's lead Secret Service agent. Fromme was only an arms-length away from the President when she raised her pistol. Seeing the gun come up, Larry—who was moving along the rope line immediately preceding the President—instantly jammed his hand under the hammer and prevented the pistol from firing. Secret Service agents quickly subdued her and rapidly led the President to shelter. Larry was later honored for this by the Department of the Treasury, which, at that time, had jurisdiction over the United States Secret Service.[2]

Fromme and Moore were both convicted of attempted assassination of a president and sentenced to life imprisonment. Interestingly, they served many years of their time together at the federal prison in Alderson, West Virginia. Sara Jane Moore was paroled in 2007 after being imprisoned for thirty-two years, and Squeaky Fromme was paroled two years later.[3]

But back to 3:30 p.m. on September 22, 1975.

For several seconds after the shots were fired everyone stood still.

---

2 Since 2003, the Secret Service has reported to the Department of Homeland Security.

3 Moore passed away in late 2025; as of this writing, Fromme is still alive.

Oddly, I remember, there was a hushed silence. My immediate reaction was that it must make the Secret Service nervous when they hear firecrackers near the President.

Everyone from the President to the Secret Service agents to the rest of us looked toward the shooter. Then pandemonium broke out.

Two Secret Service agents, Jack Merchant and Ron Pontius, forced the President down to the sidewalk next to the limo. Then they grabbed and pushed the President into the back seat. Don Rumsfeld, the President's chief of staff, and the two agents piled on top of the President and the car door slammed shut. Somebody yelled, "Go, Go, Go." The limo, preceded by a half dozen California Highway Patrol officers on motorcycles, took off at a high rate of speed for the airport.

At the same time, four of us traveling with the President immediately jumped into the control car. If we hadn't reacted within seconds, we would have been left standing on the sidewalk in front of the hotel. As far as we could tell, we were the last car in this truncated motorcade as several cars from the California Highway Patrol quickly pulled behind us. Immediately following them were two White House press vehicles and a White House staff car, all straining to keep up.

In a presidential motorcade in those days, the control car was the third car in line directly behind the limo and the spare limo. Control was the only vehicle other than the limo and the spare that was driven by a Secret Service agent.

Normally those who rode in the control car were the president's personal aide, the president's photographer, the president's military aide, and sometimes the lead advance. All four of us dove into the control car just before it left the curb with tires squealing.

We all had radios connected to others in the traveling party and to WHCA's command center, but in an emergency situation like this we had been told to maintain radio silence. The agent driving our vehicle asked someone to turn on the car radio and try to find a local broadcast reporting from the scene in front of the St. Francis Hotel.

We quickly found a station that had a live report. The reporter said that "a good-looking member of the President's staff had been shot." The four of us in the control car looked around and said that couldn't be true since each of us thought that we were the best-looking member of the President's staff! Then we immediately imagined that the reporter was talking about Don Rumsfeld. Luckily, that wasn't true either.

Nobody knew whether this was a conspiracy, an attempt to attack the head of our government, or something else entirely.

Those of us in the control car didn't know precisely what had happened or the status of President Ford. We did know, however, that in a situation like this the Secret Service's first objective was to get an unharmed President on Air Force One and in the air.

A routine presidential motorcade trip from the St. Francis Hotel in San Francisco to the airport was a forty-minute drive. Not this time. We made it in about twenty minutes.

As soon as our motorcade screeched to a stop alongside Air Force One, we raced up the rear stairs of the plane.

During the flight back to Andrews Air Force Base,[4] somewhere over the middle part of the United States in clear sunny skies, Air Force One unexpectedly dropped about two hundred feet. That doesn't seem like much flying at thirty-five thousand feet, but imagine that you are in an elevator on the sixth floor when, without notice, it drops to the fifth floor. Same sort of feeling.

Nobody on board was hurt, and we quickly resumed our flight toward the East Coast. "It was an air pocket" the pilot told us later

---

4 Now called Joint Base Andrews, Andrews is the home of Air Force One and is located in the Maryland suburbs of Washington, DC.

using laymen's terms. The way in which he casually explained this, I couldn't tell if he had been concerned or not. He probably was.

A number of months earlier Rumsfeld had initiated a no martini rule on board Air Force One. But after our flight stabilized, Don went forward to the President's cabin and said, "Mr. President, today you were shot at and a few minutes ago we just dropped in the sky. If ever there was a day when you deserved a martini it is today." And Don asked the military steward to bring the President a martini!

Without the quick response of a Secret Service agent in Sacramento and a random bystander trying to do the right thing in San Francisco, political history in our country could have changed dramatically in September 1975.

DAVID HUME KENNERLY,
White House photographer:

Before President Ford left the hotel that afternoon, I had checked out the crowd across the street, especially since many of them were demonstrating against the President. A feeling of dread came over me. It was the kind of sensation I'd experienced in Vietnam, like the alarming thought I'd had the day I told a driver to turn around on a deserted road outside Phnom Penh, and we avoided an ambush. It was the same sense I had when I decided against getting on a helicopter that ended up being shot down. It was a finely honed perception of self-preservation that I developed during the war that was always worth heeding.

I told Lead Secret Service Agent Ron Pontius about my premonition and to please not let the president cross the street to greet the crowd. Pontius knew my background and took me seriously. I'm sure he wouldn't have let Ford go anyway.

When President Ford walked out from under the hotel marquee,

I was on the other side of his car. He strode the short distance to the limo and waved at the people across the street. At that moment, a shot rang out, and the President winced in reaction. It's worth noting that he had been the gunnery officer on a carrier in the South Pacific during WWII and was under fire many times. He knew gunfire when he heard it.

Having been through my own share of gunfire I instantly knew what had happened and kept photographing. I then ran around to the other side of the bulletproof limo to try and take more pictures, but they had already shoved the President into the car, along with Chief of Staff Donald Rumsfeld. They kept him on the floor until they got well out of the area, and at one point, according to Rumsfeld, the President said, "C'mon Rummy, you guys get off. You're heavy!"

As the motorcade started to screech away, I barely made it into the control car. We had a wild ride to the airport, where the President was rushed up the stairs and into his compartment on Air Force One. Mrs. Ford was coming in from another event, so we waited for her. The President was understandably tense, so I broke up his dark mood by paraphrasing an old joke: "Other than that, how'd you like San Francisco, Mr. President?" He fortunately thought that was funny and relaxed a bit. (The original joke was, "Other than that, how did you like the play, Mrs. Lincoln?") Mrs. Ford arrived a few minutes later. She had not been told of what had occurred and innocently said, "How did they treat you?" We all laughed, which puzzled her, then President Ford took her hand and told her what happened.

When we got back to the White House that night, Susan Ford was there to give her dad an emotional hug. My photo of that moment captured the mood of the day.

It's a story all Americans of a certain age know only too well: The day President Ronald Reagan was shot, March 30, 1981.

Having just given a speech, the President was shot by John Hinckley Jr. outside the Washington Hilton Hotel in Washington, DC, as he was returning to his limousine. Hinckley fired six shots from a revolver, wounding the President, White House Press Secretary James Brady, Secret Service agent Tim McCarthy, and police officer Thomas Delahanty.

Reagan was seriously wounded but recovered after emergency surgery. James Brady suffered permanent brain damage and died from his injuries thirty-three years later. Delahanty was shot in the neck, causing permanent nerve damage to his left arm, which resulted in him retiring from the police force. McCarthy, who is credited with saving the President's life by stepping in front of him, was shot in the stomach but made a full recovery. Now retired, he became chief of police in Orland Park, Illinois, after he retired from the Secret Service in 1993.

Hinckley was deemed mentally ill and confined to an institution. He was released in 2016 and now lives in Virginia. He claimed the assassination attempt was to impress actress Jodie Foster.

Longtime Reagan friend and staffer Rick Ahearn was the lead advance man the day of the shooting, standing next to the President when he was shot. Rick stayed at the scene with Jim Brady until medics arrived. (The Secret Service had pushed the President into his limo and sped to George Washington University Hospital.)

Rick died in 2023, so since he cannot tell his story, a number of Reagan staffers—both those at the scene and those back at the White House—offered to tell theirs, painting a vivid picture of the day they will never forget.

JIM HOOLEY:

I was at the Hilton that day.

Secretary of Labor Raymond Donovan accompanied the President from the White House to the Hilton since it was a speech to the Building Trades unit of the AFL-CIO. And since I was then Donovan's chief of staff, Rick Ahearn suggested I be a volunteer site advance man.

I was just coming out of the presidential entrance of the Hilton, leading the staff out to the motorcade, when the shots were fired. I tried to assist Rick, who was helping Jim Brady—who was face down against a grate in the sidewalk—by helping Rick collect handkerchiefs to use as a compress. We literally were calling out, "I need handkerchiefs!" as mundane as that sounds.

I also ran back down to the holding room and picked up the WHCA phone and called the Advance Office. Marti Frucci answered, and I told her to turn on the TV and get Steve Studdert, advance director, on the phone so I could tell him what had happened.

At the time, we had no idea what the President's status was. Was he hit?

Secretary Donovan had stayed behind to meet with the labor guys but heard about what was happening and started to go up the stairs. As melodramatic as it now sounds, I stopped him and reminded him that he was in the line of succession, and we didn't know if it was a widespread attempt to decapitate the government or not.

I then went back upstairs as Rick was getting into the ambulance with Brady. I told them I had notified the office and off they went.

DAVID PROSPERI:

At that time I was an assistant press secretary, and I had accompanied the White House press pool to the President's speech at the Washington Hilton. Larry Speakes, who was deputy press secretary, was planning to accompany the President, but at the last minute, Jim Brady decided to go instead of Larry.

The President delivered his speech, and then the entourage returned to the motorcade. I moved the press pool through the hotel lobby and out the door to where the motorcade was waiting. Along the rope line that was between the hotel and the motorcade and facing the President's limo was a mixture of media and onlookers.

Judy Woodruff was the pool television reporter representing NBC. I was standing on the left side of the motorcade waiting for the President to exit the hotel. Judy came up to me and asked if I could take her up to Jim when he came out with the President, and I said yes. As the President, Jim, Mike Deaver,[5] and others walked toward the motorcade, I heard a pop, followed by five more pops. Even though I had never fired a gun, I instantly knew that those were not the sounds of balloons popping, so instinctively I ducked and pulled Judy down with me.

It seemed to me that almost immediately after those noises, the motorcade took off, leaving the press pool and other WH staffers behind. When the motorcade had moved out of the hotel area, I ran to where people were congregating and yelling. The Secret Service had already pinned Hinckley to the wall of the hotel, and ironically, several had guns drawn as if to protect him from being shot by someone else.

I saw DC police officer Thomas Delahanty down on the ground with a wound, and the same for Secret Service agent Tim McCarthy. Then I saw Rick Ahearn kneeling over Jim Brady and holding a handkerchief to Jim's forehead to stanch the bleeding. Jim was face down on the ground. Rick's handkerchief was soaked with blood.

Rick yelled something to me along the lines of whether I had a handkerchief. I did—it was a personally monogrammed handkerchief that my grandmother had given to me from her work in a linen store in Chicago. I threw my handkerchief to Rick and then turned to run into the hotel lobby to notify the White House.

5　White House Deputy Chief of Staff.

When I entered the lobby, all the coin pay phones were being used by people—my guess is that none of them knew what was going on outside mere feet away from them.

The only available phone was a credit card phone, so I pulled out my personal card and called the White House press office. Flo Taussig, one of the administrative assistants in the press office, answered the phone. I said something along the lines of, "Flo, this is David. I need to talk to Larry." Flo must have sensed something was up as she immediately got Larry on the phone. I told him that "the President has been shot at, and Jim's been hit." (I will never forget those words). Larry said something like "Got it," and immediately hung up the phone.

Years later, I was interviewed by the History Channel about the events of that day. When the broadcast aired, I was watching it with my oldest son, and after they previewed my comments, my son turned to me and said something along the lines of, "I hope you said the right things." For a moment, I panicked because I could not recall exactly what I had said to Sam Donaldson and others. Fortunately, when they showed the actual footage, I was greatly relieved by how I responded at that time.

I left the White House in February 1982 to return to my former role in the private sector. Shortly afterward I was walking on K Street when I heard a car backfire. I immediately ducked for a second or two, and then stood up, wondering if anyone had noticed.

JIM MILLER,
White House staff:

During breakfast that morning at the White House Mess, I chatted with President Reagan's press secretary, Jim Brady. Later I attended a staff meeting in the Roosevelt Room about policy priorities, and as the meeting ended and I followed Larry Speakes out, a lady opened the door to the press office across the hall and wailed, "Larry, the President has been shot at, and Jim Brady has been shot!"

Quickly, Presidential Assistant Dick Darman picked up a phone, connected to the Secret Service, and demanded a report. Within a minute, White House Chief of Staff Jim Baker arrived and also demanded answers.

"If he's OK, then why is the motorcade being diverted to George Washington Hospital?" Baker boomed. Eventually, Baker, David Gergen, and Ed Meese left the White House and joined Mike Deaver at the hospital.[6]

At that point, there was an air of gloom and concern, but no panic. All presumed the President was unhurt but that as a precaution he was going to be examined by physicians at GW. Jim Brady's condition was grave, and that depressed us all.

The staff within the White House complex continued to do their jobs, but most were preoccupied with the President's situation. Nearly all of us were in a state of shock. The last memory I have of late that evening is the lone jeep in the parking area along West Executive Avenue: Jim Brady's. I couldn't hold back the tears.

Over the next few days reports from the hospital were serious, but still upbeat, partly because of the President's skill in setting people at ease. "I hope you are all Republicans," he said to his surgeons.

"Today, we're all Republicans," responded the chief surgeon.

Several of the Reagan staffers referenced in their original essays the actions of Vice President George H. W. Bush that day. We'll let one of his staffers tell that part of the story.

---

6 David Gergen was director of White House Communications; Ed Meese was counselor to the president. He would be appointed attorney general in 1985.

CHASE UNTERMEYER,
executive assistant to Vice President Bush:

Vice President Bush was enjoying his first trip back to Texas since the inauguration. After he gave a speech to cattle raisers in Fort Worth on behalf of President Reagan's economic program, he was scheduled to fly to Austin to address a joint session of the Texas Legislature. As Air Force Two—a four-engine Boeing 707 that had been President Eisenhower's Air Force One—lifted off from Carswell Air Force Base in Fort Worth, word was flashed to the Secret Service detail on board about an attempted assassination of the President back in Washington.

The Vice President was immediately informed. It was decided to continue on to Austin but only to refuel. The speech was canceled; the plane would return to the capital.

During the flight back to Washington, two things of special note occurred.

One was the fateful statement by Secretary of State Alexander Haig (which the Vice President had watched without comment on a TV in the plane's lounge) that "I am in control here at the White House pending the Vice President's return to Washington."

The other was Bush's rejecting the advice of both the head of his Secret Service detail and his military aide that the Marine Two helicopter fly from Andrews Air Force Base to the South Lawn of the White House for security's sake.

At that point, no one knew if there was some larger plot against ranking officials. The Vice President said, "Only the President lands on the South Lawn."

Further, he was concerned that Nancy Reagan, perhaps trying to rest after a terrible day, might be disturbed by the chopper's noise. So, Marine Two flew instead to the grounds of the US Naval Observatory, where the vice-presidential mansion stands, and he traveled by motorcade to the White House.

The day ended as well as possible, with President Reagan on his way to recovery and Vice President Bush praised for his dignity and restraint in a time of grave crisis.

A much happier day for President Reagan was his now famous "Mr. Gorbachev, tear down this Wall!" speech on June 12, 1987. The speech—and that line—is widely considered one of the more iconic moments of and a turning point in the Cold War with the Soviet Union.

ANDREW LITTLEFAIR,
advancing President Reagan:

Although it was not the height of the Cold War, 1987 was still a tense period as democracy was beginning to break out in Eastern Europe and the Soviets were on their heels. President Reagan was pushing their new leader, Mikhail Gorbachev, to reform.

So he decided to head to Berlin to make a major speech.

For the advance office, it was all hands on deck. The preadvance team was led by Jim Hooley, now director of Presidential Advance, and Gary Foster, deputy director of Press Advance.[7] For the advance itself, I took the lead and was joined by Joe Brennan and Bobby Schmidt.

Jim had a keen eye for imagery and history, and the Reagan Advance Office was well known to be able to take the policies the President was trying to accomplish and turn them into well-crafted, theme-oriented events.

---

7 Preadvance teams were the advance to the advance. The job of the preadvance team was to iron out the more substantive and thornier issues of the president's trips so that when the advance team hit the ground, they hopefully had a smooth path to finishing the job.

This trip would be no exception.

The Germans were pushing for President Reagan's speech to take place at the Charlottenburg Palace, which would have been a beautiful location. But as we toured the Reichstag—the German equivalent of a parliament building—we went onto a balcony that literally overlooked the Wall. You could see guard towers with armed East German police and military.

I think it was at this moment Jim got the idea that the Wall, at the Brandenburg Gate, was the perfect location for President Reagan to confront the Soviets about freedom.

Jim warned me that it could be challenging. The Germans hadn't had a large rally in Berlin in years—and never near the Brandenburg Gate. Keep in mind that in 1987, the divided city of Berlin was located deep inside East Germany.

How to raise a crowd? Who to invite? We were receiving plenty of pushback from the State Department and the Germans.

As you might expect, the Secret Service was concerned. We would be a couple of hundred yards from East Berlin. Tensions were high. This was, after all, the time of Checkpoint Charlie and the occasional shooting of an East Berliner trying to escape to freedom in the West.

Jim and the preadvance team left us behind. Now the detailed work began. Over the next two and a half weeks, we received great support from the Americans on the ground, including Richard Burt, the US ambassador to Germany.

After a few days, it occurred to us that we could use security measures to our visual benefit. We incorporated bulletproof glass into the stage, so the Wall could be seen as the President spoke.

Crowd-building was indeed difficult. This type of event was foreign to the Germans. But we realized that West Berliners knew there was an opportunity with this event, and through radio and newspaper advertising and fifty thousand invitations mailed, we managed to build a lot of excitement.

An even more interesting phenomenon was occurring on the east side of the Wall. Each day, hundreds of German youths gathered. Every day more came. Through the grapevine, they had learned President Reagan was coming. On the day before arrival, and maybe the day of, East German police used water cannons to disperse the crowd, which numbered in the thousands. On the night before the speech, we added sound amplifiers and pointed them east so President Reagan could be heard in East Berlin.

I passed back all reports of the unrest at the Wall to the White House speechwriters. Peter Robinson, who was on point to write the speech, came to Berlin himself for a few days to survey the site. The location selected by the advance team allowed Peter to write the famous line, but it was hotly debated among Reagan's senior team at State and the National Security Council (NSC), as they thought it was too provocative. It was the President who made the final call on what he would say.

Of course, as I remember it, the trip was flawless. Huge crowds along the motorcade. An iconic picture of the President on the balcony of the Reichstag. A beaming Chancellor Helmut Kohl onstage, and thirty thousand people cheering at the Brandenburg Gate as President Reagan challenged Mikhail Gorbachev to "tear down this Wall."

Even the cynical White House press corps praised President Reagan for his confidence and boldness to speak out against Soviet tyranny in such a dramatic setting.

I was proud to have played a small role in this historic event.

At some point on Thanksgiving Day 2003, Americans were shocked to learn that as they were eating turkey and watching football, the President of the United States had secretly flown to Iraq to boost morale among the troops; eaten dinner with them; and was already on his way back home.

It was no easy feat.

GREG JENKINS,
director of advance for President Bush 43:

"We're going to do something that's never been done in the history of the presidency and you're going to help organize it. Sign this."

What I signed—in the White House Situation Room—alone with my boss, Deputy Chief of Staff Joe Hagin, was a form committing me to secrecy and elevating my security clearance to help me get the job done.

What was that job? Spirit the President into and out of Baghdad, in the middle of a war, on Thanksgiving Day 2003, without anybody knowing anything about it until it was all over.

Huh?

These days, presidents fly in and out of war zones under the cloak of secrecy all the time. But there's always a first time. This was it.

Joe told me to concoct a cover story to explain my sudden absence. The office knew I liked to fly fish, so I told my assistant that I was going bone fishing in Belize for a couple of days while everyone else was at the President's ranch in Texas. I don't know if she believed me, but she didn't ask any questions. The next day, off I went the other direction around the globe with a small band of Secret Service agents and one of the President's military aides.

Joe made it clear that if at any time word leaked that the trip was happening, it would be canceled. If word leaked while the President was in the air, they'd turn around. If word leaked while he was on the ground, they'd immediately leave. This was not a game.

Upon landing at Baghdad International Airport, we were met by some CIA officers who had made Saddam Hussein's former VIP terminal their base. They housed and fed us for the duration and provided Humvees and pickup trucks for a makeshift motorcade. On our first night, the lead agent, military aide, and I stood outside our shipping container/bunkhouse looking at the stars and figuring out our plan for the next day. Overhead, an AC-130 gunship flew by releasing chaff meant to confuse inbound missiles.[8] I asked the military aide if they were doing that for practice. "No," he said, "they don't usually do that for practice in an active war zone. A bad guy has probably locked on to them."

"So that means a bad guy is nearby with a ground-to-air missile?"

"Probably."

"Well, that's just fantastic."

The next day we headed into Baghdad to meet with the only three people in Iraq who knew about the President's upcoming visit: General Ricardo Sanchez, commander of the military Joint Forces in Iraq; Ambassador Paul Bremer; and Brian McCormack, who was an advisor to Bremer.

I ran through the schedule: The President would land just as the sun was going down, motorcade to the mess hall, give a few remarks, have Thanksgiving dinner with the troops, meet with some Iraqi leaders, and then head back home.

I asked for somebody at the airport who could make things happen. I needed to get a lot done in two days, a lot of seemingly odd things. Sanchez said that General Martin Dempsey (future Chairman of the Joint Chiefs of Staff) was running the airport and that he'd get me whatever I needed. I said that I couldn't tell him who I was, who I worked for, or why I needed what I needed and that he would almost certainly have some awkward questions.

Sanchez smiled and said, "Son, officers in my command tend not to question my orders. Tell him what you want and you'll have it." If only it were that easy in Detroit, Des Moines, and Denver.

Back at the airport, I met with Dempsey and ran through some of my immediate requirements:

---

8   In a military context, "chaff" refers to small strips of aluminum foil or other reflective material released by aircraft.

- An awful lot of jet fuel—enough for a 747—to be stored and guarded around the clock.
- The mess hall would have to be secured by some of the guys who came with me. (Yes, the Secret Service.)
- And the troops had to unload their weapons before entering the mess hall.

I cringed, waiting for an expected, "HAVE YOU LOST YOUR MIND? THIS IS A WAR ZONE! YOU WANT MY TROOPS TO UNLOAD THEIR WEAPONS?"

No such reaction was forthcoming.

The next night, the CIA put the motorcade in position as Sanchez and I stood alone on the darkening tarmac waiting for Air Force One. Security was so critical and unconventional that there was no military fighter escort for the President's plane, the most recognizable plane on earth—any escort pilot would know immediately what it was and who was on it. If word had gotten out, the jig would have been up. So Air Force One flew hundreds of miles through an active war zone unescorted—another first.

Once the President landed, we motorcaded the short distance to the mess hall where Sanchez and Bremer would introduce a surprise visitor. I stood next to the President backstage peering through the camouflage netting. It occurred to me then—too late now—that since this entire exercise was so unlikely, troops might think the President was an impersonator like Dana Carvey was to his father. Laughter wasn't the reaction we were going for.

As nervous sweat poured down my face, Bremer and Sanchez on stage asked if "there was anybody more senior than us back there." I crossed all my fingers.

The President emerged and the room went berserk. Hundreds of soldiers leaped to their feet to cheer their commander in chief.

When we were done with the mess hall, we motorcaded a few

blocks to a building on the airport grounds for the President to meet with Iraqi leaders. I am not sure when the Iraqis were informed about the visit.

President Bush is more familiar with how advance works than probably any other president, having been up close and personal for his and his father's campaigns and presidency. He asked me on the flight home what was different about this one.

"Sir, I think we may have written a new chapter for the Advance Manual tonight."

White House Deputy Chief of Staff Joe Hagin had a couple of very interesting PS's to Greg's story:

JOE HAGIN:

I don't believe that the Iraqi leadership was informed that the President of the United States was coming to visit until we were on the ground. They either had been invited to come to the Thanksgiving celebration or to meet with Bremer—or both.

Getting the press together to cover this trip was rather complicated. There were two tranches of press that made up the pool:

The first was a few members of the press contingent covering the president in Texas over the holiday.

The second was a small group of senior reporters who joined the trip in Washington when we landed at Andrews Air Force Base. We had to change planes to the second Air Force One, which was fully fueled and waiting for us, in order to have the range to make it all the way to Baghdad nonstop, which we couldn't do from Texas, so it was an opportunity to get additional reporters and a few staff, including Chief of Staff Andy Card, on board.

The Texas press group was met and briefed individually by the deputy head of advance, Steve Atkiss, and me at various locations around Crawford, Texas. They went to the meetings thinking they were meeting Steve because if they knew they were meeting with me, they would have known something was up before we had the opportunity to lay out the rules regarding secrecy.

I believe the same tactic was used to brief the Washington contingent. They went to a meeting with White House Communications Director Dan Bartlett—and found Andy Card there, too.

We told them they could tell no one where they were going: not their family or their boss, no exceptions. They also were told we were going to confiscate their cell phones.

We promised them that we would let them file their stories from Air Force One once we had cleared Iraqi air space on the way home. We also told them that they didn't have to go if they were worried about their safety, but that they needed to tell us that before we left the meeting. Lastly, we pointed out that if they violated our rules and there was a leak, there was a chance that, at best, the trip would be canceled and, at worst, we might not survive the trip.

I was pretty confident it wasn't going to leak. And it did not.

President Obama made several trips to Afghanistan, also done under the cover of secrecy.

PETER NEWELL,
advancing President Obama:

The call came from my boss, Alyssa Mastromonaco, on Thanksgiving weekend 2010: "Pack your bags. Andrews Air Force Base tomorrow. Afghanistan."

My family was told "undisclosed location, out of contact for eight days."

Secretly, I was exhilarated. An advance junkie, I envied colleagues who had planned presidential trips to the world's most dangerous regions, and now it was my turn.

Soon I was in a sleeping bag on the floor of a C-130 cargo plane, surrounded by military vehicles, MREs,[9] and a group of thirty bearded operatives—the bravest, most capable men I'd ever seen.[10] I felt unworthy of their company, yet determined to add value to this highly secretive, ambitious visit.

Our mission: President Obama's second visit as commander in chief to Afghanistan, a year after announcing the surge of thirty thousand more troops. He wanted to thank the military and civilian personnel sacrificing so much; receive an update from General David Petraeus, commander of US and NATO forces in Afghanistan; and ideally, visit a forward operating base.

We landed at Bagram Air Base and were whisked to a CIA annex, cloaked in anonymity and strictly forbidden from revealing our White House affiliation. My bunkmate, fellow advance colleague Grant Campbell, and I slept close enough to the base prison to hear the unsettling howls of Taliban prisoners each night. This was unlike any advance trip I'd ever known.

Plans shifted constantly in the volatile environment. While Air Force One safely landed in total darkness, high winds ultimately grounded the President's helicopter options, forcing the cancellation of his planned face-to-face with President Hamid Karzai in Kabul and his tour of a forward operating base.

Instead, he spent extended time making remarks to four thousand troops gathered in a Bagram hanger and a walk-around to shake hands at the tables in the Bagram Mess.

After his remarks, the President requested a visit to the Bagram

---

9 Military Ready-to-Eat meals.
10 We would tell you who these "operatives" were but then we would have to shoot you.

Hospital. Breaking the news to the medical staff minutes before his arrival, I watched their faces transform with smiles, their exhausting, emotional shifts momentarily forgotten. The energy in the hospital elevated, remaining sacred amid the grave injuries. President Obama moved slowly, deliberately, into each room. I saw his senior military aide hand him a small box as he entered to greet patients. Peeking around an open door, I realized the boxes held Purple Hearts.

In one room, a gravely injured member of the 101st Airborne lay unconscious, the only sounds the chiming of machines aiding his recovery. The doctor and military aides shared his story, and in that moment, the immense weight of this visit crashed over me.

MAJU VARGHESE,
advancing President Obama:

On Friday morning, December 14, 2012, I was at a community college in Portland, Maine, with an advance team, preparing for an upcoming presidential visit. Routine work, routine meetings, routine conversations.

Then I got the call.

It was Pete Selfridge, the White House director of advance. Our calls—even the work ones—usually started with a joke and a laugh. Not this one. He told me the trip was being pulled down and that we should notify our hosts. Something had happened in Connecticut that morning—a school shooting. I should be prepared to travel to Newtown that day to begin planning for a potential visit by the President. He didn't have many details yet but said two other team members would be joining me. More information would follow.

As we hung up, I began to catch up on the news: a shooting at Sandy Hook Elementary School. The details were still coming in but first graders were among the victims. It was worse than I could have imagined.

Twenty schoolchildren—six- and seven-year-old first graders—and six adult staff who entered Sandy Hook Elementary School that morning would never come home.

Lives were forever changed. A community was shattered. And a small town in Connecticut and its elementary school would become shorthand for tragedy after a mass shooting.

At the time, my son Evan was a first grader. That fact was just beginning to seep in. I imagine millions of parents across the country felt the same. I couldn't stop picturing Evan's face, his classroom, his friends, his teacher. The tiny desks. The artwork stapled to the bulletin boards. The small reading nook in the back of the room. The tragedy was both unthinkable and instantly personal.

I headed for Connecticut along with Stephanie Temaat and Patty Park. They were terrific advance staffers—but even better humans, the kind of colleagues you want beside you when you're doing something really hard and unprecedented. We listened to updates on the radio, each story more heartbreaking than the last.

When we arrived in Newtown, we checked into the hotel, and the lobby was swarming with advance team members from the Secret Service and the White House Military Office who had just arrived. Reporters were also checking in as the national media began to descend on the town and satellite trucks began to dot the streets. The front desk staff were polite but solemn as they handed out our keys.

We later learned that, as we arrived that evening, victims were still being recovered from the school and parents were being reunited with surviving children at the local volunteer fire station. Some parents were just getting confirmation that their children had been killed. Just under two weeks from Christmas, this small town had been turned completely upside down.

When our full team assembled on Saturday morning at the hotel, we had very little sense of when the President would arrive and what he would do. There were vigils being held in town, but our White House colleagues were working with the Governor's office and local stakeholders on which event was appropriate for a presidential visit.

It was determined that the President would attend an interfaith vigil at Newtown High School on Sunday. The families of the victims and other members of the community would be invited. Much of the logistics and planning would fall on us as local officials were dealing with more pressing matters, supporting a town that was still reeling and families that needed help.

There were trips that reminded me just how remarkable my colleagues were. This was one of them. They very deftly balanced their compassion for this community with their determination to get the work done. Michael McSwain, a member of our team, took the lead in thoughtfully setting up classroom space for the families to have time with the President. He worked closely with the Secret Service and the Connecticut State Police, who had assigned an officer to support each of the families in the aftermath of the shootings, particularly with information flow and logistics.

When I woke up on Sunday, with the President scheduled to arrive in several hours, I remember thinking about the parents of the children lost in this senseless tragedy. Could I muster up the energy and strength to attend this event if I were in their shoes? Would I want to? At that moment we weren't sure which families would choose to attend. Before we left the hotel that day, the television in the hotel restaurant had a graphic from the local news with the photos of the children killed at Sandy Hook. The light in their eyes, their smiles, their innocence. All gone in an instant. It made absolutely no sense.

The sights and sounds from that visit will stay with me forever. The look in the President's eyes when he exited the limo at the high school. He looked at me and said "This is going to be a tough one, Maju" as he entered the building. The faces of the families as they gathered at the school before meeting the President. The tears in the eyes of the White House staffers waiting in the hallway.

The President went room to room, each containing three to four families, so he could have time with each of them. Some cried, some told stories of their loved ones that brought them laughter. Some siblings of the victims posed for photos with the President. President Obama took a brief pause before entering each room, preparing himself to look those families in the eye and comfort them by following their lead as they processed this immense grief.

Then, at the vigil, President Obama addressed the community and the nation. His words were filled with empathy, sorrow, and a quiet strength. He said something that stopped me cold:

"Someone once described the joy and anxiety of parenthood as the equivalent of having your heart outside of your body all the time, walking around."

The President read the names of each of the victims. At times, after the name of a victim was read, you could hear the families cry. At one point, after a child's name was read, I heard a family member wail. It was visceral and raw. It was the sound of pain. I'll never forget it. I stood backstage with a lump in my throat.

After the President boarded Air Force One and departed, I drove back to the hotel from the airport with my Secret Service counterpart. He, too, was a father, and we both talked about our kids, their schools, our hopes, and our fears as parents. That night I packed up my things preparing to depart Connecticut the following morning. I spoke to my wife, Julie, about the day. She told me she cried watching the President's remarks and that she hugged Evan a little tighter that night. She squeezed him tight enough for both of us. Before I fell asleep that night, I broke down for the first time since the shooting.

I was going to see Evan the next day, but I don't remember ever being more eager to see him while at the same time feeling guilty about getting to go home to my child.

As promised, we are going to end with a story from 9/11.

Brian Montgomery was head of White House advance for George W. Bush and was traveling with the President that day. The main item on the President's agenda: visiting an elementary school. Brian often is asked to speak at 9/11 commemoration ceremonies, and he shares with us some of his memories of that day.

BRIAN MONTGOMERY:

It was going to be a good day.

We left the Colony Inn Resort in Sarasota, Florida, around 8:20 a.m. heading to Emma Booker Elementary School. The President was excited to get to talk to the students and to talk about one of the signature proposals of his presidency: education reform.

As the presidential motorcade arrived at the school, one of my White House colleagues, who was on his cell phone behind me, leaned forward and said an airplane had just hit the World Trade Center. When we slowed to a stop and jumped from our cars, Mark Rosenker, head of the White House Military Office, intercepted me to say that National Security Advisor Condoleezza Rice, who was back in Washington, needed to talk to the President immediately on a secure line.

Following a quick greeting with the school principal and several students, who were oblivious to what was transpiring 1,180 miles to the north, we quickly took the President to his holding room, which was equipped with a secure telephone.

After he hung up with Dr. Rice, the President ordered us to "get Dick [Cheney] on the phone ASAP."

After speaking with the Vice President, without knowing there were more hijacked planes out there ready to attack, President Bush went out to meet with the students.

And then the second plane hit the other tower.

White House Chief of Staff Andy Card immediately said: "That's it. I need to tell the President." I pointed to the door he should walk through and warned him: "You'll be walking into the camera shot."

He turned to me with an "I know" look and entered.

Here is how he described that moment—a television image that went around the world: "I walked up to the President, leaned over, and whispered into his right ear: 'A second plane hit the second tower. America is under attack.' I stood back from the President so that he couldn't ask me a question and inched my way back to the door."

The President quietly and calmly concluded his visit with the students and left the classroom. He then delivered brief remarks in the school cafeteria where more students, faculty, and some parents had gathered. He told them the news, reassured them that "terrorism against this nation will not stand," and asked for a moment of silence before quickly heading to the motorcade and Air Force One.

Even before we could get to our seats, we were rolling down the taxiway. Air Force One is a modified 747; that morning we took off like an F-18. The Air Force military aide told us we'd soon be joined by a fighter escort and an Airborne Warning and Control System (AWACS) aircraft to monitor any airborne threats.

Our first destination was the heavily guarded Strategic Air Command (SAC) center, located at Barksdale Air Force Base in Shreveport, Louisiana. As soon as we landed, Mark Rosenker and I hurried down the rear steps to get off ahead of the President.

We were met by the base commander, who resembled the George C. Scott character, General Buck Turgidson, from the Cold War–era movie *Dr. Strangelove*. He looked at the two of us and asked, "Who is in charge?"

Before we could respond, he pointed to several rows of B-52 bombers, parked wingtip to wingtip. "You see those planes? Every one of them is loaded with nukes—just tell me where you want them!"

While I had my own opinion as to where he should drop the bombs, President Bush was descending the airplane stairs, so we told the General, "You need to tell that to your commander in chief!" as we pointed to the President. And it appeared the General did as we instructed him.

(By an odd coincidence, our nation's strategic nuclear forces were participating that very day in an annual readiness exercise known as "Global Guardian." By established protocols, the B-52s were in position and ready to take off—each armed to capacity with Air Launched Cruise Missiles.)

After President Bush held several secure telephone conversations, each of us were given the opportunity to call our families, although we were not to tell them where we were.

Before departing Barksdale, President Bush delivered brief remarks to the press pool that was traveling with us. While remarks to the press pool are not unusual, that day they signaled so much more. Not only was President Bush providing more details of the attacks, he also was showing continuity of our American government. That was important for all Americans to hear and see.

Minutes later, we again took to the skies.

Next stop: Offutt Air Force Base in Omaha, Nebraska, better known as the headquarters of United States Strategic Air Command (SAC). As we motorcaded to the base, it was obvious the base was on full alert as dozens of heavily armed airmen protected our route.

We slowed to a stop in front of an office building, but instead of entering, we headed across the street to what looked like a small concrete bunker with a door. Two armed airmen waved us in, and down, down we went.

I never thought I'd see in person the SAC war-fighting center that

I had seen only in the movies, but there it was before me, many floors underground inside what resembled a small city.

After participating in secure video teleconferencing meetings with national security advisors and members of his cabinet, President Bush had finally worn down the objections of the Secret Service and Vice President Cheney, who wanted him to stay in this very safe location.

Instead, we flew back to Washington, DC, escorted by two F-16 fighter jets just off each wing tip of Air Force One. The President was determined to address the nation from the Oval Office before the day ended.

One of my colleagues leaned over and said something that none of us had considered: "We are the only airplane with civilian passengers flying within the entire United States." (Earlier in the day, all commercial air traffic in the United States had been grounded.)

As we landed at Joint Base Andrews and boarded helicopters for the White House, we could see in the distance large plumes of smoke rising from the Pentagon.

I managed to squeeze in a couple of hours of sleep at home and headed back to work around 5:30 a.m. The White House was on full alert and bustling with staff. I received a call from the deputy chief of staff advising me that the President wanted to visit the Pentagon later that day. We quickly assembled a small site survey team and headed over.

After a brief visit with Secretary of Defense Donald Rumsfeld's chief of staff, who described to us in great detail the previous day's events, we headed back to the vans for the quick drive to the opposite side of the Pentagon where the plane had plowed into the building. The van was quiet, and I suspect my colleagues were similarly contemplating what we would soon see. This crash site was the very embodiment of America's military might, now exposed as penetrable.

I was asked in a press interview weeks later to describe what I saw. It was at once physically surreal and emotionally intense.

Tents had been put up overnight for HAZMAT teams, firefighters, the FBI, ATF, clergymen, provisions, and a temporary morgue.

Dozens of FBI agents in their familiar blue jackets were combing the crash site. A massive crane was being pulled alongside the impact site. The smell of smoldering plastic, metal, wood, fuel, and worse hung heavy in the air. Teams of firemen were still going into the building looking for survivors and remains of those who tragically perished.

The oddest part of what we were witnessing was what we could not see—the airliner.

It was burrowed into three of the five rings that make up the Pentagon and had largely melted in the inferno. Fifty-nine passengers and another 125 persons perished inside the Pentagon.

After forty-five minutes we were ready to return to the White House. Unlike a normal presidential site survey where you scope out every move and prop, here we would clearly call an audible.

The Secret Service informed us where the limo would arrive and depart, and we cobbled together a loose plan on what the President should do.

Later that afternoon the limo pulled into the crash site and President Bush stepped out, surveying the scene before him.

This was going to be President Bush's longest public appearance since the prior day's events, and his presence became a rallying cry of sorts. The rescue workers were not shy in their opinions about what we should do next.

As President Bush grew closer to the impact site, he paused and stood there in silence alongside Secretary Rumsfeld.

Seconds later, several soldiers and firemen unexpectedly unveiled a large American flag just to the right of where the American Airlines 757 had pierced the Pentagon's exterior. As the flag unfurled, a wave of emotion and pride rippled throughout the assembled throng. Everyone applauded and cheered for a few moments and then grew silent once again.

After briefly speaking to the press and shaking hundreds of hands, President Bush stepped back into the limo for the ride back to the White House.

Two days later, the morning of September 14 began with a solemn ceremony at the Washington National Cathedral, followed by President Bush's much anticipated visit to Ground Zero in New York City.

That afternoon, as we helicoptered into Manhattan from McGuire Air Force Base in New Jersey where Air Force One had landed, our sense of smell was put to the test as soon as the New York skyline came into view.

Our military helicopter circled over Ground Zero for a few minutes so that we could see the horror wrought by the collapse of the Twin Towers.

Once we got to Ground Zero, there wasn't much of a detailed plan except for President Bush to greet and thank as many people as possible.

With the Secret Service as close to the President as I had ever seen, except on September 11, we moved around within the assembled crowd.

There was debris and chalky paste everywhere. Pieces of the fallen towers were strewn about as were several crushed vehicles. I especially noticed a flattened fire department vehicle that appeared to be an SUV. It, too, was covered in grime, and you could barely make out its bright red paint.

But of all the visual scenes at Ground Zero, the one I recall most was the look in the eyes of the firefighters, policemen, construction workers, and other first responders who after three days numbered in the hundreds.

Within minutes of arriving, Andy Card told Karl Rove—a senior adviser to the President—and me to find a place from which the President could speak. We headed back toward the flattened SUV, which by then had several firefighters standing atop it. It seemed sturdy enough, so I made my way back to Andy who was standing near President Bush. Within seconds Andy handed President Bush a bullhorn and we headed toward the SUV.

The firefighters saw us heading in their direction and started jumping off the vehicle, except for one man who appeared older than his colleagues. We told him to stay put. President Bush stepped onto the makeshift platform with his Secret Service detail leader right behind him.

He put his arm around the senior fireman and began to speak through the bullhorn about America and our prayers for those whose lives were lost, the workers at Ground Zero, and the families who mourn.

However, for those in the crowd, many could still not hear his remarks. In the distance, you could hear single voices yelling, "We can't hear you," and immediately President Bush responded with the now historic phrase that has since been repeated countless times:

"I can hear YOU! I can hear you! The rest of the world hears you! And the people who knocked these buildings down will hear all of us soon!"

A wave of euphoria overcame us amid the chants of "USA! USA!"

Standing on the site where the lives of close to 2,800 men, women, and children violently ended, you could not help being overcome by the emotion of the moment.

We got back in the motorcade and sat there in complete silence.

We then headed to the Javits Convention Center, where we visited with many of the rescue workers who had made their way to New York from Cincinnati, Philadelphia, Chicago, and dozens of other cities. President Bush had that magic touch that could make someone feel instantly at ease. He made each person feel special and conveyed to them they were the only person on the entire planet who for that moment in time had the attention of the President of the United States.

That trait was put to the ultimate test when we entered a small cordoned-off room within the cavernous exhibit hall. Inside were dozens of family members of policemen and firemen who were missing and presumed dead. We could hear the cries and occasional nervous laughter as each person told President Bush of their loved ones.

One woman gave President Bush the police badge of her fallen son, and he vowed to carry it with him throughout his presidency. And he did. President Bush stayed with the families for close to two hours, offering words of comfort.

When we later motorcaded back to the helicopter landing zone, we passed through an enormous crowd of well-wishers holding candles and applauding as we rolled by. After boarding the helicopters, the President asked to circle Ground Zero one more time.

He was headed for Camp David where he would meet with key members of his team and his senior military advisors throughout the weekend.

I returned home, exhausted from the most demanding week of my life. I spent September 11 with the President; visited the Pentagon crash site twice; and helped plan the National Cathedral event as well the visit to Ground Zero, where I accompanied the President.

I sat on the edge of my bed and stared at the floor. This was the first time in four days I rested. I took off my black dress shoes, which were caked in the chalky paste from Ground Zero, and a loaner FEMA jacket that I still had on from earlier that day.

Despite my best efforts over the next few days, I just could not bring myself to clean the shoes. One evening I wrapped the dirty shoes and placed them in a plastic container where they remain untouched to this day.

CHAPTER FOUR

THE PRESIDENT AND FIRST LADY GO ABROAD

*T*he world of advance gets a lot more complicated when the president and First Lady decide to head overseas.

And who better to explain why than former advance man Robert M. Gates.

Yes, that Bob Gates. Most of you know him as the former Secretary of Defense or, before that, head of the CIA.

But everybody has to start somewhere. Secretary Gates did advance for both Presidents Ford and Carter as a member of their National Security Council (NSC) teams, detailed to the White House from the CIA. He specifically participated in the preadvances, part of the team whose job it was to iron out the big problems before the advance teams hit the ground.

Sometimes it worked; sometimes it didn't.

ROBERT M. GATES,
as an advance man:

Whatever the challenges of preparing presidential travel inside the United States, they are magnified significantly when the president ventures overseas. Measures to ensure the good health and security of the president as well as access to high quality communications must be arranged. Where he sleeps and where and what he eats, sites he may visit, motorcade routes, and more all are in play—just like in the United States. However, unlike travel inside the United States, answers and solutions in each case require the cooperation and permission of the host foreign government.

Some are completely overwhelmed by the logistical demands of an American presidential visit: Some countries just don't have the infrastructure; host government bureaucracies are often slow, resistant to American requirements, or just plain incompetent; and sometimes national pride bristles at Secret Service demands that the US presidents fly only in US helicopters or ride in Secret Service limousines.

To tackle all these and many other details associated with presidential travel internationally, a "preadvance" team visits each country—time permitting—well before Air Force One departs Andrews. Consisting of thirty to forty people, the team includes representatives of the Secret Service, WHCA, presidential medical staff, support staff for Air Force One (the president's pilots often flew the preadvance team so they would be familiar with each airport), the White House press office, the State Department, and members of the NSC. Each preadvance was hectic, with different elements of the team fanning out to meet with counterparts, visit whatever hospital might be needed, meet with security and communications officials, and consult with government officials to work out preliminary agendas, ceremonial site visits, and timetables.

During the presidencies of Gerald Ford and Jimmy Carter, from 1974 to 1979, I often was the NSC staff member on preadvance trips, reporting back to national security advisors Henry Kissinger and then Brent Scowcroft under Ford, and Zbigniew Brzezinski under Carter. What follows are simply my recollections of some of the most memorable personal experiences on those advances.

My first preadvance was to prepare for President's Ford's meeting with French President Valéry Giscard d'Estaing on the French island of Martinique on December 14–16, 1974. The team was quite small, only four as I recall. Upon our arrival at the resort where the meeting would be held, we were immediately taken to a meeting with Giscard's team, led by his chief of cabinet. Still in our suits and ties, we were escorted to an open-sided cabana right on the beach. As I would later confess to Scowcroft, my notes of the meeting were both incomplete and somewhat disjointed because the cabana was in the middle of a topless beach densely populated by young women escaping the European winter. It was all very distracting.

The only substantial disagreement between the two sides was one of protocol: Giscard insisted that Ford fly to the meeting site in the French president's helicopter. The Secret Service adamantly objected, and we were at an impasse when the meeting ended. Ultimately, as usual, the Secret Service prevailed. That hiccup notwithstanding, Ford and Giscard's get-acquainted meeting went very well, focusing on Western economic problems, energy, and détente with the Soviets. The two established a strong personal relationship that would last through Ford's presidency. I never did learn, though, whether they had met in the cabana on the beach.

My second preadvance was to prepare for Ford's May 28 to June 3, 1975, trip to Europe, with visits to Brussels for a NATO Summit; Madrid, Spain; Salzburg, Austria, for a meeting with Egyptian President Anwar Sadat; and Rome and the Vatican. The preadvance visits to Brussels and Madrid were pretty cut-and-dried.

I've always thought we were lucky some of us didn't get arrested in Salzburg. The challenge there was to find a spectacular setting for the meeting between Ford and Sadat. There were many such sites, but we were dealing with an unusual problem: Sadat had a heart condition, and we were told we needed to find a castle or some such awesome place without more than three or four steps. Good luck with that. We learned about a beautiful château just outside of Salzburg in the mountains that fit the bill in every particular; indeed, it was the château where several scenes for *The Sound of Music* had been filmed.

The President's appointments secretary, one other member of the team, and I were driven to the château by a young Austrian assigned to us, whom we quickly concluded was highly anti-American. He seemed determined to kill us on the mountain road. We finally arrived in one piece—but without having called ahead to say we were coming.

Relying on my primitive recollection of college German, I knocked on the massive front door. A very stern man answered, and I tried to explain that we were looking for a place for a high-level meeting and his château seemed just right. Well, it turned out the château had been turned into a very exclusive school for girls. The stern man at the door was the headmaster. Clearly not understanding the unique opportunity we were offering, he ordered us off the property before he called the cops and proceeded to slam the door. The preadvance plainly needed its own preadvance to avoid embarrassment. A place was finally found in Salzburg for the meeting and, go figure, Sadat had no problem navigating the steps. We saw no need to share our misadventure at the château with our bosses back at the White House.

The other notable stop on that trip for the preadvance was the Vatican. Our instructions were that the President should motorcade to the Vatican and then leave by helicopter. Getting the cardinals to understand that the President would arrive and depart by different modes of transportation proved to be nearly beyond our negotiating talents. Also, with the long institutional memory of the Vatican Curia, we were told that the President could not depart the Vatican by helicopter because the last time that happened, Lyndon Johnson's helicopter rotor wash nearly destroyed the Vatican gardens. We found another landing spot, so Ford ultimately did arrive at the Vatican by car and depart by helicopter.

My one other memory of the preadvance involved the head of Ford's advance office, Red Cavaney. Red had a mop of red hair and—it was the mid-seventies—a maroon double-knit suit. I really enjoyed Cavaney, who had a great sense of humor and was also very competent. He had a disarming candor and dry wit. I'll never forget walking down the halls of the Vatican palace behind Red and Cardinal Casaroli, then Vatican secretary of state, and hearing Red, as we walked past the great art treasures on the walls, tell the cardinal, "This place is done in really nice taste." I never figured out if Red was pulling the cardinal's leg or just making an honest observation.

Ford's visit to the Holy See went a lot smoother than President Nixon's in 1970 when, in a US delegation meeting with the Pope, Secretary of Defense Mel Laird's cigar—stuffed in his suit pocket at Kissinger's insistence—reignited. According to Kissinger's memoirs, Laird began slapping his pocket to put the fire out, at which point others in the American party thought they were being cued to applaud the Pope and did so. As Henry later wrote, "Only wisdom accumulated over two millennia enabled the Vatican officials to pretend that nothing unusual was going on." The best laid plans . . .

Next up was a preadvance trip to Europe to plan for Ford's visit in July 1975 to attend the Conference on Security and Cooperation in Europe summit, to be held in Helsinki, followed by visits to Poland, Romania, and Yugoslavia.

It was my first visit to Warsaw, and I was struck by how gray and drab everything looked—and how awful the Stalinist architecture was—except for the reconstructed historic inner city, which was beautiful. While the preadvance went well, the President's visit was marred by his stumble and fall on the stairs of Air Force One as he was disembarking. I would later only half-jokingly tell the first President Bush to be cautious about visiting Poland—presidential visits there were jinxed.

Upon Nixon's arrival in Warsaw in 1972, the Polish military

band marched right under Air Force One, their lines splitting around the engine pods, and they repeated the same performance on the President's departure.

And then there was Carter's visit, when he delivered a speech to the Polish nation that, due to a mistranslation, instead of expressing his admiration and affection for Poles had him "lusting" after them.

The preadvance to Nicolae Ceaușescu's Romania was particularly stressful for me. Ceaușescu was the most internally repressive of all the dictators in Eastern Europe, tolerated and even wooed by the United States only because of his independence of the Soviet rulers in Moscow. Thus, Romania's inclusion in Ford's itinerary. Soon after our preadvance team landed in Bucharest, the local security services went out of their way to make it clear that they knew I worked for the CIA, even if on loan to the NSC. Once my official passport was in their hands, it "mysteriously disappeared." During that night, I received several ominous phone calls, asking if I had my passport and describing in rather lurid terms what might happen if I did not.

By the time our first meeting with the Romanian officials rolled around the next morning, I was livid over the harassment. So much so that our Ambassador told me that if I did not stop glaring at the Romanian security participants it might well affect the President's visit. Ultimately, the embassy had to issue me a new passport so I could leave the country. Just as the door of our presidential aircraft was closing, I waved goodbye to the Romanian security police with an uplifted middle finger. I admit that my gesture as the preadvance team departed did not set an encouraging tone for the President's subsequent visit, although it did take place without incident or difficulty.

A couple of months later, the leaders of France, Germany, Italy, Japan, the United Kingdom, and the United States agreed to hold a summit meeting in mid-November 1975, focused mainly on economic issues. This "G-6" summit would be the first of what would become annual affairs. The meeting would be held at Château Rambouillet, not too far outside Paris. The preadvance team had to deal primarily with two issues:

The first and most important was telling the French hosts that President Ford felt very strongly that Canada should be invited. The French refused to entertain that possibility, but we pushed at every turn. Since all the leaders would stay at the château, we constantly pressed our hosts about which suite would be for the Canadian Prime Minister. They became quite exasperated with us and, unsurprisingly, they ultimately prevailed. (The United States hosted the summit the following year; the Canadians were invited and afterward the meetings would be the "G-7.")

The other issue we faced was that both Secretary of State Kissinger and Treasury Secretary Bill Simon wanted to stay at the château with Ford.

Unfortunately, given the limited accommodations in the château, the space set aside for the US President and his staff had only one spare bedroom. The preadvance could see only two options: Either the two secretaries stayed overnight at a hotel in Paris and helicoptered to the meetings, or they had to share a bedroom. (The preadvance team knew that neither secretary would agree to stay in Paris while the other remained with Ford at the château.) And, by the way, the only bathroom available to the occupant(s) of the spare bedroom was down the hall and would be shared with the Japanese delegation. I confess that the image of either or both of the secretaries padding down the hall in their pajamas, toothbrush in hand, and waiting their turn for the bathroom gave rise to much hilarity among the preadvance team.

Needless to say, both stayed in Paris. A consistent challenge in preadvances for overseas travel was proximity to the president by senior staff and cabinet officials—as I'm sure was also the case for domestic travel.

The most daunting of the preadvance trips I made was in the fall of 1977 for President Carter. In twelve days, we went to Venezuela,

Brazil (both Brasilia and Rio de Janeiro), Nigeria, Liberia, Iran, India, Poland, Belgium, and France (both Paris and Normandy). Upon the strong recommendation of the preadvance team, Carter would later hit all these places but on three separate trips.

There were several memorable experiences on this "Flying Dutchman" journey. In Caracas, Carter was to meet with President Carlos Andrés Pérez. What sticks in my mind about that trip had nothing to do with official business but rather the long drive from the airport up to the capital and mile after mile of tin and cardboard shanties on both sides of the highway as far as the eye could see. I had never seen such poverty, especially in an otherwise rich country.

The challenge for the preadvance in Rio was finding a suitable private residence where Carter could stay. One of the mansions we visited (unlike Salzburg, prior arrangements had been made for us to view the building) we were told belonged to a famous plastic surgeon. On a mountainside, it had a beautiful view of the beach and ocean, a cantilevered tennis court hanging over empty space, and a mahogany-paneled, open-sided building for practicing martial arts. But it was the inside of the house that caught our attention. In one large room for entertaining there was a modest-size indoor swimming pool. When we went down a floor, we were in another space for entertaining complete with large windows in the wall of that indoor swimming pool. The housekeeper informed us that during parties, the owner arranged for young women to swim nude in the pool for the viewing pleasure of guests. Then we toured the master bedroom, the walls and ceiling all mirrored. While we on the team were much taken with the house, we were unanimous that it would not be to President Carter's taste or liking. We subsequently settled on a far more traditional mansion for his stay.

The next stop was Lagos, Nigeria. Our Air Force pilots were somewhat dismayed when, on our approach, the airport runway lights blinked off. Even so, we made a safe landing. If I thought the outskirts of Caracas were desperately poor, that memory would be eclipsed by Lagos. Poverty was everywhere. The state of the country was symbolized by the multistory Foreign Ministry, where we held all our meetings. All the elevators and the air conditioning were inoperable. Still, Nigeria was (and is) one of the most important countries in Africa, and its leader, Olusegun Obasanjo, was reform-minded and moving the country toward a closer alignment with the United States. So Carter wanted to visit, and despite a lot of logistical challenges, we figured out how to make it work.

There was a moment, though, when we on the preadvance team all thought we were going to die. My general rule of thumb when eating in developing countries on official trips is to limit intake to food and drink that is burned or brewed. On a multicountry preadvance where you are basically doing a different country every day, you cannot afford to risk being down sick for a day. So we were all very cautious.

Except when we had no choice—and that was the lunch hosted for us by the Nigerian foreign ministry. It was in a fancy restaurant where we broke every cautionary dietary rule. The lunch began with a green salad, the appetizer was shellfish, the main course was filet mignon with a mushroom sauce, and dessert was ice cream. With each course, we all looked at each other resignedly, confident we were all going to be very sick. Turned out, not one of us got so much as a stomachache. It was with great relief we headed to our next stop, Monrovia, Liberia.

Two memories remain of the visit to Liberia. The first is that the capital city was a long distance from the airport and the road was unbelievably bad. We speculated that the Secret Service might need to substitute an all-terrain or tracked vehicle for the presidential limousine. Second, the presidential palace—an all-white monstrosity—in Monrovia was just gigantic. It was then that I came up with the axiom that the poorer the country, the bigger the residence of the head of state.

The next stop was India. Upon arrival, we went to our hotel for a little down time and then proceeded to the embassy to begin working on the arrangements for the President's visit. The first order of business, however, was a warning from the embassy staff not to drink the bottled water in our hotel room refrigerators—it likely came straight out of the tap. So, for the next six hours we all—having, of course, had some of the water to drink—sat in meetings waiting for our insides to explode. Time never passed so slowly. As in Nigeria, we were all okay.

Then, it was off to the darkest stop on our seemingly endless adventure—Tehran. Demonstrations against the Shah began in October 1977, and as we motorcaded from the airport through the city to our hotel in the early evening, we could sense the tension. The streets were empty except for a significant police presence. It was just eerie.

One of our several stops the next day was the Shah's Niavaran Palace, where Carter's meetings and the state dinner were to take place. I had never seen such opulence, including mosaic fountains embedded in the floor, the surface of the water sprinkled with rose petals. At the state dinner on December 31, 1977, President Carter toasted the Shah with words he would later deeply regret: "Iran, because of the great leadership of the Shah, is an island of stability in one of the most troubled areas of the world." (A good advance or preadvance cannot prevent a presidential gaffe.) A year and two weeks later, January 16, 1979, the Shah flew into exile, then fifty-two Americans were taken hostage that November. I think that those of us who had been on the preadvance, reflecting back on the atmosphere when we were in Tehran, were not terribly surprised.

The last legs of this endless preadvance—to Warsaw, Brussels, and Paris—were uneventful and unmemorable, no doubt because the entire team was exhausted and sick. Everyone had a cold, bronchitis, or the flu, probably due in no small part to too much time on the airplane, constantly changing climates in the various countries, and no sleep.

But our last stop had a big impact on all of us: the American cemetery at Normandy, where more than nine thousand soldiers killed during D-Day and the campaign thereafter are buried. We each went our separate ways on a windy and rainy afternoon, walking down the rows of white crosses, alone in our thoughts and emotions. Finally, we were driven to Cherbourg where our plane awaited and then flew home. The preadvance from hell was over.

Many years later, when I would travel as secretary of defense to 109 countries, and if things didn't go perfectly, my recollections of my time on preadvances served as a constant reminder that something unexpected always happens or goes wrong, and it is almost never the result of an oversight or mistake of the advance team. Stuff happens! My advance people probably wondered why I rarely was perturbed when something went awry. It was because I had once upon a time had their job and remembered nearly going to jail in Salzburg.

By far the most challenging place for these fearless advance teams to do their job was Russia. Even when the Cold War ended, the Russians continued to be . . . well, difficult.

BOB GOODWIN,
advancing President Nixon:

In June 1974 1 was sent to Minsk, the official capital of Byelorussia in the Soviet Union, to plan a brief one-day visit by President and Mrs. Nixon.[1]

Nixon was to be in Minsk on July 1 to celebrate the thirtieth anniversary of the Soviet's recapture of that area from the Germans during World War II, and he would be arriving from Yalta following a meeting with Soviet leader Leonid Brezhnev.

---

1 Byelorussia is the historic name for the country Belarus.

Minsk was a dreary industrial city of about one million people situated about midway between Moscow and Warsaw.

On this occasion our advance team included a nonworking observer. He was a young US Army Major who had recently been selected to be the next army military aide for the president.

Military aide positions at the White House were/are highly sought after and very competitive. Each branch of the service has a representative assigned to the president. These are normally three-year assignments.

This young Major was due to succeed his predecessor in about a month. In fact, he didn't even bring his uniform with him. He dressed in a coat and tie like the rest of us.

Our Soviet hotel was drab at best. We ate most of our meals in the hotel's dining room. One reason for doing this was because the State Department paid for meals at our hotel and not elsewhere. Every advance person over the years liked that formula. It allowed us to pocket most of our per diem.

On our third evening, as we were walking from the dining room to the elevator, we heard loud music coming from the hotel's basement. We followed the music down the stairs and discovered a Soviet disco. We stood in the doorway and looked inside. It was packed with mostly young people. It was loud. It was noisy. Strobe lights were flashing everywhere. It had a strong odor due to the type of cleaning fluid the Soviets used on their clothing at that time. After a few minutes we left.

Several nights later I was in our office when the Major walked in. He asked, "Could you get me a bottle of scotch and a carton of cigarettes from the Control Room?"

"Sure. Be happy to. What's up?"

The Major responded, "Well, I was down at the disco tonight and I met this nice Russian girl who speaks a little English, and she has invited me to go back to her apartment to listen to some music."

I told him I didn't think that was a good idea. He said that he would be fine. She had a car and would drive him back to the hotel later.

I reiterated my opinion that I didn't think it was a good idea, but I told him since he didn't work for me, he was free to do whatever he wanted. I gave him the scotch and cigarettes.

I wanted to see his new friend in person so we both got on the elevator to the lobby. To even the most casual observer she was wearing more makeup than needed and it seemed to clash with her colorful disco outfit. He could see that I was dubious about the entire situation but off they went into the cold Soviet evening.

The next morning he showed up on time with the rest of our team for the first meeting of the day. I didn't mention his sojourn the night before and he didn't volunteer anything about it either.

All was well until several days later when some "interesting" photos of the Major and his "disco friend" showed up on the doorstep of the US Embassy in Moscow.

When we returned to the United States, he was reassigned and never served a day as a military aide at the White House.

DR. LAWRENCE MOHR,
White House physician, advancing President Reagan:

In early May 1988, I traveled to Moscow with a White House advance team a month before President Reagan's summit meeting with Mikhail Gorbachev. As White House physician, the purpose of my participation was to coordinate medical support for the President should he become sick or injured and require hospitalization while in the Soviet Union.

Following an initial meeting with officials from their Ministry of Health, a visit to the so-called Kremlin Hospital was arranged. The morning of the hospital visit, I was met by a black ZIL government limousine outside the old Rossiya Hotel. In addition to the driver, a man who wreaked of tobacco smoke sat in the right front seat and an attractive young woman sat in the back. The driver opened the large back door, I took my seat next to the woman, the door slammed shut, and off we went. The woman politely introduced herself as Tatiana and told me that she was my interpreter. I then asked her what the man in the front passenger seat did. As it turned out, he also spoke English and turned around to introduce himself. He told me that his name was Dr. Ivan Lebedev and informed me that he "used to be a cardiologist." I then asked him what he did now. He replied, "now I put on programs." Upon attempting to have a basic physician-to-physician conversation with "Dr." Lebedev, I realized that he had not been educated as a physician. I deduced that he was my KGB "handler."

Soon thereafter, Tatiana started a conversation with me. I was very surprised and dismayed to hear how much she knew about me and my career. After thanking her for her multiple compliments about my demeanor and my accomplishments, she began to ask probative questions about the health of President Reagan. She was well-versed in his medical history, which was a matter of public record, and asked me for updates about how he was doing. I repeatedly assured her that President Reagan was doing very well and was in excellent health. This was also the truth. It soon became apparent that Tatiana was more than an interpreter. She was my KGB "interrogator," as I had been warned by the Secret Service. I was careful not to say anything that could be construed as anything other than the President being in robust good health.

As we rode through the streets of Moscow, I was following our route on a map provided by the US Embassy. After several minutes it became apparent that we were not heading in the direction of the

Kremlin as I had expected. I then asked "Dr." Lebedev where we were going. "To the Kremlin Hospital," he replied.

When I asked why we were not driving toward the Kremlin, he said "because the Kremlin Hospital is not in the Kremlin." Tatiana then chimed in to explain that the official name of the hospital was the Central Clinical Hospital, but it was called the "Kremlin Hospital" because it was the hospital that provided medical care to senior government officials, communist party leaders, and their families.

At one point I assertively asked where this trio was taking me. "Dr." Lebedev then turned around and matter-of-factly said that "the hospital is not on the map." "Why not?" I asked. He replied, "for security reasons." My concern further increased on hearing this explanation. Being taken to a "Kremlin Hospital" that was not in the Kremlin and was not on the map for "security reasons" did not make me feel "warm and fuzzy."

We continued to drive away from downtown Moscow. After another thirty minutes or so, our ZIL limousine turned onto a narrow road, lined on both sides with white-barked birch trees. The road seemed to disappear into a forest. I was not surprised this road was not on my map. I had no idea where we were or where we were going, but I decided to remain calm, focused, and alert. After driving into the forest for another twenty minutes, we encountered a large metal gate that was guarded by a squad of soldiers bearing rifles and machine guns. "Dr." Lebedev got out of the limo and talked to the guards. After a brief conversation, he returned, the guards opened the gate, and we continued.

We came upon a large clearing containing multiple large buildings. We pulled up to the main hospital and entered the building through a door that led to an elevator. The elevator doors opened, and I was ushered to an ornate couch inside the elevator. I sat down and we ascended slowly for several minutes. The elevator doors opened to a large, opulently furnished room. I was greeted by several physicians wearing green scrubs and starched white coats. We exchanged pleasantries, as translated by Tatiana, and sat down to partake of small pastries and tea.

A few minutes later I was told that it was time to take a tour of the hospital. I was also told I would have to change into hospital attire before taking the tour. Well, I was not about to take my clothes off and was very assertive in refusing to do so. We negotiated this matter for several minutes. I eventually agreed to put hospital scrubs and a large white coat over the suit that I wore that day. I felt very hot in this bulky outfit and am sure that I looked ridiculous. However, there was no way that I was going to leave my clothing unattended in a Soviet Union government facility. Once I was appropriately attired, my physician hosts proceeded to lead me on a hospital tour, accompanied by "Dr." Lebedev and Tatiana.

My tour began in the intensive care unit, which was staffed with two nurses per bed and equipped with the most advanced patient monitoring devices. There was a major glaring deficiency, however. There were no patients in the unit. We then toured a state-of-the-art suite of operating rooms. However, there were no patients undergoing surgery. The radiology department contained the most modern Western imaging devices. Once again, there were no patients getting imaging studies. I had never seen anything like this before. I was touring a modern, well-staffed, state-of-the-art hospital and had yet to see a patient. It became apparent that my hospital tour was a carefully orchestrated "dog and pony show" that was designed to impress me with medical equipment while preventing me from observing the way in which the equipment was used to care for patients. This did not inspire confidence in the ability of this hospital to provide top-notch medical care to the President of the United States should he become ill or injured while visiting the Soviet Union. I decided that should the President require hospitalization while visiting the Soviet Union, it would be best to get him stabilized on Air Force One and fly to a US military hospital in Germany as quickly as possible.

LUCY LAMB,
advancing President Bush 41:

In July 1991, the call came into the advance office that officials from the United States and the Soviet Union had agreed on a date for President Bush and President Gorbachev to sign the historic Strategic Arms Reduction Treaty, known as START. The summit would take place in Moscow in less than two weeks.

The director of White House advance told me to pack my bags: "You are leaving for Istanbul, Turkey, tomorrow."

Why Istanbul? you might ask. Because President Bush was already overseas on another foreign trip, and we needed to fly to Istanbul to pick up our remaining team. We hung out in Turkey for a few days, becoming part of the presidential motorcade to the airport on July 22. The motorcade, with over seventy-five vehicles, made its way along the twenty-mile route, packed with people hoping to catch a glimpse of the American president. One amusing note: During the departure ceremony, Prime Minister Süleyman Demirel of Turkey was knocked off his feet by the jet engine blast from Air Force One.

Once Air Force One was in the air, our advance team boarded another air force jet, along with a Soviet official sent to accompany us on our flight as a navigator (or to monitor our every move). I found out later that our USAF plane was not kept in Moscow for security reasons. The pilots flew the airplane to Helsinki, Finland, and would return to pick us up.

Another security note: The Secret Service told us to inspect our hotel room for listening devices; and yes, a bug was found in one of our rooms.

Over the next week, our team would visit all of the various sites multiple times to determine the logistics of President Bush's visit: the US Embassy; Spaso House, the US ambassador's residence; the Ministry of Foreign Affairs Press Center, which would be the site for a joint press conference; Mezh Hotel, site of the International Press Center; the Radisson Hotel, site of the Soviet Businessmen's Breakfast; the Moscow Institute of International Studies; and, of course, the Kremlin.

The countdown was on. President Bush's arrival date was Monday, July 29; the treaty ceremony was scheduled for Wednesday, July 31.

President Bush would also visit Kiev, Ukraine, on this trip. So we had to squeeze in a day trip to Kiev to map out the details for this portion of the official visit.

On Tuesday, July 23, our advance team made our first visit to the Kremlin. It was surreal to be allowed inside the inner sanctums. We were given a tour of the Hall of St. George, St. Catherine Hall, the Palace of Facets (built in 1491 with religious murals covering all of the walls), and Vladimir Hall, where Ivan the Great had a bedroom off to one side. Vladimir Hall is where Presidents Bush and Gorbachev would sign the treaty.

The Kremlin made the White House seem plain and ordinary.

Advance team member Meghan O'Neill and I were tasked with site advance at the Kremlin for the state dinner. The KGB agents would not let us inside despite showing them our official credentials. What are two girls to do in this situation? We found an unlocked and unmanned door and snuck up a back staircase. We hid in St. George Hall until closer to the start of the state dinner. We were envisioning years of hard labor or the front page of the newspaper if the security breach was discovered. Thankfully, it was not.

KELLEY GANNON,
doing press advance for President Bush 41:

It was late December 1992. President Bush had lost to Bill Clinton, and I was still suffering from postelection blues when I got a call: President Bush was going to Moscow to sign a START II treaty agreement with Russian President Boris Yeltsin, and I was to be the press lead for the trip.

When the team arrived at Joint Base Andrews, we learned even before departure that President Yeltsin wanted the treaty-signing event to be held in the small, then-unknown town of Sochi (yes, the town that would host the 2014 Winter Olympics).

Sochi had a small airport and no facilities large enough to accommodate the approximately ten US aircraft and five Russian planes that would be flying in for the event.

After meeting with government officials in Moscow, the Russian leaders insisted we visit Sochi. Bill Sittmann, executive secretary of the NSC, agreed. He told us everyone would fly to Sochi, but he would do the walk-through alone with the Russians. Once we were back in Moscow, Sittmann planned to inform the White House senior staff and Russian officials that it would be impossible to hold the signing event in Sochi.

So off we went to Sochi on New Year's Eve 1992. We landed and sat on the tarmac all day while Bill conducted the walk-throughs.

After a long day, we were ready to head back to Moscow, but the airport at Sochi did not have the runway crew or deicing capabilities to accommodate our plane, much less the many aircraft flying in for the signing. After two failed takeoff attempts, we finally made it off the ground.

Our pilot flew over Red Square during New Year's Eve fireworks to celebrate the New Year and for getting back safely. Before getting back to the hotel I bought a hat from a kid in the middle of Red Square, I was so cold. I still have it today.

Normally, a foreign advance trip takes two weeks to prepare. We had two days to create a press office and filing center,[2] negotiate press coverage, and plan and accommodate pool movements—the list went on.

Where did the signing ceremony take place? At the Kremlin, not in Sochi. Bill Sittmann won the day. In Russia, that was never an easy feat.

CAPRICIA MARSHALL,
special assistant to First Lady Hillary Clinton:

President and Mrs. Clinton traveled so extensively they often brought Chelsea with them on foreign trips. I was entrusted to manage Chelsea's logistics. The First Lady knew that even if her daughter's movements were "off the record," nothing was *really* off the record and that she would be monitored by the press and others when traveling separately from her parents. The visits to museums and most cultural locations—which Chelsea loved—were exciting but also brought a lot of attention. Security and staffing were necessary.

One of my favorite trips was to Russia. Staying in the Kremlin was extraordinary,[3] and walking the streets and visiting St. Petersburg Square was breathtaking.

This was certainly a big visit for the administration as it was President Clinton's first trip to Russia to meet with President Yeltsin.

---

2 When the press travels with the president, one of the advance team's responsibilities is to set up a press filing center—usually located in a hotel ballroom or somewhere at the airport—where the press can work and file their stories.

3 If ever there was a sign that the Cold War had ended, the fact that the President and his family stayed at the Kremlin instead of Spaso House would be one.

But this trip was unique not because of the geopolitics of the day or the exciting schedule that the Yeltsins proposed for Chelsea—it was because of what happened on our departure from the Kremlin.

Departures from a historic government building like the Kremlin present their own challenges. Getting in touch with our team was nearly impossible. Our rooms were very remote; our flip-phones and pagers often didn't work; and every time I picked up my room phone to call other staff rooms, a person would answer with a loud "Hahloow," and that was the end of his English.

Hence, if you wanted to find out any new information, you needed to run through the halls, which had a lot of Russian security, to find the operations hub or anyone from our delegation with information.

On departure morning, the Clintons were scheduled to meet with President and Mrs. Yeltsin for a formal farewell. Chelsea was not required to attend. After speaking with the trip directors for *both* the President and the First Lady, as well with the Secret Service, it was decided that Chelsea should wait at a designated door, where the motorcade would pause for her and the rest of us to jump in the motorcade. This would allow her to miss the open press departure that was planned for her parents. (The Clintons routinely tried to shield her from press coverage.)

At the appointed time, Chelsea, myself, a Secret Service agent, and his Russian counterpart, along with the President's valet—a wonderful man named Lito Bautista who had a mound of the First Family's luggage—stood on the walkway outside the designated doorway awaiting the motorcade's arrival. The motorcade approached, and the Beast limousine with the President and Mrs. Clinton came and then . . . went.

I thought, Huh? That's odd. Perhaps they want Chelsea to ride in the staff van with me? Several cars and vans later the staff van approached. It came and went. Then Staff 2 whizzed by. We started to wave our arms to get someone's attention because it was now crystal clear that the motorcade was *not* stopping!

We finally saw the taillights of the last Russian police vehicle and turned and looked at each other in amazement. What just happened?! How could they not stop for us? How did no one see us?

As I mentioned, I had no communications tools; our Secret Service agent had no communications with his team; and for reasons I still am unclear about, our assigned Russian security had no communications with her team either.

All heads swung to look at me: What do we do?!

I spotted a truck that was not far away. We needed a vehicle that was large enough to transport all of the luggage, and this was a laundry truck. I mimed to our Russian security—who spoke very limited English—that we needed to go to the airport and we needed that truck. She got it, and quickly and very fervently spoke to the driver. He agreed to help. Both agents gave the truck a hard review before we started to load the luggage, after which we boarded, too. Our agent gave me a look that said it all: Really?! This is the plan?! I shrugged and thought this is very likely my last day on the job.

Our Russian security person was amazing. She pushed the driver to speed down the roadways, and once we arrived at the private gate of the airport, she convinced the airport guard—again in a very stern, commanding voice—to open the gate!

A few hundred yards ahead was the end of the President's motorcade. The driver pulled up right behind the last police vehicle; the officers were quite alarmed by our presence. They halted us with loud voices and gestures to stop and pull away. Our wonderful Secret Service agent and Russian security again came to the rescue. She immediately conveyed who she had with her to her counterparts, and our agent was finally able to communicate with the other agents about who he had in the truck.

We were given permission to move close enough for the stewards to begin to unload the luggage from the truck and onto the plane but were still quite a distance from where Chelsea's parents were bidding final farewells to the protocol line of dignitaries. Chelsea, who was patient and calm—a real champ—throughout this hysterical journey, made her way to the bottom of the staircase, with the rest of us directly behind, and waited for her parents to board.

White House staff almost never gets the opportunity to one-up their boss when things go awry—but the President's daughter can! When her parents arrived at the stairs to board Air Force One, Chelsea stood in her parents' path with a quizzical face, hands on hips, and said, "Uh, did you forget something?"

THÉRÉSE BURCH,
advancing President Bush 43 and First Lady Laura Bush:

In May 2002, during a state visit to Russia, Vladimir Putin invited President George W. and First Lady Laura Bush to spend the night at Novo-Ogarevo, which is similar to our Camp David. The visit didn't go as smoothly as the President and Mrs. Bush thought it would.

I was the overnight staff person for the visit, so I went with a Secret Service agent to meet with President Putin's staff and do a walk-through of the residence. They were very accommodating and even offered me a coat of President Putin's because they thought I would be cold walking the grounds. We then went to a guesthouse where the senior staff would stay, and they offered me and the Secret Service agent candy and told us we could relax in the house until the arrival of the President and Mrs. Bush.

Something just didn't feel right, so I asked the agent if he thought we should go to the arrival site. But the Russians wouldn't let us and said we had to wait there. So I called Brian Montgomery, head of advance for 43 and who was in the motorcade, and told him the situation and suggested they delay arrival until we could figure out what was happening.

We figured out that Putin was planning to take the President fishing and didn't want us to know because he was afraid we would not let it happen. The motorcade arrived and they closed the gate after the spare limo, leaving the senior staff including Secretary of State Colin Powell outside. (Apparently this move was in retaliation for how many Russian cars had been allowed—or not allowed—inside the gate when Putin visited President Bush at his ranch.)

We had to negotiate one car at a time to get everyone through the gate. At one point I went to find Condoleezza Rice, who was then the National Security Advisor and fluent in Russian, to help me negotiate the entry of the President's valet, who had the President's bags.

The senior staff later arrived at the main house for the planned dinner, and President Bush asked how they were all doing. Everyone smiled and said "great." The President had no idea that his staff and security and Putin's staff and security had just engaged in an all-out battle. At the end of the day, that's exactly the goal of every advance person.

We will end the Soviet-Russian series with a story about the fact it might have been the Americans who were misbehaving.

GENE GIBBONS,
Reuters News Agency's White House correspondent:

I can't personally vouch for the authenticity of this story since I wasn't there, and the supposed participants are no longer with us. But . . .

The story is legendary, so it must be told. It involves a White House advance team that was in Moscow to lay the groundwork for the historic May 1972 summit between President Richard Nixon and Soviet President Leonid Brezhnev.

After a long day's work, members of the team went out for dinner during which copious amounts of vodka were consumed. When they returned to their hotel, it seemed like a good idea to go to somebody's room for a nightcap. It didn't take long for speculation to start about where and how the KGB was listening in, and a search began for the electronic bug everyone was sure was hidden somewhere.

There was nothing behind the mirror, or under the cushions or any of the chairs. Then someone pulled up the rug and there, cut into an indentation in the floor, was a nest of wires surrounding a large nut and bolt.

"Aha, gotcha!" said the discoverer, who began to unscrew the device. Suddenly there was a large crash as a glass chandelier fell to the floor of the ballroom below . . .

Advancing France could also be difficult . . .

PAUL COSTELLO,
advancing President Carter:

The Élysée Palace could be very difficult.[4] I'm sure the French would say the same about the White House.

I was part of the advance team for President Carter's second overseas trip in December 1977 and January 1978. I was the lead advance person for press on the Paris team. My job was choosing the best coverage and camera shots that would showcase President Carter.

---

4 The Élysée Palace is the official residence of the president of France.

The Élysée Palace assigned one of their spokespeople, Evelyne Richard, to be my counterpoint and to walk me through the places where President Carter would be with French President Giscard d'Estaing. The sites were many: Élysée Palace, a walk down the Champs Élysée, a state dinner at Versailles, a speech at a convention center, and a trip to Normandy to commemorate the D-Day invasion.

I'm not sure the French had ever dealt with the modern American presidential trip requests for rope lines, press risers, flatbed trucks, and press pools. As my many requests grew, I think Ms. Richard wished I would just go away.

But I was determined.

One memorable example: The two presidents were to walk down the famous French boulevard, Champs Élysée, to the Arc de Triomphe, one of the most venerable monuments in France, honoring those who fought and died during the French Revolution and the Napoleonic Wars. To me, this would be the most important photograph of the visit in Paris, and I wanted to make sure cameras (broadcast and still) could capture the two presidents with the monuments at their backs. We need a flatbed truck, I told my counterpoint. Now Evelyn was quite an elegant woman—I don't know what designer she wore, but for sure, it was top drawer. A flatbed truck on the Champs Élysée horrified her, and I was told, "NON."

As we proceeded to all of the other sites, I kept on coming back to the flatbed truck on the Champs Élysée. Finally, I pleaded, "How are we going to have the two presidents on the cover of *Time* magazine if we don't have a flatbed truck and give the press the best elevated shot?" I don't know if that convinced her or if it was my persistent annoying American behavior, but we got a flatbed truck.

One week later? Carter and Giscard appeared on the cover of *Time* with the Arc de Triomphe in the background. Score one for press advance.

PEGGY DOOLEY,
White House speech researcher for President Bush 41:

In July 1989, France was celebrating not only its bicentennial but also was hosting the annual G-7 Economic Summit, inviting world leaders to share in its landmark anniversary.

Fireworks. Parades. Opening of a new opera house. Excitement was high.

I was very lucky to be part of the preadvance team to help put all the plans in place, and then came home to help write one of the President's speeches for the festivities.

It was a heady time. The President and First Lady made stops in Poland and Hungary en route to Paris, where the forces of democracy were bubbling and the communist hold on power was dwindling. (The Berlin Wall would fall only months later.) It was in this spirit of "fraternity, equality, and liberty" that President Bush decided to hand over the Key to the Bastille to French President François Mitterrand in a small ceremony at the Élysée Palace.[5]

The Key to the Bastille, you ask? How did that get into America's hands? Good question.

The Marquis de Lafayette, the young Frenchman who served under George Washington in the American Revolution and then went home to play a leading role in the early days of the French Revolution, gave the key to Washington as a gift, a mark of the two nations' bond in liberty. It had been on display at Mount Vernon, Washington's beloved Virginia home, for many years.

Enter the Mount Vernon Ladies' Association. The Holders of the Key.

---

5 The Bastille was a medieval fortress in Paris used as a prison. Many consider the storming of the Bastille on July 14, 1789, as the beginning of the French Revolution.

On the preadvance I visited the room where the ceremony was to take place, noting interesting aspects of the setting and other pertinent details. Then, back in DC, as part of my research for the speechwriter who was to write the President's brief but very friendly and meaningful remarks, I spoke to the Mount Vernon Ladies' Association.

I don't remember who I spoke with but I do remember the chill. There was none of the usual muted delight that would greet me when I would start a call with, "Hello, I'm calling from White House speechwriting office." No sense of wanting to be helpful. None. There was only one word that came to mind: difficult. This lady was a pill.

But we deal with all kinds, right? We prepared the remarks. The President went off to Paris. The time for the Key to the Bastille ceremony arrived. And another word comes to mind: hijacked. The head of the Mount Vernon Ladies' Association hijacked President Bush's ceremony.

Eugenia Seamans was her name. Not the name of someone you'd want to mess with, is it? And apparently the President did not. The plan was for Eugenia to give a brief introduction of the President, who would then step forward to make *his* brief remarks before handing over the key. Eugenia, however, took things into her own hands. Literally. She gave her brief remarks then presented the key to President Mitterrand. She cut out the middleman, so to speak—the middleman being the President of the United States.

Today the key is back at Mount Vernon, and has been for a while. Bicentennials may come and go, but the Mount Vernon Ladies' Association's claim to the key (apparently) is forever!

One of the challenges of foreign trips was protocol, including who arrived first; who arrived last; who stood where, especially in photos. One rule of thumb: Don't arrive before your host.

RUSS CANCILLA,
military aide to President Bush 41:

During the summer of 1991, I was the military aide responsible for accompanying President Bush to France so that he could present the Legion of Merit, Degree of Chief Commander to French General Michel Roquejeoffre, commander in chief of the Daguet Rapid Action Force during Operations Desert Shield and Desert Storm.

I was aboard Marine One with the President as we made the flight from Charles De Gaulle airport to Rambouillet, France, the location of the award ceremony. When we were approximately ten minutes from the ceremony site, I listened in my earpiece to the Secret Service and advance folks as they provided updates of the activities on the ground. It was being reported that President Mitterrand had not yet arrived at the ceremonial location. When I inquired about the delay, no one had an answer about how long it would be before our host's arrival.

I decided to switch to the Marine One pilot's frequency to ask the pilots to stay out of range of the event site and remain in the air. They agreed to circle and delay our landing. Given President Bush had a zillion hours of flying time, he quickly detected we were not making the usual approach for landing. I could see the puzzled look on his face, and before long he asked, "What is going on, Russ?" I looked at him and told him that since President Mitterrand had not yet arrived at the event site, I didn't think it was appropriate to land our President if the host was not yet present. President Bush looked at me, winked, and smiled. A few moments later, we made our final approach and Marine One landed. President Mitterrand was there to greet President Bush, and the event was carried off without a hitch.

Here are some "around the world" stories, starting with a Secret Service agent with whom Manuel Noriega was obsessed.

BARBARA RIGGS,
advancing President Carter:

Many people have asked me over the years what was the most frightening event that happened in my thirty-one-year career with the Secret Service.

It was not an incident but a person, a Panamanian strongman by the name of Manuel Antonio Noriega.

First, a little history lesson:

When President Teddy Roosevelt oversaw the building of the Panama Canal in the early 1900s, the Isthmus of Panama was then part of Colombia. Colombia refused to ratify a treaty granting the United States use of the territory in exchange for financial compensation. In response, President Roosevelt supported a Panamanian movement to secede from Colombia and declare independence. In November 1903, the United States recognized the Republic of Panama and quickly proceeded to sign a treaty with Panama granting the United States exclusive and permanent possession of the Panama Canal Zone.

The canal opened on August 15, 1914, and the right of the United States to control and operate the canal remained unchanged until the 1970s.

Many Panamanians considered the original treaty of 1903 illegitimate from its inception, leading to ongoing tensions between the United States and Panama for most of the twentieth century. Several presidents tried to negotiate better terms with the Panamanian government but with no success.

President Carter ultimately negotiated two treaties that would (1) give the United States the right to defend the canal in perpetuity, and (2) relinquish the Canal Zone to Panama in 1979, and the entire operation of the canal by the end of 1999.

President Carter accepted an invitation from General Omar

Torrijos to visit Panama in June 1978 to officially sign the protocols confirming the treaties.

The treaty and presidential trip to Panama were very controversial, both in the United States and Panama. In the Unites States, many were opposed to relinquishing a significant military and economic possession. In Panama, nationalists believed the canal treaties still gave too much control to the United States.

This was the political environment the White House and Secret Service advance teams faced when we landed in Panama two weeks ahead of the President's visit.

I was twenty-six years old and had been an agent for less than four years.

I had only been assigned to the Secret Service's Intelligence Division (ID) for about four months. I was quite naive and uneducated on how to deal with authoritarian regimes, strongmen, and dictators.

I was assigned to this trip in a training capacity and because I was fluent in Spanish.

The Panamanian intelligence chief, in charge of coordinating the presidential visit to Panama—not just for the intelligence coordinators but for the entire Secret Service and White House advance teams: Lieutenant Colonel Manuel Noriega.

Noriega had risen through the ranks of the Panamanian National Guard through his close and loyal relationship with his senior officer and boss, General Torrijos. In 1968, Noriega was instrumental in assisting Torrijos mount a successful coup and take control of the country. Noriega was known to carry out the dirty work for Torrijos, including intimidation, harassment, beatings, murder/assassination, rape, and bombings. He was suspected of coordinating bombings against US interests in the Canal Zone.

In short, he was one bad hombre.

We also learned Noriega was both an ally and nemesis for the US government. Even though the United States knew he engaged in drug smuggling and other illicit activities, the CIA placed him on their payroll, considering him an asset because he provided information on the Cuban government. (Later, the United States learned he was also selling information to the Cubans about US activities, serving as a "double agent.")

I was warned by the CIA before I left for Panama that Noriega was a notorious womanizer who loved blond, blue-eyed, young women, so to take care.

In our first meeting, Noriega took an immediate interest in me. The CIA briefers were not wrong about his instant attraction to blonds. And he liked that I spoke Spanish.

The CIA took note of Noriega's interest in me, and that he was meeting with me in offices they had never been in. They wanted access to these locations, and they wanted to assign a CIA officer to serve as my interpreter when I met with Noriega to access these different venues. I flatly refused as I explained he already knew I spoke Spanish.

As standard operating procedure, the CIA was eavesdropping on Noriega's communications. This was a main source of our intelligence information regarding Panamanian thinking and operations. (The CIA informed me that Noriega had been discussing me.) And Noriega's intelligence service was doing the same against the US government, including the US advance team communications.

I soon realized his men were following me in and around Panama City, and a Panamanian man had been posted on a balcony in close vicinity to my hotel room. I complained about this to one of my colleagues during a call to headquarters and soon the person was gone. That confirmed what I already suspected—that my phones or hotel room, or both, were tapped. But that did not stop his men surveilling me when I was out and about in Panama City.

The first weekend in the country the American advance teams hosted a poolside picnic at the Hotel Panama for our Panamanian counterparts. Noriega attended with two of his aides, Captain Moises Cortizo, a West Point graduate, and Captain Luis del Cid, known as Lino, who I soon learned was Noriega's henchman. On several occasions throughout the evening, Cortizo told me Noriega would like to take me dancing at a discotheque he owned called Numero Uno. I ignored this, but as the evening ended, he mentioned it once again more forcefully.

Everything the advance team requested in Panama for the President's visit had to be approved by Noriega, so I feared my declining would embarrass and anger him. So, I made a plea to fellow agent Pat Miller, who was lead advance for the Secret Service, to accompany me as I did not feel comfortable going alone. Ultimately, several of the USSS and WH advance team members joined the entourage going to Numero Uno. My thinking was safety in numbers.

Driving to and arriving at Numero Uno with Noriega resembled a presidential movement. There was no stopping at red lights or intersections, and the club manager met us curbside and escorted the Colonel and his guests to a seating area on a balcony overlooking the main dance floor and bar. The place was packed, and I was thinking some patrons must have been hurriedly evacuated from this area when the staff learned "the boss" was en route.

Not long after we were seated, several very attractive women appeared and made advances toward my male colleagues. Noriega invited me to dance. As I was departing the balcony on his arm I whispered to Pat Miller, "If you leave me, I will kill you."

Pat himself was under siege by a woman, Vicki Amado, who would later in 1989 become famous as the mistress with whom Noriega allegedly went into hiding when the US 89th Airborne was searching for him after invading Panama. This proved to be a false rumor, but she indeed was his mistress at the time.

Panama is in the tropics, and it was June. The weather was hot and humid. Everyone dancing generated a lot of sweat. While I was dancing with Noriega, he was pressing his sweaty body against mine, with his face near my bosom. Simultaneously, he was rubbing his legs against mine. It was *gross*, plain and simple.

The Panamanians mockingly referred to Noriega as "La Cara de Pina-Pineapple Face" because his face was severely pockmarked. After being up close and personal with the man, I can attest the moniker is befitting. He was one ugly man. Throughout our dance sets, I kept saying to myself, "Barb, this is for God and country . . . for God and country," because he was quite aggressively pushing his body against mine.

Pat Miller kept his word and stayed put on the balcony. It seemed Noriega was trying to separate me from my colleagues by distracting them with honeypots, but his ploy failed. He offered to drive me to my hotel, but I was determined to leave with my colleagues, which I did. Knowing his history of raping women, I was scared to death to be left alone with him.

As the President's visit approached, and as predicted by CIA analysts, huge demonstrations and riots broke out throughout Panama. Anti-American sentiment ran high, primarily because by treaty agreement the United States retained the right to defend the canal in perpetuity. The University of Panama campus was near our hotel, and every night we could hear constant gunfire.

A few days before the President's arrival, *The Washington Post* carried the headline, "Panama in State of Anarchy on Eve of President's Visit," or something to that effect. *Post* columnist Sally Quinn followed with an article describing the violence and suggesting the President should not make the trip.

I was out jogging one morning when a van pulled up alongside me. Noriega's lackey, Lino, asked if I could accompany him as the "Colonel wants to talk to you." I resisted a bit because I was in jogging attire and did not think it appropriate to meet with Noriega attired as such. But Lino insisted, so I got into a van, which in effect was an arsenal. There were several AK-47s hanging on the van's walls, plus other sundry firearms. These guys were ready for combat. As we pulled away from the curb, a hand grenade rolled across the floor in front of my feet.

At the Panama City airport, the Panamanian military was holding a dress rehearsal in preparation for the state arrival ceremony for President Carter.

I was driven to a building at the airport and escorted into a room, where I was confronted by not only Colonel Noriega, but General Torrijos.

Holy crow, I was feeling out of my depth and in diplomatic hot water.

Torrijos, who appeared drunk, very visibly checked me out from head to toe, a virtual undressing for a very uncomfortable minute or two as I stood there in my jogging shorts. He then launched into a tirade about *The Washington Post* headline and Sally Quinn and her article:

How could the US government allow such an article to be written?

What was the United States doing about Sally Quinn?

Was the President canceling the trip?

I answered him in Spanish and told him:

In the United States we respect the free press, so the news media could write what they pleased.

As far as I knew the President was still scheduled to make the trip.

I explained to him I was a US Secret Service agent, not involved in foreign policy decisions, and that he should address his remarks to the US Ambassador.

He had calmed down somewhat by the time I finished answering his questions. Noriega never said a word. Once I was "excused," I had the Panamanian driver drop me at the US Embassy so I could immediately report to the Ambassador this most unusual encounter with Panama's "Maximum Ruler."

The CIA reported to me they had intercepted Noriega directing his men to "tráigame la rubia" ("bring me the blond"), prior to them scooping me off the street. Why did they not give me a heads-up?

Those were the days of no cell phones, and I was out for a run, so they did not know where to locate me.

As the day of the President's arrival approached, the Panamanian government increased its enforcement on opposing groups that had been protesting the President's visit. After a gun battle on the campus of the University of Panama left two dead and dozens injured the night before the visit, the government shut down the university and other institutions throughout the city. The spokesperson for the Panamanian government announced the authorities would not tolerate any further opposition efforts to disrupt President Carter's visit.

The President arrived on June 16, 1978, for a twenty-three-hour visit. The visit included signing the treaties at the New Panama Coliseum; giving a speech in front of hundreds of thousands of Panamanians at the Cinco de Mayo Plaza; and visiting the canal and US civilians and military in the Canal Zone.

The usual custom after a president's visit is for the US Embassy to hold a "wheels up" party to thank the US advance team members, embassy staff, and host country counterparts. As I was departing the Panamanian Command Post after the President's departure, Lino advised me Colonel Noriega would like to escort me to the Ambassador's party that evening. I replied that I was exhausted, and my plan was to take a nap and pack as I was scheduled to depart early the next morning for Guatemala. I told Lino to relay to the Colonel I would see him at the embassy later that evening, but I did not know what time I would arrive.

Later that evening, as I was walking out through the lobby of the hotel, Lino approached me and told me Colonel Noriega was waiting for me in his vehicle in the hotel parking lot. Are you kidding me? I did not know how long he had been waiting, but I did not have a good excuse not to go with him, so I arrived at the US Embassy on the arm of Lt. Colonel Manuel Noriega. The Ambassador greeted us, and I quickly passed Noriega off to him.

The next morning I could not get to the airport and out of Panama fast enough.

Editors' note: *Noriega seized power in 1983 and ruled like the brutal dictator he was, including harassing American military living in the Canal Zone. On December 20, 1989, President George H. W. Bush launched Operation Just Cause, sending twenty thousand troops into Panama to oust Noriega. He surrendered on January 3, 1990, and died in a Panamanian prison in 2017 at the age of eighty-three.*

PAUL COSTELLO,
advancing President Carter:

I was lead press advance for President Carter's trip to Lagos, Nigeria, in 1978. Among his events would be a visit to Tin Can Island. I arranged for a boat for the press pool, which would head out before the President. But when we got to the dock, our boat was nowhere to be found. There was a Nigerian press boat sitting there, and I told the pool to hurry up and get on. The engineer didn't know who belonged on the boat, so I told him to take off. As we were pulling out, the Nigerian press came running down to the dock, screaming, "That's our boat. That's our boat." All I could yell back was, "Sorry."

WENDY WEBER FINK,
advancing First Lady Nancy Reagan:

This is a story about how we lied to the Pope when the First Lady paid a visit to the Vatican while the President was attending the G-7 meeting in Bonn, Germany.

Vatican Security was built on the basis that the guests of the Pope would honor the Vatican's rules, and so it did not use background checks or magnetometers to screen the guests. After all, who would lie to the Pope?

Oh, and Secret Service agents were not allowed.

So we made two agents, including the Director of the Secret Service, members of the First Lady's official party. First Ladies get much less security than the president, so whenever his wife traveled overseas independently of the President, President Reagan always asked the Director of the Secret Service to accompany his wife. After the assassination attempt on President Reagan in 1981 and the shooting of the Pope himself just a few weeks later on the Vatican grounds, we weren't going to take any chances. So we (the advance team) identified and pinned the two agents as staff members. One actually carried a concealed weapon into the Papal Library. No one was the wiser and everyone slept more easily.

JIM HOOLEY,
advancing President Reagan:

We once left Secretary of State George Shultz in the bathroom at the President's temporary residence in Brazil and departed without knowing he wasn't in the President's limo.

When we arrived at the US Embassy for a farewell event with the employees, Shultz was announced several times while the President was held offstage. We scrambled, including his security team, to find him. Then the President remembered that "George went to the bathroom" and when it was time to roll, no one remembered.

Back at the guesthouse, Shultz tried to get one of the Brazilian contract drivers to take him, but they all said, no, only "Senhor Hooley" could authorize it. He ended up getting there, I think in a taxi, and he told President Reagan: "I don't know who this Senhor Hooley is but he must be important."

DAVID DEMAREST,
White House staff, President Bush 41:

I would say that this story is a good example of how sometimes we're too smart, too clever, or too creative for our own good.

Toward the end of 1990, leading up to Operation Desert Storm, which would commence in January 1991, we knew the President would be headed to Saudi Arabia to see the troops for Thanksgiving.

We also knew that he'd be making several stops in Europe en route, the first being Czechoslovakia.[6] There he would make two major speeches: Upon arrival he would address the Czech Parliament, and later that day he would make an outdoor public address in Prague's Wenceslas Square.

This would be President Bush's first trip to a country newly freed, and its citizenry would likely welcome him as a liberator.

It seemed fitting that the President should make some kind of special gesture during his speech in Wenceslas Square. It turned out that bells—church bells and the like—have a special significance in Czechoslovakia. Their tolling signified important civic, religious, even political events. Our team came up with the idea of having the President reflect on the symbolism of bells in his speech and then present the Czech people a beautiful brass bell mounted on a wooden frame. He would close his speech by dramatically ringing the bell three times.

---

6 Czechoslovakia split into two countries at the end of 1992: the Czech Republic and Slovakia.

We anticipated a sizable crowd even though it was mid-November and a distinctly chilly day. It exceeded everyone's expectations. It was the largest crowd in the four years of the Bush presidency, with estimates as high as 1 million people.

I realized at some point during the day that we had added the whole bell theme, as well as the gift, late in the game. No one had briefed him on the plan for him to *actually ring the bell!*

I asked the advance team when there would be the opportunity to quickly tell him the plan. Unfortunately, they said the President would have no down time between his last meeting and his arrival at Wenceslas Square.

Dang! This might be awkward, but not as awkward as it would be if he didn't follow the script and ring the damn bell three times. I imagined him getting to that point in the speech, fumbling around, wondering if he was really supposed to bang on the bell with the little mallet lying next to it, and losing the moment we had so creatively prepared. My imagination painted that not-so-pretty picture.

One might think I could have just called him and explained it over the phone, but this was 1990. We did not have cell phones yet, and there was no texting. I could have had an advance man radio to another advance man who was near the President and try to relay the whole plan that way. But remember the game of "Telephone," how information gets garbled the more people it goes through? The President could have ended up ringing the bell to open the speech, as if calling a meeting to order. Or, on an open mic, asking, "What the hell is a bell doing here?" No thanks. I had to go over this with him myself.

I determined that when he arrived, I would have to get between him and the speaker's platform even if just for a minute, maybe just for thirty seconds. That's problematic as the President typically bounds out of a motorcade and his focus would be to simply get to the platform and do his speech thing. I actually thought to myself that I may have to tackle him.

I got myself to the steps leading up to the platform and waited. The motorcade pulled up, and here comes the President, heading my way at a brisk clip. He's got that quizzical look on his face, clearly wondering why I'm in the way.

Again, there are an estimated one million people waiting to hear him speak. They've been here for hours. He knows it. I know it. I can feel every one of them, and my head feels like it will explode, but I do my best to ignore the crowd's anticipation.

I've got the appropriate speech cards in my hands, pointing to the relevant lines. In a rapid fire of staccato verbal bullets, I'm in the zone:

"Mr. President, quickly . . . in the closing of your speech . . . right at the end"—damn I already said in the closing, move it along!—"the closing . . . it's about bells, bells are a big deal to the Czechs, there's a bell up on the platform, on the table next to you, it's your gift to the Czechs, it's got a little mallet, you're going to ring the bell three times—once after each of three phrases: once for your courage (ding), once for your country (ding), once for your children (ding). OK?"

He gave me that familiar "whatever" look and off he went.

To him my words might have just come across as a lot of babbling about bell ringing. But when it came time to present the gift, it worked, and in Wenceslas Square that day freedom rang clear as a bell.

In the meantime, members of the White House press team were up to mischief behind the stage.

KELLEY GANNON AND LAURA MELILLO BARNUM:

We were standing with our Ambassador, Shirley Temple Black, when a group of protesters showed up and somehow stormed the backstage. We were trying to bargain with them and finally got them to stand down until after the event. We promised them they could use the entertainment stand after we left. What we didn't tell them—we owned the generators. Before we left, we pulled the plug, so they were in the dark with no working microphones.

ROBBIE AIKEN,
advancing President Bush 41:

As my friend Brad Blakeman tells it, we kidnapped the President.

Now I'm not sure I would go that far, but the story of George H. W. Bush's visit to Brazil in 1992 was full of unusual twists and turns, literally and figuratively.

Brad was the staff lead for the trip to the Rio Earth Summit,[7] while I served as press lead.

We were excited to be heading to Brazil, and once we arrived, we began our usual logistical planning around the official events. There was a lunch that the President would host for the US delegation; the main plenary session, which included remarks; the ceremonial signing of the "Earth Pledge" wall; a group photo of world leaders; and dinner at the home of the President of Brazil.

Oh yeah, we also had to avoid any run-ins with Fidel Castro, who was attending the meeting.

During one of our countdown calls with the White House the week before, Director of Advance Ed Murnane noted that we had not identified a good OTR stop that could bring some color and interest to the trip, something that the press pool could capture. Brad and I realized that the only time we could pull off an OTR was on the way back to the hotel after the plenary. The timing of this also served the added

---

7 The official name was United Nations Conference on Environment and Development, and it was attended by representatives from 179 countries.

purpose of exiting before Castro spoke, thus allowing the President to sidestep any confrontations and potential international headlines.

For that to all work, we needed to make sure we had a credible place to visit, to justify the President's early exit. So we came up with a bold idea—let's tour the rain forest that was at the top of a nearby mountain. Murnane was intrigued but told us to advance the route and the spot. We had our local driver take us and the Secret Service up to the site, which was absolutely perfect. The movement up the mountain to get to the spot was less than perfect. The roads zigzagged and the entire route was not very conducive to moving fast with a large motorcade.

The plan, once we got there, was for our driver to give the President, Mrs. Bush, and the President's chief of staff, Sam Skinner, a tour. There were lots of logistical nuances with this one, and with them, sensitivities. Like many OTRs, though, the sphere of people in the know was pretty small. Beyond me, Brad, and Murnane, no one knew exactly what we were doing. And looking back, that wasn't ideal. But our plan was approved and once the President finished his plenary remarks, we exited to the motorcade.

White House Press Secretary Marlin Fitzwater joined us for the visit. He knew we were going to go to an OTR stop in the rain forest, but he didn't know how long the trip would take. Unfortunately for the advance team, we didn't either. We anticipated fifteen minutes based on our own run-through, but because the Secret Service underestimated the movement of a scaled-down motorcade (led by the presidential vehicle known as the Beast) up the mountainous switchback road, the trip took twice as long. And as anyone who has done advance work well knows, taking more time to move is the worst.

After roughly twenty minutes, the comments started coming back over the radio. Murnane asked Brad if we were still in Brazil. Fitzwater reported that he could see the Pacific Ocean after starting from the Atlantic.

Lucky for me, things went perfectly once we arrived. Our driver led the President, who at one point was punching the spongy side of a eucalyptus tree while the press pool captured the moment, around the rain forest. He greeted a family enjoying a picnic; one man even offered him a beer. The backdrop was spectacular, and the President and Mrs. Bush enjoyed the experience. After the tour, we assembled the team for departure, and with that, we headed back down the mountain. Happy ending, or so I thought.

Fitzwater was not happy, and he let us know. He indicated that we had really messed up the visit and our actions could have serious ramifications. I was a bit confused by his ire but responded that the rain forest visit had been vetted and approved. I guess he assumed the President was angry the trip took so long and wanted to channel that anger toward something. I was that something. Marlin's unhappiness seemed to permeate the entire presidential party, too. Blakeman asked me, "Did we kidnap the President? Is that what people think we did?" I went to bed that night wondering whether my advance career was over.

The next morning provided a bit of vindication though. Tom Brokaw had opened his NBC Nightly News broadcast the evening before with a report on the President's visit to the Earth Summit and his stop in the rain forest. All the video and photos shown were from our OTR. *The New York Times* also ran a story and photo about the visit. I was beyond relieved. Our visit was a grand success.

A quick Barbara Bush story from her travels abroad.

PEGGY SWIFT WHITE,
aide to First Lady Barbara Bush:

Mrs. Bush chose not to travel with "an entourage" (as she liked to say), so one of my jobs and that of the advance team was to find the First Lady a hairdresser.

While in London for the 1991 G-7 Summit, the US Embassy team arranged for her to use Princess Diana's hairdresser. He appeared on the first day with long, stringy hair and a scruffy beard. The staff thought he was very chic and European. Mrs. Bush was not a fan of facial hair and told him so. He told her she sounded like his mum. By the final day of the meetings, he arrived clean-shaven with shorter hair. She managed to accomplish what his own mother and Princess Diana had not—and within four days!

Suffering from a bad case of the flu, President George H. W. Bush threw up on Japanese Prime Minister Kiichi Miyazawa during a state dinner on January 8, 1992. Here are behind-the-scenes details from a Secret Service agent on duty that night.

BARBARA RIGGS:

While en route from Akasaka Palace to the Prime Minister's residence, DSAIC Rich Miller,[8] who was riding in the right front seat of the President's vehicle, radioed to me in the follow-up car: "Make sure we know where the bathroom is at the PM's residence as soon as we arrive."

What I did not know at the time was the President was feeling ill and nauseous. Upon arrival, I conferred with Sam Tong, who was the site advance agent, and he showed me the location of the bathroom.

The President and First Lady proceeded to a reception room where they participated in a receiving line. Miller was close to the President when they both suddenly bolted from the room and headed to the bathroom, where the President threw up, staining his shirt and tie. The White House steward always brings extra shirts for the

---

8 Deputy Special Agent in Charge.

President, but he had no extra tie. Special Agent Tom Farrell whipped off his tie and gave it to the President.

While the wardrobe change was taking place in the men's bathroom, I returned to the receiving line where I whispered to Mrs. Bush what was happening. The President did eventually return to the receiving line, then proceeded to the dining room for the state dinner. The dining room was a large, enclosed room with window panels on each side of the doors so those of us outside in the lobby could see inside the room.

None of the guests knew the President was ill or that he had thrown up in the bathroom. Miller was inside the room seated as a guest, as was the White House doctor, Burton Lee. The guests were seated at tables arranged in a U shape, with the President, Prime Minister, and First Lady at the "head dais" of the configuration at the far end of the room from the entrance doors.

The dinner was in progress when Miller noticed beads of perspiration forming on the President's brow. He got up to approach him with the intent of escorting him to the bathroom. He was standing behind his chair as the President vomited into the lap of the Prime Minister, fainted, and fell over, pulling the Prime Minister to the floor with him.

The shift agents flew into the room, where all the guests had stood up. The agents signaled to the guests to sit down by raising and lowering their arms. No words were spoken, and all guests complied. Can you imagine that type of compliance in the United States, after witnessing the President of the United States collapse?

When the shift members approached the head dais table, the President was on the floor, entangled in his chair that had tipped over on top of the Prime Minister. Special Agent George Robinson leaped over the table to assist Miller in untangling the President from the Prime Minister. The President was under the table, unconscious and ashen gray. He looked dead.

While the agents were attending the President, I communicated by radio to the agents in the motorcade to have the ambulance brought forward. And as Murphy's Law would have it, Dr. Lee had left the dining room to use the bathroom. As he was returning, the President regained consciousness. He was lying under the table, now disengaged from the chair and the Prime Minister, with Miller and Dr. Lee assisting him. As the President began to realize the situation, he quipped to those attending him, "Roll me over and let me sleep this one off." He knew this was not a good optic and a public relations disaster in the making.

The President had been scheduled to give remarks after dinner, so the media had prepositioned cameras on the balcony overlooking the dining room. All cameras were supposed to be off, but a Japanese network, with a feed to ABC-Tokyo, had left a camera rolling. So the entire incident was captured by their camera, much to the embarrassment of the Japanese government and nation.

The medical decision was made by Dr. Lee for the President to return to Akasaka Palace and not go to the hospital. I communicated to the motorcade personnel to have the limousine ready as we were departing immediately for the residence, not the hospital.

Before we left the dining room, Mrs. Bush pulled me aside and advised me she would like to stay at the dinner. I told her we would plan for this, which required the Secret Service to quickly assemble a second motorcade package to leave the Prime Minister's residence for her use.

As we prepared to depart from the dining room the President apologized to the guests.

American and Japanese media had been prepositioned in the lobby of the residence, waiting to enter the dining room to cover the President's speech. The press knew something had happened as they had seen the ambulance brought up, then dismissed from the departure area, to be replaced by the President's limousine. To move to the motorcade we had to pass right through them. The President was informed the press was in the lobby, and he stopped dead in his tracks and asked for a comb. Tom Farrell once again came to the rescue and the President combed his hair. We proceeded out the dining room door and into the lobby, hurriedly moving to get the President through to the motorcade.

It was a crush of humanity. Press members were crowding in yelling questions, and camera shutters were in rapid fire mode. I also vividly remember hearing bodies and camera equipment crashing, as the Japanese security was throwing newscasters, photographers, and film crews against the walls to make a path for the President.

Mrs. Bush gave remarks on behalf of the President. She said: "You know, I can't explain what happened to George because it has never happened before. But I'm beginning to believe it's the Ambassador's fault.[9] He and George played the Emperor [Akihito] and the Crown Prince in tennis today, and they were badly beaten. And we Bushes aren't used to that. So, he felt much worse than I thought."

A PS from one of the White House staffers traveling with the President:

PHIL BRADY:

The next day, when the President came out of the palace to the motorcade, the advance team all had vomit proof ponchos on with smiles on their faces. The President's comment, with a smile on his face: "I assume you all have lined up other jobs."

Editor's note from Jean: *During the years when I was President Bush 41's chief of staff, he used this story often to help calm people down.*

---

9 Ambassador Michael Armacost.

Many times I listened as someone would confide in him how embarrassed they were by this or that happening, often adding, "You have no idea how it feels," to which he would always reply: "I threw up on the Prime Minister of Japan." Mic drop.

RICK JASCULCA,
advancing President Clinton and First Lady Hillary Clinton:

After fifty years of advancing presidents, First Ladies, and vice presidents, I always emphasize when conducting advance training workshops that advance is as much about strategy, teamwork, savvy, taking care of people, and thinking quickly on your feet as it is about logistics.

Ghana, for me, will forever be a mix of all of the above.

On March 23, 1998, President and Mrs. Clinton touched down in Accra, Ghana, on the first stop of their twelve-day, four-nation visit to Africa. While they first visited a farm to showcase a US-supported agricultural program, it was the public event at Independence Square that created the headlines and made history, including the fact that no other sitting American president had ever visited the country.

Our advance team arrived in Accra approximately two weeks before game day. I was a tad surprised when I learned from our Ambassador, Edward Brynn, and our State Department Control Officer, Steve Nolan, that we'd be meeting directly with Ghanaian President Jerry Rawlings.

President Rawlings made it very clear from the get-go that he had a vision for this visit. It would be at Independence Square, because of its historical significance;[10] it would include traditional

---

10 Completed in 1961, Independence Square was built to celebrate Ghana's independence from the British Empire.

Ghanaian ceremonial elements; Ghanaians would be making a pilgrimage by foot to Accra to attend; and he expected "over a million" to be there.

I smiled, expressed our gratitude, and proceeded to explain the logistical requirements of a presidential event that varied significantly from a traditional Ghanaian ceremony at Independence Square. We would need a main stage, sound system, press riser, mult box,[11] cutaway press riser, and rope/barrier line surrounding the stage because President Clinton always descended the stage and spent significant time shaking hands with attendees.

Now it was President Rawlings's turn to smile, as he designated his Information Minister and several other ranking officials to visit Independence Square "and work out the details" with our team.

Once we got to the site, their team explained that normally President Rawlings or other leaders would speak from the grandstand. We explained why that wouldn't work in this case. They told us where the Ghanaian musicians usually performed. And we shared with them why having them on a platform elevated only a foot off the ground was going to prove to be impractical here. Press set-up, sound, security protocols—we painstakingly went through every element. Yes, it was about logistics, but it was more about negotiating a blended event strategy that would be viable for everyone.

As we tediously went through each piece, I asked my deputy advance lead, Shanan Guinn, to take copious notes and then do a very thorough set of diagrams we could share with our hosts and whatever vendor they'd be using to build out the site.

Shanan did an outstanding set of very detailed diagrams. But when we visited the Information Minister, it turns out that his team had created a diorama of the event site, with each item in it to scale.

---

11 Also known as a press box, a mult box is an audio device that allows a single audio source to be split and distributed to several audio hookups.

That diorama remained on the coffee table where we met regularly up until game day.

As work commenced, I decided to join our event team at Independence Square to see if construction meshed with both the diagrams and diorama. As Shanan and I arrived, we were met by our site duo and informed that President Rawlings's wife, Nana Rawlings, was there personally supervising the event site buildout, which was being done by hand, including all carpentry, by a huge team of Ghanaians.

And there she was, sitting in a chair out on Independence Square, holding a parasol to protect herself from the scorching sun. I introduced myself and Shanan, and before I could get a word out of my mouth about the site, Nana noticed I was wearing a Chicago Bulls Championship cap; talked about how she loved Michael Jordan and the awesome team; and asked if she could have a cap, too. I took mine off and started handing it to her, and she smiled and asked, "Can I possibly have one that isn't used?"

I immediately dispatched a member of my team to return to our hotel, grab a fresh hat from my room, and bring it back to the square. (On major trips, it was my habit to bring gifts—T-shirts and caps—for our advance team. I brought Bulls caps to Ghana because the Bulls were months away from securing their second "three-peat" of the Jordan era.)

And so it went for the next week, as issues popped up almost daily, including logistical concerns by the Secret Service about security measures. Because President Clinton always worked a rope line following remarks, they were worried about an enormous crowd pushing forward, with not the heaviest, most stable of bike rack barriers being able to withstand the pressure. They wanted to use additional bike racks to create sections that would relieve pressure near the main stage.

Our press lead had to address who would be sitting in the

grandstand directly behind the stage, so the head-on press shot didn't have a vacant backdrop, and then the careful placement of the cutaway cameras, so when the Clintons and Rawlings turned to greet those in the grandstand, we'd have dramatic images of the anticipated huge crowd.

We also had to address the intense heat and humidity. With tens of thousands of Ghanaians attending, I asked that we have as much water on site as possible, with access to that water for all.

I honestly thought President Rawlings was talking a bit like an advance guy when telling me that Ghanaians would come from all over, many hiking long distances, and that we'd have a million people attending because this was a historic moment.

Come game day, I wanted to get to the airport early, so I could focus on the arrival ceremony and note cards for President Clinton.

My jaw dropped en route as I witnessed throngs of Ghanaians, including entire families, hiking toward Independence Square. Maybe President Rawlings wasn't exaggerating.

The event came off without a hitch, save for an incident on the rope line that I'll get to in a moment. After President Clinton spoke, the Rawlings presented the Clintons with beautiful kente cloth wraps,[12] which the Clintons put on, waved to the assembled crowd in front of them, and then, as if choreographed, turned and waved to those in the grandstand, with the cameras on the cutaway riser capturing the iconic photo of the Clintons and Rawlings, adorned in kente cloth garb, holding up their hands in unity, with the enormous crowd behind them.

The only hiccup? As President Clinton worked the rope line, the crowd was so energized and excited that they surged forward, the bike rack broke, and a five-foot-tall woman, who was right up front, fell to the ground and was in danger of being trampled. A few early

---

12 Ghanaian textile made of hand-woven strips of silk and cotton.

press reports said that President Clinton "angrily" was shouting at the crowd to back up. He did yell at the crowd to back up, but urgently, not angrily, as the woman was being trampled. President Clinton and our Secret Service agents swung into quick action that likely saved her life—with the President and one of our agents reaching down and pulling the woman up as the other agents found a way to resecure the rope line.

What did President Clinton do next? He spent another fifteen minutes calmly, and with a big smile, finishing shaking hands.

GREG SAIKIN AND CURTIS JABLONKA,
advancing President Bush 43:

In his January 2003 State of the Union, President Bush announced PEPFAR, which stood for the President's Emergency Plan for Aids Relief, a significant part of his legislative agenda.[13] In July, the President traveled to Africa to assess where PEPFAR could have the most significant impact. I was sent to Pretoria, South Africa, where the President would overnight before heading to Uganda the following morning.

My job was to ensure that the traveling White House press corps—all two hundred of them—were transported to their United Airlines 747 press plane in a timely fashion to leave for Uganda. I was working under my advance mentor, Curtis Jablonka, who would be transferring to the President's 2004 reelection campaign after this trip, so I told him to relax and let me handle everything.

---

13 PEPFAR is credited with having provided lifesaving HIV treatment for over twenty-six million people, including millions of children, across fifty-five countries in Africa and around the world. While implemented in 2003 by President George W. Bush, PEPFAR was adopted and carried forward by three successive presidential administrations.

For example, I took responsibility for checking all of the credentials as the press corps boarded the plane. Standing at the foot of the stairs, I did not let anyone on the plane until I saw their press credential. Also checking credentials were the Secret Service and United Airlines personnel. After all two hundred press members were on board, I ran up the plane stairs and confirmed to Curtis that we were "all good, boss" and he could put it on cruise control for the rest of that trip. I recall Curtis drifting off to sleep just before takeoff.

I'll let Curtis take the story from here . . .

We landed in Entebbe, Uganda, and, yes, I was well rested as Greg explained. But I never could have imagined what was to come. We arrived at the Imperial Botanical Beach Hotel, near Lake Victoria, where the President was to speak. The press was primarily stationed in their filing center just fifty yards away down a winding pathway.

As the press were buzzing around, a diminutive man approached me and with an accent asked, "What is the area code for South Africa?" He did not have a press credential, so I asked him where he was from. He said, "South Africa," in a soft, meager voice. This seemed sketchy—he doesn't know the area code of his own country? Or that, like most countries, it has multiple area codes?

He then said he was with ABC. Because the networks sometimes contract with locals, I walked him over to the ABC producer, Vija Udenans, who likewise could not identify the man. After asking him to identify himself once more, he changed his story and indicated that he was with SABC, the South African Broadcasting Company. But when I asked him to produce any credential, he said he left it in his bag on the plane.

After a few more story changes, enough was enough. I asked, "Sir, who *are* you?" He opened his jacket, pointed at his Manchester United soccer jersey emblem and said, "I am with the choir, I'm here to sing for President George Bush."

At this point, I walked the man over to the Secret Service agent who flew with us on the press plane. I explained everything to the agent, who indicated that the man had actually sat behind him on the plane. The agent was as perplexed as I was: Why has the man changed his story so many times? What are his intentions? How did he sneak through so many security checkpoints? And why is he not running away at this point?

The agent disappeared to get backup and returned with ten heavily armed Secret Service agents—all members of the Counter Assault Team (CAT)—who came briskly walking toward us, down that winding path. I nudged the man and said, "Check it out, you are in big trouble now." The man did not even blink until the agents grabbed him, at which point he started screaming at the top of his lungs: "They are going to kill me, they are going to kill me!!!"

Members of the press corps rushed over like in a feeding frenzy, asking all kinds of questions about what the agents were doing to this man. Unfortunately, this incident tended to overshadow the President's event, with headlines in *The New York Times*, Reuters, and *The Washington Post* about a stowaway making it within yards of President Bush—and one member of the press claiming in a story that he first observed the stowaway on the press plane in business class eating an egg frittata.

We headed back to the airport and unloaded every bag on the plane so that the Secret Service K-9 unit could clear them. I will never forget when I saw a beat-up black canvas bag and knew that it had to be his: no tag, faded, stained.

I have told this story over one thousand times and only one person has guessed what we found inside. Can you guess?

When we opened the bag after a thorough K-9 search, we discovered a Costco-sized amount of condoms, some of which were the oversized female variety. It wasn't until about a year later that we learned this man had met a woman online and decided the night before that he would jump on our flight for a rendezvous. He somehow made it through the press filing security at the hotel, the buses, three layers of check-in at the airplane, and finally to the press center in Uganda.

And no, we still aren't sure how he managed to do that.

And unfortunately, there was no romantic ending to his story. He spent quite a few years in a Ugandan prison.

THÈRÉSE BURCH,
advancing President Bush 43 and First Lady Laura Bush:

The President and First Lady visited Botswana in 2003, taking their daughter Barbara with them. Included on the schedule was a visit to the Mokolodi Nature Reserve. We were all so excited when several elephants came out, until the male elephant, Shaka, mounted one of the females, Thandi, in full view of the group. The press fell out of the truck laughing so hard. President Bush took off his hat and covered Barbara's eyes with his hand. After a few minutes, the elephants stopped, and President Bush applauded their performance. The joke began to swirl that we were breeding Republicans in Africa.

Lesson learned by the advance team: Find out when mating season is.

CHARITY WALLACE,
traveling with First Lady Laura Bush:

A little-known fact is that Laura Bush is the most well-traveled First Lady to date. She traveled to seventy-seven countries and all fifty states.

On a visit to Jerusalem in 2005, Mrs. Bush visited the Western Wall (also known as the Wailing Wall), inserting tiny papers filled with prayers into that ancient wall, which holds centuries' worth of prayers. The crush of people around us was uncomfortable—and extremely unusual. Our lead Secret Service agent held his arm in the air to direct our little gaggle around the site so that we did not get lost in the crowd. As we departed this holy site, Chief of Staff Anita McBride was slammed into the limo due to the crowd of security and dignitaries.

From the Wailing Wall, Mrs. Bush immediately headed for the Qubbat al-Sakhra mosque, formerly known as the Temple Mount. The Palestinians provide security for the mosque, which required a hand-off of security forces from the Israelis to the Palestinians. The tension was palpable.

There was a scuffle on our walk toward the mosque with the security group closing in around us. Unlike the Secret Service, who create a wide security perimeter, security in the Middle East creates a tight bubble. I found myself ducking under the linked arms of the security to go ahead to view the next site and then ducking back under their arms to get closer to Mrs. Bush and our team. Several local press aggressively pushed against the arms of the security to get photos and shout questions.

When I looked at Mrs. Bush, she was unfazed and seemed to be floating above the chaos. Her grace, confidence, and peace changed the atmosphere. As we approached the entry for the mosque, I kept loudly reminding the US press and our team to remove their shoes and cover their heads out of respect.

Several photographers were trying to get photos of Mrs. Bush as she entered the mosque, and they were pushing against our small group of staff to get the photo. One man kept pushing against me, so I decided to push my back into him a little bit more, which I assumed would make him back off. Instead, to my surprise and alarm, he jumped on me piggyback. I began twisting my body trying to get him off, which worked. I found myself laughing at the ludicrousness of the situation.

There were other incidents that felt slightly more threatening, and, during an interview, one of the reporters from CNN asked Mrs. Bush if she had been afraid and if President Bush had called to check on her safety. Mrs. Bush replied, "Well, no. I wasn't afraid. Were you?" The reporter seemed to be trying to sensationalize the trip and deflect from the purpose of our visit.

Mrs. Bush also visited Jordan and Egypt on that trip. The visit to Egypt, where she appeared on *Alam Simsim—Sesame Street* in Egypt, went off without a hitch. She joined the Muppets, standing next to their version of Big Bird, to count in English and recite the ABCs.

In Jordan, Mrs. Bush gave keynote remarks at the World Economic Forum at the Dead Sea. The logistics of such occasions are complicated, with interpreters, ever-slipping timelines, and countless dignitaries moving through the halls.

When Mrs. Bush began her remarks—which were displayed on large screens around the convention hall—an infamous Dead Sea fly landed on Mrs. Bush and walked around her face, crawling on her eyebrows, and down her cheeks.

Most people would have swatted or had a strong reaction, but Mrs. Bush discreetly and calmly swiped her eyebrow—to no avail.

As the advance director, you try to plan for all contingencies, but I had never thought of a *fly*! I scrunched down in my seat in horror and nervously laughed with the speechwriter at the circumstance that was beyond our control.

But, once again, Mrs. Bush taught us how to react to unexpected, uncomfortable possibilities. When she came off the stage, she turned and said, "Did you see that fly!? It wouldn't go away. Do you think people could see it?"

Um, *yes*, but her understated reaction made it almost invisible to the audience.

Soon after the fly incident, we drove in a small motorcade up to Mount Nebo. In the Bible, there is a story of Moses standing at the top of Mount Nebo to overlook the Promised Land. As we wound up the mountain, the motorcade became slower and slower. Finally, Mrs. Bush's limo completely stopped. We were all bewildered. Why were we stopping? This didn't seem like a particularly safe thing to do. Then, we realized that the limo (a heavier car than most) had overheated. We were stuck on the road to Mount Nebo, trying to figure out how we would make it to the top.

Once again, Mrs. Bush was gracious, laughing off what the Secret Service found embarrassing and a bit of a security issue. We eventually made it to the top and were overwhelmed by the knowledge that many centuries before, a holy man was shown by his God what was promised to be a land "flowing with milk and honey" for the wandering Israelites.

We learned another lesson—sometimes your trip to the heights takes a little longer than expected—something the Israelites knew only too well.

PETER NEWELL,
advancing President Obama:

June 6, 2009, found me at Omaha Beach in Normandy, France, a twenty-nine-year-old staffer amid thousands of American flags, awaiting remarks from world leaders. "Was this really my life now?" I wondered.

Just two years prior, I was a $125/day "press lead" on the Obama campaign, a gig I grabbed onto after volunteering nights and weekends at campaign HQ as an email sorter who'd raised his hand to take a week off work and "help with events in Iowa." I never left.

Now, as director of the White House Travel Office, the stakes and travel demands were infinitely higher. My second day on the job, I was thrust into President Obama's ambitious 2009 international schedule. While earlier trips to Canada, G-20, NATO, and the Summit of the Americas felt like a whirlwind, this June trip was different—a meticulously planned diplomatic tour centered on his "A New Beginning" speech in Cairo, aimed at bridging divides with the Muslim world. It was to be a diplomatic "sandwich": King Abdullah in Saudi Arabia, the landmark speech in Egypt, a somber visit to Buchenwald in Germany, and then the D-Day commemoration in Normandy.

The challenge felt enormous: tracking three time zones (local, destination, and, crucially, East Coast morning and evening news) for more than one hundred media and support staff. With press costs exceeding $20,000 per journalist for chartered flights, buses, internet, and hotels, ensuring they could go live with the President's movements was paramount.

Our odyssey began at 12:30 a.m. in Riyadh (6:30 p.m. the day prior in New York), setting up for TV network hits at the Ritz Carlton. From there, four shuttle buses whisked us to King Abdullah's vast, deserted private airport to jump ahead of Air Force One on our chartered 747 to Cairo.

I knew escorting one-hundred-plus journalists through three countries and customs processes was far from a guaranteed success. The recent detection of H1N1 Swine Flu in California had already resulted in tense negotiations and delayed arrivals due to surprise temperature screenings for each journalist a day earlier in Saudi Arabia, where our hosts were already skeptical of the herd of international journalists we were bringing into the kingdom.

Furthermore, my nerves were still raw from the incident two months prior in Istanbul, where I learned even White House–chartered 777s can have mechanical issues. In that scenario, we discovered the issues after we had already checked out of all our hotel rooms and stamped the journalists' passports out of the country, thus needing to find a fresh set of one hundred hotel rooms across Istanbul and allow the journalists to remain in the country (illegally) for an extra twenty-four hours, creating a lively diplomatic fight on the Istanbul tarmac with senior members of our State Department and their Turkish counterparts before we were allowed to leave.

So, yes, I was nervous.

After his speech in Cairo, while the President snuck in a quick tour of the pyramids, we raced back to the airport for more live shots, constantly eyeing our schedule to ensure we'd be in Dresden by 11:30 p.m. Germany time for the East Coast evening news. Thanks to the meticulous planning and incredible support from Saudi, Egyptian, and German hosts, as well as our embassies and military, we achieved the "hat trick"—three continents in one day. We landed safely, a relaxed and jovial group, buoyed by the equally exhilarated flight attendants who had delivered hard-earned heavy pours to the thirsty passengers on the day's last leg.

Sitting at Normandy a day or two later, coffee and adrenaline still coursing through me, I watched the President and First Lady nearby, marveling at a life I couldn't have fathomed just two years prior. The D-Day tribute concluded, one last live shot to New York, and a bus back to Paris, but there was no time to savor the moment. On the flight home, my focus already pivoted to the next major international swing: Russia, Italy, and Ghana, just four weeks away.

CHAPTER FIVE

THINGS THAT HAPPEN IN THE SHADOW OF THE WHITE HOUSE

*C*ommon wisdom might say that planning or working an event within the walls of the White House must be easier than anything you do in the Soviet Union or the middle of Africa.

Well, the commute is shorter, that's for sure. But that doesn't necessarily mean everything happens exactly as planned.

We'll begin with one of the more infamous incidents on the White House lawn.

GORDON JAMES,
advancing President Bush 41:

I, unfortunately, am the man behind the "talking purple hat."

In May 1991, there was a long-awaited state visit scheduled for Queen Elizabeth II. State visits by foreign dignitaries are a big deal no matter who they are, but this was the Queen.

Each president has a podium built to suit his height so he can read his remarks without bending over. The podium even has a name: "The Blue Goose."

President Bush was six two (a full eleven inches taller than the Queen). There is a step built into the bottom that could be pulled out to allow shorter people to be seen.

At almost all events the President speaks last so the tray can be pulled out ahead of time and then he can kick it in when he steps to the podium. But for a state visit he speaks first, welcoming his guest to the United States.

President Bush gave a warm welcome to the Queen, and she stepped to the podium and completely disappeared. All you could see was her white gloves and purple hat. In Mrs. Bush's memoir, *Barbara Bush: A Memoir*, she wrote, "You literally could not see her face, just the hat bobbling up and down."

I was standing just to the right of the stage and could have easily crawled up on the stage, politely tapped the Queen on the knee, and pulled out the tray, but I was frozen in place. It was the Queen of England for goodness' sake.

The next day she gave a speech to a joint session of Congress and said at the top, "I do hope you can see me today from where you are." Got to love her for that.

The British tabloids had a ball with this. "The Talking Hat" was the headline all over England. I was mortified, and while this was clearly my fault, my boss—Ambassador Joseph Verner Reed, Chief of Protocol—took the heat. My apologies were profuse, but he brushed this off as no big deal.

Well, I thought all was forgiven and I had heard the last of this disaster. It turns out Ambassador Reed did some interviews a few years before he passed away, and when asked what his worst day at the White House was, he exclaimed, "The day the Queen disappeared!"

To make matters even worse, his obituary in *The Wall Street Journal* in 2016 had his quote and a photo of her at the podium. I will never live this down.

JAY PARMER,
advancing President Bush 41:

When I started doing advance in 1981, I was told repeatedly to never allow myself to become part of the story.

But nobody is perfect.

Early in 1989, President Bush went to the Department of Housing and Urban Development to participate in a swearing-in ceremony for Secretary Jack Kemp. At the ceremony, the former Buffalo Bills quarterback gave the President an NFL football as a gift. The ball ended up in my hands, and when we returned to the South Lawn of the White House, I walked toward the Oval Office side door to hand it over to the personal aide, Tim McBride.

The President saw me carrying the ball and gestured for me to toss it to him. He then proceeded to gesture for me to go out for a pass. Keep in mind, I am wearing a suit, overcoat, leather-soled shoes, a radio, and an earpiece. I ran down the driveway and the President let loose a long pass, accurate but a little out of my reach and veering out onto the wet lawn.

I had the choice of diving for the ball and making a complete idiot of myself or coming up a little short. Suffice it to say, I didn't catch it, and the President threw up his arms in mock frustration. I carried the ball back to him and apologized for my poor effort. He laughed and walked inside the Oval.

When I turned around, I was told by the traveling press aide that the travel pool wanted to talk to me. I tried to get away, but it didn't work. The pool had witnessed the entire scene, and a reporter asked me if it was a bad pass. Realizing that "no comment" would be a terrible response, I said, "It was a good pass, I am just a lousy receiver." One of the reporters said that it was a good answer, although a "kiss ass" one. I believe this episode made it into *The Washington Post*, because I received a lot of phone calls and got a good roasting from my boss, John Keller. "I told you guys to stay out of sight," he reminded me sternly.

LAURA MELILLO BARNUM,
press aide to President Bush 41:

A lot was at stake when President Gorbachev came to town in May 1990. There were high hopes that the Cold War itself might be coming to an end, so all eyes were on the two world leaders.

My job was fairly simple.

All I had to do was escort the press pool into the Oval Office to catch that all-important photo of the visiting head of state sitting with the President of the United States in front of the Oval Office fireplace. You have seen the photo a hundred times.

I escorted the press in, then stepped back out of the way. But I noticed that President Bush kept gesturing at me, trying to tell me something I could not quite understand. Finally, he had to whisper aloud: "Laura, you have a little something there stuck to the back of your dress."

Then he says to President Gorbachev: "She has toilet paper stuck to the back of her dress!"

I was mortified. President Bush was pointing to my derriere, which then President Gorbachev started staring at. The entire press pool then turned and started clicking furiously at my backside as I grabbed at the toilet paper adhered to my dress!

And that is how the summit meeting began.

You might say this is how the summit ended . . .

JIM CICCONI,
White House staff secretary to President Bush 41:

Do you ever wonder how the sausage is made?

I was with President Bush and President Gorbachev as they were waiting in the Green Room of the White House to walk out to their highly anticipated announcement to the world of what had been agreed on. My main job was to hand the President his speech cards.

Then he suddenly started negotiating a couple points with Gorbachev. I tried to keep up with what I thought Gorbachev agreed to and started editing the speech cards, writing on a coffee table while on my knees. As they went back and forth, I ended up having to scratch out words and then add new ones. Their conversation ended and they both stood behind me as I edited President Bush's speech, with me still on my knees. When I handed the cards to the President, I apologized for what looked like a mess. He gave me a look like "How am I supposed to decipher this?"

I said, "Mr. President, just read everything that's not crossed out." He started laughing and thanks to the interpreter, so did Gorbachev, who made a joke about the situation, and they both started laughing. Loudly. Outside in the East Room (there was no door to shut), the audience heard them laughing and started applauding before the two of them even came out the door. Little did they know this wasn't about détente, it was about two presidents laughing at a staffer trying to keep up with them!

Actually there is one more story to tell from this summit meeting . . .

PEGGY SWIFT WHITE,
aide to First Lady Barbara Bush:

After the hard summit work was done, the Bushes invited the Gorbachevs to Camp David for the day.

Mrs. Gorbachev always dressed pretty formally and with very high stiletto heels. Mrs. Bush commented once that it was important for Raisa to project a certain image while traveling overseas—which was applicable to all spouses, really.

Mrs. Gorbachev would have received a suggested clothing protocol prior to the visit, which included guidance that Mrs. Bush would be sporting typical "Camp David casual"—slacks and a sweater. Mrs. Bush's attire also included her signature Keds sneakers. (President Bush had gifted her thirty pairs for a birthday after she had mentioned that you couldn't find Keds anymore. She loved to mix and match her collection to see people's reactions.)

After lunch, the small entourage of the two First Ladies, interpreters, and security set off on a walking tour. Mrs. Gorbachev obviously got the memo regarding slacks but sure enough was wearing her signature stilettos.

After a while it was painfully obvious she was suffering from walking in high heels on concrete. Mrs. Bush suggested she borrow some bowling shoes from the Camp David facility. I am not sure how that was translated but there was a firm head shake "no." We continued on, and it was really dreadful to watch. Mrs. Bush quietly asked me to arrange a golf cart so we could continue the tour more comfortably.

We returned to Aspen Lodge (where the president stays at Camp David) and had more time to fill while the official discussions continued between the principals. It was just the three of us and the two interpreters.

The discussion was fascinating and personal. Mrs. Gorbachev shared details about their daughter and her lifestyle. She was intrigued to learn how different my experience was as a young woman compared to their daughter in the Soviet Union. While I could afford to share a rental home with friends, her daughter and her family lived with the Gorbachevs because they could not afford a place of their own. Mrs. Gorbachev was inquisitive about the cosmetics in my purse—the sheer variety of brands such as Revlon, Chanel, L'Oréal—and commented that when they went into a store, there was usually only one option in one color of lipstick available.

Later that day, Mrs. Gorbachev joined the group for another activity and was wearing a pair of bowling shoes.

BOBBIE KILBERG,
White House staff for President Bush 41:

Most Americans know that every Thanksgiving, the president of the United States pardons two turkeys, provided by the National Turkey Federation. It's a fun little event, organized by our office. What possibly could go wrong?

For years, the turkeys were lightly sedated so that they would not try to fly away during the Rose Garden ceremony. However, in 1991, an animal rights group mounted a major campaign to convince the White House not to sedate the birds since they viewed it as cruel treatment. For whatever reason, the White House agreed. (I am not sure who the "White House" was, but it was a big mistake.)

The day of the event, the turkeys' handlers brought them to the Rose Garden early so they could walk off any "anxiety." As it happened, my four-year-old son, Andrew, and Doro Bush's four-year-old daughter, Ellie LeBlond, had also arrived early for the ceremony, and they were playing together on the outskirts of the Rose Garden. Well, the turkeys spied them and proceeded to chase them all around the garden and out onto the South Lawn. While observers thought it was funny, Doro and I certainly did not. Nor did the kids, who were terrified. President Bush was informed and brought the kids into the Oval Office to calm them down, mainly by giving them candy.

The event itself went off without a hitch—the turkeys also managed to calm down. But my son Andrew had the final word. As the turkeys were being pardoned by President Bush to be sent to a farm, he tugged on my skirt and told me that the President was very nice to send the turkeys to a farm but that was not necessary. They could move in with us.

BRIAN JONES,
advancing President Bush 43:

"The President's Dinner" is one of those DC fundraisers that pulls the biggest names in Republican politics—House and Senate leaders, party dignitaries, and, of course, the President. The years I worked it, the dinner took up most of the sprawling Walter E. Washington Convention Center. It was so big that a friend and I tossed a football from room to room during the walk-throughs.

I always enjoyed this event because I was a congressional staffer long before someone made the misguided decision to let me work at the White House. The chance to see the rock stars of Congress up close was pretty cool. One year, the dinner was particularly exciting for me because several members of the President's family were in attendance, including his parents and his siblings Jeb, Neil, Marvin, and Doro.

The event went smoothly as planned. My advance mentor, Robbie Aiken, served as the staff lead while I ran point on the site. That meant positioning greeters and then handling the photo line, which seemed endless at fundraising events like this. But the speech was well received, and despite the massiveness of the venue and the audience, we had no problems.

As the President headed to the motorcade, Robbie radioed and asked me to come to the departure elevator immediately.

When I arrived, President Bush was stepping onto an elevator, already filled with his family members, that would take him to the garage level where the motorcade was positioned. Confused as to why I was summoned, Aiken moved me onto the lift and whispered, "You're going to take everyone down. But you are not, under any circumstances, allowed to leave until we have Dirk Kempthorne on this elevator. Do you understand?"

"Roger that," I responded as he jetted away in search of the Governor of Idaho and future Secretary of the Interior.

So, there I was, on an elevator with the President of the United States and his family. Pretty typical night. No, it was an incredible, albeit intimidating, *Forrest Gump* moment. Heeding Aiken's call to not leave for any reason, my finger held firm on the secret elevator button that controlled my fate, one that rested in the hands of a man named Dirk. I wondered how I came to be here.

Regardless, I had my orders. Every second that passed without Kempthorne, however, seemed to last hours. And after a few minutes of waiting, President Bush felt the same way. He turned to me and asked, "What are we waiting for? Let's go."

I responded, "Yes, Mr. President, we are waiting for Governor Kempthorne, who is traveling back in the motorcade to the White House."

That appeased the President for a few moments, but after sharing a quick word with his sister Doro, he came back to me.

"C'mon, we have to go," he pressed.

As I processed what to do and say in that moment, the white noise of Bush family conversation came to a screeching halt with just two words that didn't come from me. Instead, a constructive suggestion surfaced from the back of the elevator for the President to "calm down." I never realized that two one-syllable words could be stretched for so long, but I knew that the tone they were delivered with meant that they came from a sibling. It's one I had heard countless times from my brothers and one I had doled out to them.

The words "Oh. My. God. Who said that?" didn't actually escape my mouth, but they certainly ran through my head in the deafening silence of that moment.

I turned around, with the rest of the elevator's occupants, and stared in disbelief at the guilty brother, who I will not incriminate. The look President Bush gave said brother, though, was one I would describe, borrowing a phrase from the military, as a "proportionate response."

Before things escalated any further, George H. W. Bush—now a father and not a former president—brokered an armistice with a very simple and loving, "Now boys, c'mon now." And just like that, it was over. The President removed his stare from his brother, focused it back on me, and asked in a very calm tone, "Can we go please?"

That was enough for me. I released the hold button, the doors closed, and we made our way down to the motorcade. As I watched the President leave and the always calming "Trailblazer departs" announcement from WHCA echoed in my ear,[1] I paused to process the moment. Every experience that I was afforded to serve President Bush, in the very small way I did, was humbling. But this one was special in a different way—I got to see the President and his family just being, well, a family.

Because I disobeyed his order, I was relieved to learn that Robbie Aiken never located Dirk Kempthorne. His search continues to this day.

---

1 Trailblazer was the Secret Service code word for President George W. Bush.

STEPHEN GOODIN,
aide to President Clinton:

Sometimes you forget that you are working for a president and you see him as a person. A real person doing real person things.

I got to witness one of those moments on September 28, 1995.

Israeli Prime Minister Yitzhak Rabin and Palestinian leader Yasser Arafat made history by signing the Oslo II Accord, expanding Palestinian self-rule in the West Bank. Flanked by Egyptian President Hosni Mubarak, King Hussein of Jordan, and President Clinton, they gathered in a White House hallway before the signing ceremony. The President's photographer, Barbara Kinney, was there to record the historic moment. As the world leaders waited, I told President Clinton that his tie was crooked. As he reached up to straighten it out, the other men also reached up to adjust their ties.

A few months later, Barbara won the prestigious World Press Photo prize for her shot of the historic tie-straightening moment.

We'll end with a story about being caught hanging out in the Oval Office.

TYLER ABELL,
advance man for President Johnson:

On a beautiful Saturday in May 1964, my wife, Bess, who was White House social secretary, suggested we take our two children, Dan and Lyndon, to lunch in the White House Mess. Dan was dawdling over his food, so Bess suggested that while she stayed in the Mess to encourage him to finish, I take Lyndon to show him the Oval Office.

And while I was doing just that, the President walked in through a door leading to the Rose Garden.

Uh-oh.

I was a little worried that he might not like being surprised by uninvited guests in his office, but I summoned up my composure to say, "Hello Mr. President, let me introduce you to your namesake, Lyndon Abell."

Lyndon, a month shy of turning four years old, dutifully stuck out his hand, and President Johnson led him out the door, saying "Lyndon, come out here and have your picture taken with the President."

Then, to make the situation all the more interesting . . . former President Truman showed up. He had been visiting with the President in the residence. He stuck out a beckoning arm to me, saying, "Here, you get in this picture."

The picture was snapped, and then President Johnson said, "Tyler, you get out of this picture and let Lyndon have a picture taken alone with two presidents."

What a lucky four-year-old!

CHAPTER SIX

THE SURPRISING LIFE OF VICE PRESIDENTS

*T*he role of the Vice President of the United States is one of the most
misunderstood and underappreciated roles in the world.

Many vice presidents have been the target of ridicule and sarcasm while
they navigated the shark-infested waters of Washington, DC. If they work
quietly behind the scenes, they are considered irrelevant. If they make news,
they are accused of upstaging the president.

It is not the purpose of this book to explain and defend the forty-nine
men and one woman who have occupied the office. But by telling a story
or two through the eyes of advance, you might have a greater appreciation
for the role of the person who is one heartbeat away from the presidency.

We will begin with a trip that Vice President George H. W. Bush took
to Poland in September 1987, a trip that most likely hastened the end of
the Cold War.

CRAIG FULLER,
chief of staff to Vice President Bush:

On September 28, 1987, Vice President Bush managed to outfox the
communist regime of Poland while delivering a message directly to

the freedom-seeking people of Poland that made it clear America stood with them.

All was made possible by his personal resolve, but also by an advance team that never quit against all odds.

First some background:

Poland was dangling between communism and freedom in the form of a labor movement called Solidarity and led by a worker who one day would become president: Lech Walesa.

Communist regimes across Europe were faltering. Leaders like Walesa were putting their lives on the line with the hope that the West would support them.

President Reagan responded to the favorable movement in Poland in February 1987 by lifting all sanctions against Poland. This was an important next step in a process that had started with some sanctions being lifted in January 1984.

Vice President Bush, seeing an opportunity in the global contest with communist regimes, quietly had suggested a presidential visit to Poland after the 1984 reelection. That was not to be, but President Reagan liked the concept and encouraged his Vice President to make the trip, which he did.

The morning of September 28 began in Warsaw with a briefing around the three significant events on the schedule for the day:

- The Vice President would visit an important shrine honoring Father Jerzy Popieluszko, who had been killed by the Polish secret police in 1984.
- He would attend a reception at the US Embassy with Americans and our Polish hosts.
- He would then address the Polish people sitting at the table where the daily television news was broadcast.

Each of these events had been crafted by the Vice President's advance team weeks earlier. While they remained in frequent contact with trip planners in Washington, their creative ideas about what was possible contributed much to this historic event. As an example, when the Polish government offered an address to the nation, the advance team insisted it be a live broadcast. They knew that once the remarks began, the government could only decide to let the broadcast proceed with the remarks of the Vice President or kill the transmission. Winning approval for a live broadcast proved an inspired decision.

The first event that day was the visit to the shrine. What the Polish government did not know was that the advance team had carefully coordinated Lech Walesa's secret arrival to the guesthouse where the Bushes were staying so Walesa could accompany the Vice President to the shrine.

The visit was a somber event. The Vice President knew that at some point as we were leaving the church, his hosts would turn left. At that moment, he and I would turn right, go up steps to a balcony, and join Walesa to address the Polish people who had been encouraged to show up by those in the Solidarity movement.

With thousands in the crowd, Walesa and Vice President Bush spoke over a sound system secretly put in place by our advance team the night before. The images and the messages of that day were broadcast around the world. The crowd chanted, "Long Live Reagan!" "Long Live Bush!"

With the television address to the Polish people that evening remaining, our Polish hosts were pressing for a copy of the Vice President's remarks. Having been pushed to the limits, they were insistent. Eventually, we shared the draft press release quoting from the remarks, but it was not marked "draft." This proved helpful later.

With cancellation of the broadcast threatened, we shared the Vice President's remarks in full before going to the US Embassy reception. That relaxing moment proved brief as the head of the US Embassy,

US Chargé d'Affaires John R. Davis Jr.,[1] was told to deliver the Vice President's chief of staff to a meeting at Communist Party headquarters to discuss the speech.

Telling Vice President Bush where I was headed and why, I told him: "Follow the lead of the advance team as I have no idea where I will be and no idea whether your live address to the Polish people will happen." He understood and wished me luck.

The meeting was held in the darkest and greenest building I have ever entered. And it was held with four very unhappy Polish officials. They did not like our stunt with Lech Walesa. They did not like the delay in getting the remarks. And they did not like that we had, or so they assumed, already issued the press release. And, of course, they did not like some of the planned remarks.

Davis was eager to avoid a conflict and wanted to explore elements in the remarks that were a problem. We started down that path until I suggested to our Polish hosts that they could either broadcast the remarks the Vice President had written as we had agreed or cancel the broadcast. What they could not do was edit his remarks.

That ended the meeting.

A short time later, as Vice President Bush sat down in the chair in the studio, we had no idea whether what he was about to say would be broadcast. But it was.

Understanding the historical significance of their work in Poland in 1987, members of the advance team wrote a book called Advancing History, *to tell their behind-the-scenes stories of what happened during those two weeks in September. The authors: Gary E. Fendler, lead press advance for the trip, and John G. Keller, director of advance for Vice President Bush.*

Robert Athey, lead staff advance man on the trip, was a significant

---

1 The post of ambassador was vacant, making the chargé d'affaires officer the ranking embassy official.

contributor, along with help from the entire team, who you will meet in the story.

As they said in their book proposal: "At Bush's direction, for two weeks his staff and press advance team prepared for the approaching trip as though it was engaged in a political chess game with Polish authorities."

We are pleased to include some edited excerpts from their unpublished book.

GARY E. FENDLER AND JOHN G. KELLER:

The United States Secret Service agent straightened his posture, removed his hands from the pockets of his tan overcoat, and squared his stance when the vehicles first appeared, approaching the official Polish government guesthouse, Klonowa Villa, in central downtown Warsaw. One car trailed behind the other.

As they approached the outer-perimeter security checkpoint established around the compound, the Secret Service agent remained vigilant. The autos moved in single formation and eased to a stop directly in front of the team composed of US and Polish security. The US Embassy diplomatic license plates now came into focus. The Secret Service agent leaned down toward the rear, passenger-side window as it slowly opened, offering a glimpse of the man in the back seat. The two men acknowledged each other with a slight nod.

The agent stepped back and with his left hand adjusted the frequency dial on the small radio strapped to his belt. He simultaneously lifted his right hand toward his lips and spoke softly into his concealed hand mic. A second Secret Service agent posted inside the government guesthouse situated a hundred yards away acknowledged his colleague and repeated the message to the group of officials gathered in the reception room: "The guest has arrived."

US Chargé d'Affaires John Davis Jr. smiled, arose from his

armchair, excused himself, and silently departed the room and exited the guesthouse. Once on the sidewalk, he strode past a black armored limousine parked outside the front entrance of the building and proceeded toward the vehicle security checkpoint.

As Davis approached the security checkpoint, the rear passenger-side door opened. A stocky, mustachioed gentleman of medium height in a neat, three-piece dark blue suit emerged. The men shook hands, exchanged greetings in Polish, and immediately turned and walked back toward the guesthouse.

They moved rapidly, shoulder to shoulder, toward the main entrance. Facing forward, both men watched as a Polish security officer in the distance marched away from the limousine. Judging by the officer's rapid pace, he appeared agitated.

As the two men neared the idling limousine, the guesthouse door opened and out stepped Second Lady Barbara Bush followed by her husband, Vice President George Bush. An acknowledging smile appeared on their faces as they sighted Davis and Lech Walesa approaching from the corner, walking side by side down the concrete footway.

All staff, guests, and the traveling press pool were already sitting in their assigned vehicles in the assembled motorcade. Walesa was ushered into the back seat of the limousine where he was joined by Vice President Bush and US State Department interpreter Victor Litwinski for the brief ride to St. Stanislaw Kostka Church.

The Polish immediate response to Walesa's presence was to insist on the removal of the Polish flag from the front fender of the Vice President's limousine. When time allowed later in the day, Davis asked the Polish security leader about removing the flag. "Walesa is not an official of the Polish government. At least, not yet," Davis recalled being told by the official as the reason he demanded the flag be removed from the limousine. "It was interesting in revealing that even hardline regime loyalists were beginning to see the handwriting on the wall as early as 1987," Davis said. Craig Fuller, who witnessed the flag's removal, didn't disagree with Davis but had a slightly different take on the reaction to Walesa riding in the limousine. "The Polish authorities were flabbergasted. They didn't know what to do."

Both leaders were about to share in a remarkable, overt display of political defiance, each unique in its own way: Walesa, previously imprisoned as head of a government-banned trade union, audaciously appearing with the US leader amid thousands of Solidarity supporters at a large-scale outdoor event, and Vice President Bush boldly, warmly, and publicly embracing an "enemy" of the Polish military state against the ardent, stated opposition of the host government.

Later, while speaking to the media as the church visit ended, Walesa, as reported by the United Press International's (UPI) White House correspondent Norman Sandler, said, "It's the biggest support ever given to Solidarity. We are happy he understands our strivings and our struggle."

The Vice President's first thirty-three hours in Poland had been filled with mostly official and ceremonial events, all planned with both the knowledge and cooperation of the Polish government. But as the evening sky darkened on day two, the schedule shifted. The "unofficial" events, or events not previously organized with or formally approved by Polish authorities, were all planned and orchestrated by the advance team.

At 7:05 p.m., Vice President and Mrs. Bush departed the Klonowa Villa guesthouse on a ten-minute drive to Davis's home. The residential gate creaked as it closed behind the Vice President's limousine. With Vice President Bush inside the residence, all that remained for the night's event to begin was arrival of the remaining few guests.

"Fendler, Athey!" lead advance Robert Athey stated calmly over the radio.

Since the Vice President's morning landing the day before, all advance team members had communicated through personal radios

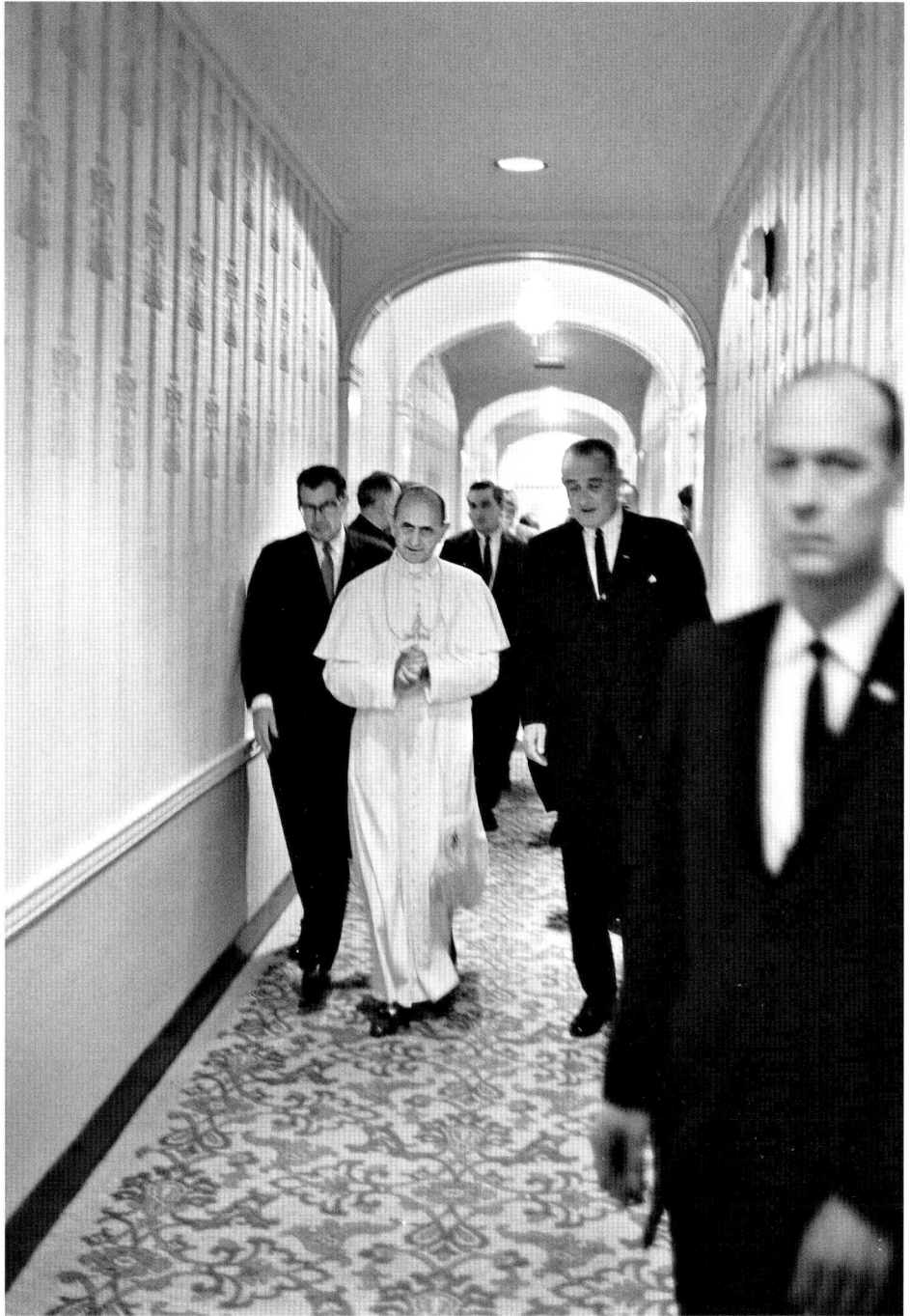

President Johnson and Pope Paul VI walk down a hallway at the Waldorf Astoria on October 4, 1965. It was the first time a pope had visited the United States.
Photograph by Yoichi Okamoto. Courtesy of the LBJ Presidential Library and Museum.

Irving Berlin sings "God Bless America" with President and Mrs. Nixon, celebrating the return of POWs from Vietnam at a gala dinner at the White House, May 25, 1973. Also pictured (*left to right*) are Phyllis Diller, Joan Weber, Joey Heatherton, Sammy Davis Jr., and Bob Hope. *Photograph by Oliver "Ollie" Atkins. Courtesy of the Richard Nixon Presidential Library and Museum.*

President Ford hugs his scared and relieved daughter, Susan, at the White House on September 22, 1975, the day Sara Jane Moore tried to kill him in San Francisco. *Official White House photograph by David Hume Kennerly.*

President Carter and French President d'Estaing strolling down the Champs-Élysées in Paris in January 1978. A photo of this walk appeared on the cover of *Time*'s international edition, which was a big "win" for the advance team. *Photograph by Karl Shumacher. Courtesy of the Jimmy Carter Library and Museum.*

A Jeff MacNelly cartoon illustrates the political fallout from President Reagan's visit to a Nazi cemetery in Bitburg, Germany, in 1985.
Jeff MacNelly cartoon published by the Chicago Tribune. *Courtesy of David Harris.*

Vice President Bush and Lech Walesa wave to thousands of Polish supporters from a church balcony in Warsaw, September 28, 1987. The huge crowd is hard to see in this photo because the Polish communist regime tried to keep them away. They came anyway, lining the streets.
Photograph by David Valdez. Courtesy of the George H.W. Bush Library and Museum.

President Reagan giving his "Mr. Gorbachev, tear down this wall" speech in Berlin, June 12, 1987.
Photograph by Pete Souza. Courtesy of the Reagan Presidential Library and Museum.

The moment Vice President Bush's chief of staff Craig Fuller (*on the far right*) spots a plane that maybe could be borrowed to get the Vice President to his speech on time. Also in the photo (*left to right*) are head of advance John Keller, Tom Collamore, the Vice President, and a Secret Service agent.
Photograph by David Valdez. Courtesy of the George H.W. Bush Library and Museum.

During the 1988 Republican primary campaign, Senator Dole meets with an interesting group of greeters at a spontaneous drop-by that had NOT been advanced. *Left to right*: Woody Woodpecker, Charlie Chaplin, Dole, and Frankenstein.
Photograph by Dennis Brack.

The perils of the campaign trail: What you can't see is that this pig peed all over Vice President Bush while he was courting farmers in Iowa in 1988.
Photograph by David Valdez. Courtesy of the George H.W. Bush Library and Museum.

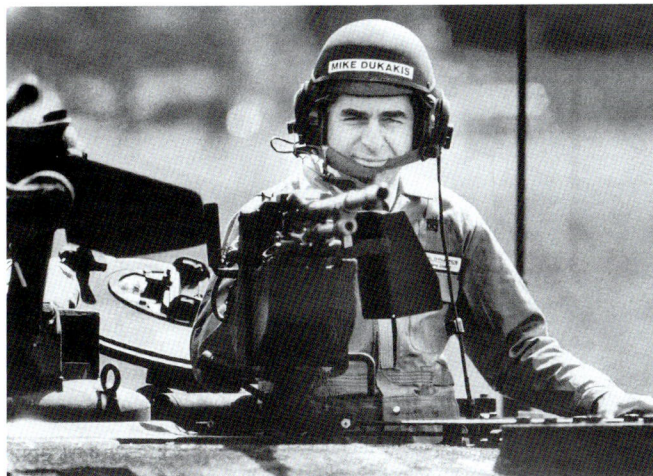

Governor Dukakis and the infamous tank photo, September 13, 1988. *Bettmann Archive via Getty Images.*

Panicked White House communications director David Demarest explains last-minute speech changes to President George H. W. Bush. An estimated one million Czechs were waiting for the President to take the stage in Prague on November 17, 1990. *Photograph by Carol Powers. Courtesy of the George H.W. Bush Library and Museum.*

"The talking purple hat" photo became fodder for comedians and critics for a few days— or years. The photo was taken during the arrival ceremony of the Queen's state visit on May 14, 1991. *Photograph by Steven Purcell. Courtesy of the George H.W. Bush Library and Museum.*

After President Clinton's aide told him his tie needed straightening before the White House signing of the Oslo II Accords on September 28, 1995, everyone in the room decided they better do the same. *Left to right*: King Hussein of Jordan; Egyptian President Hosni Mubarak; and Israeli Prime Minister Yitzhak Rabin. Palestinian leader Yasser Arafat, who stands with his back to the camera, obviously was not wearing a tie.
Photograph by Barbara Kinney. Courtesy of the William J. Clinton Presidential Library and Museum.

President and Mrs. Clinton visit Ghana in March 1998. With them are Ghanaian President and Mrs. Rawlings.
Photograph by Sharon Farmer. Courtesy of the William J. Clinton Presidential Library and Museum.

President George W. Bush consoles a firefighter during his visit to Ground Zero on September 14, 2001—three days after 9/11.
Photograph by Paul Morse. Courtesy of the George W. Bush Library.

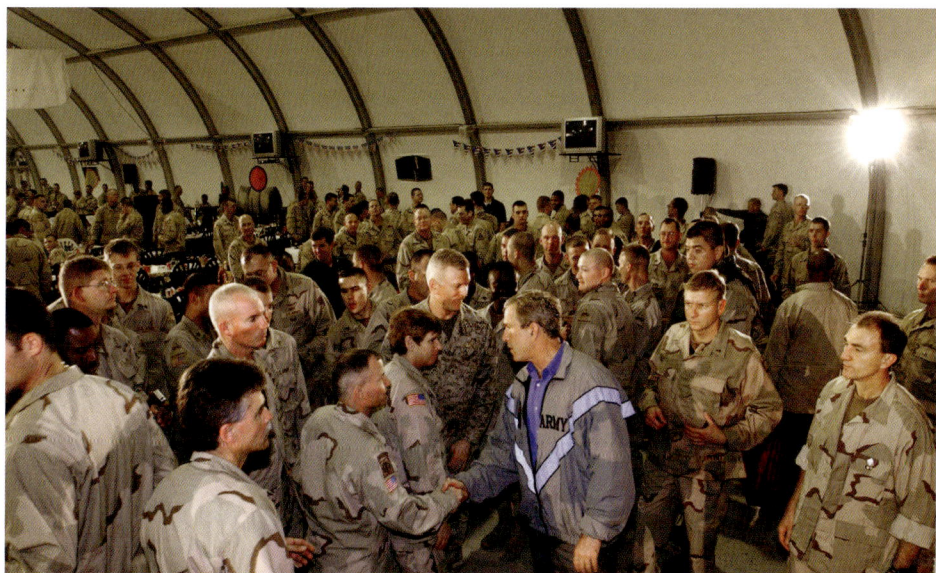

President George W. Bush greets the troops during his surprise visit to Iraq on Thanksgiving Day 2003.
Photograph by Tina Hager. Courtesy of the George W. Bush Library.

Oprah joins Senator Obama at a campaign rally in Des Moines, Iowa, on December 8, 2007.
Scott Olson via Getty Images.

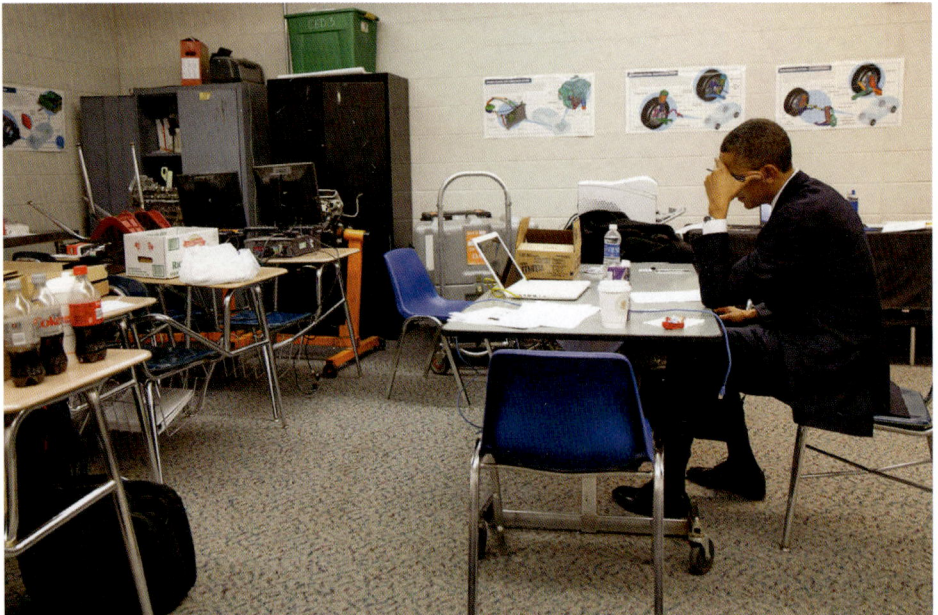

President Obama sits alone in a classroom at Sandy Hook Elementary School in Newtown, Connecticut, contemplating what to say to parents and the community after the horrific school shooting on December 14, 2012.
Photograph by Pete Souza. Courtesy of the Barack Obama Presidential Library.

using discreet earpieces and handheld microphones threaded underneath their suit coats, running down their sleeves.

"Go," responded Gary Fendler, lead press advance for the trip.

"Arrival imminent," Athey replied.

The time was 7:20 p.m.

"En route gate," Fendler responded as he walked away from the traveling press pool already prepositioned on the driveway inside the gate but outside the house. Press aide Bruce Zanca remained with the pool.

The advance team did not include many details in radio conversations. A private network was deployed by WHCA specifically for the trip, but it was unsecure. The team was working in a communist country run by a dictator, so it seemed prudent that short, cryptic messages worked best no matter the topic to thereby avoid "sharing" too much information.

Athey and Fendler met on the driveway and approached the closed, tall metal gate leading to the street. They joined staff site advance Dave Novelle and Fred Grubbe, who were responsible for facilitating the evening's private meeting and follow-on group dinner. US Embassy personnel and Secret Service agents were also at the gate.

Keller was inside Davis's home, and on hearing the radio traffic, exited the residence and walked toward the gate to observe the arrival. Coordinating the on-time arrival of Solidarity's top leadership took planning and persistence. The President of Poland, General Wojciech Jaruzelski, lived a stone's throw away, so on a normal day there were security checkpoints all along the road.

Cameron Munter, an economic officer at the US Embassy in Poland in 1987, and who thirteen years later would be named US ambassador to Pakistan, remembered events preceding the dinner with clarity.

"There were checkpoints in place in that area and anyone who came to Davis's residence was stopped and asked for ID by the Secret Police. It was a deterrent to visit us, the Americans," he said. "For the [Solidarity] leadership, it didn't bother them. It was expected." While the days of arbitrarily jailing members had ended, detainment and other methods of harassment continued and often were used to impede an individual's travel and business.

Although not detained, several of the Solidarity dinner guests were delayed and harassed at these security checkpoints before being allowed to pass and present themselves at the gatehouse, usually in ones and twos. Several vehicles arrived. Each caused a commotion in the street. Guests were escorted into the house by Grubbe and Novelle. The Polish Security Service was clearly agitated by the arrival of these particular visitors.

At 7:25 p.m., Polish agents in the street started speaking in elevated tones and motioned toward one of the security checkpoints established at a nearby intersection. A set of headlights could be seen in the distance as dusk descended on the well-manicured neighborhood. The vehicle was stopped. Polish security asked to see Walesa's identification card, which he produced. They pretended not to recognize his name or face as he sat in the back seat. Harassment, not incarceration, was their intent.

Back at the gate, Athey, Fendler, and a couple of US Embassy officials urged Polish security to let the vehicle continue. They said Walesa was an invited guest. Eventually the Polish security voices quieted, and the vehicle was allowed to pass as had the other arrivals earlier in the evening.

The car dimmed its headlights as it approached the gate and then came to an abrupt stop when a Polish security agent stepped in front of it. Several of his colleagues approached the vehicle. This maneuver on the part of Polish security was baffling. That Walesa and possibly another out-of-town guest or two would attend the dinner was previously disclosed to officials in the Polish foreign ministry. Their presence was not a surprise to security at the residence. Again, another clear example of harassment.

Having reached this point, a few yards from the front gate of Davis's home, the advance team was determined to help Walesa keep his dinner appointment.

The front gate swung open and Athey, Grubbe, Novelle, Fendler,[2] and an embassy official or two stepped into the street and jostled their way to the passenger door. With sharp elbows, smiles, and verbal assurances (in English) that everything was okay, a low-intensity shoving match ensued between the United States and Poland.

With a small group of Americans running interference, the 1983 Nobel Peace Prize recipient and outlawed Solidarity leader exited the vehicle. He slipped into the center of the small, loose-knit protective circle and maneuvered the few remaining steps through the open gate. Once through the gate, the Polish Security Service retreated because it was considered sovereign property of the United States.

By 7:30 p.m., Walesa was safely beyond the gatehouse and was escorted through the front door of the residence. Following a brief indoor greeting, the Vice President, Walesa, and Davis emerged from the house and stood on the porch for a photo opportunity for the assembled international press pool. A minute later, without comments, the men turned and reentered the house and moved to one end of the home and positioned themselves in seats in the study.

At 8:00 p.m., the Bush-Walesa-Davis private meeting concluded, and they moved to the dining room for the expanded group dinner. At its conclusion, a final unscripted photo op, including brief comments, evolved.

The press pool was once again assembled outside on the driveway facing the front door. Shortly, the right side of the two-door

---

2 Other members of the Warsaw advance team were Lauren Zanca and Steve Broadbent. Their roles also were crucial in making the events go smoothly.

entrance opened and out onto the driveway stepped Vice President Bush, Walesa, Davis, and seven members of Solidarity's top leadership for another highly visible group photo.

But the biggest impact of the trip would occur the next morning: the surprise joint visit of the American Vice President and the Polish resistance leader to the grave of a Polish hero, Father Jerzy Popieluszko.

Orchestrating the event at the church was more easily envisioned than accomplished and was made even more difficult because the Vice President and Walesa had met for the first time less than fourteen hours earlier at dinner. It was there that the Vice President had invited Walesa to join him.

The biggest challenge was getting Walesa to the guesthouse. Concern was raised that Polish security would now be watching Walesa closely and try to prevent him from arriving at the guesthouse. Davis suggested that shepherding Walesa in a vehicle with US Embassy diplomatic license plates was the best way to ensure his arrival and avoid any delay. A second automobile carrying a US Embassy film crew would follow the first car. If Walesa's vehicle was stopped, at least a film crew would capture the incident and, perhaps, act as a deterrent.

Meanwhile, back at the church, the advance and press teams had worked through the night to restructure the Vice President's visit since he was now bringing an unexpected guest.

Two microphones with wind blockers were connected to a portable sound system, their cables surreptitiously threaded along the base of the outside church wall and up to where the Vice President and Walesa would make their surprise appearance on the balcony.

Earlier in the advance, Athey had called Keller from a secure line at the US Embassy to request an extra portable sound system and thousands of handheld US and Polish flags—"Just in case they were needed." A cargo plane delivering WHCA equipment was already scheduled, and Keller arranged for the additional equipment to be delivered to the embassy in Warsaw before Air Force Two landed in Poland.

Back at St. Stanislaw, new locations to stage the traveling press pool were established to obtain advantageous TV and camera balcony coverage. These locations not only had to offer a clear view of the leaders, but also had to afford an unobstructed pathway for the press pool to the motorcade, which was departing the church immediately after the balcony appearance.

By 7:30 a.m., Poles had started to gather behind the fences installed by the government around the church perimeter. The government's intent was to limit the crowd size by placing these barriers on the opposite side of the street to keep the people far enough away so that they could not see what was to take place on the church grounds. But the government underestimated the Polish people. They would not be kept away.

As the nine-o-clock hour neared, the Vice President and Mrs. Bush stepped outside the guesthouse and were joined by Davis and Walesa, who were walking toward the couple on the pathway. Walesa was steered into the limousine.

At approximately the same time, Athey was waiting at the church, with Father Zdzislaw Krol, chancellor of the Warsaw Metropolitan Curia and acting pastor of St. Stanislaw. They were standing in the street outside the front gate along with the Secret Service site agent as the motorcade neared. Fendler was positioned several feet away off their left shoulders. All along the motorcade route, thousands of Poles stood on sidewalks and porch steps enthusiastically cheering as the limousine passed, many of them waving miniature Polish and American flags that had surprisingly appeared that morning.

Fendler and the assembled media were ready. The advance team knew what surprise awaited the crowd surrounding the church, which by now greatly exceeded the five-hundred-person limit previously dictated by the Polish authorities.

An estimated twenty-thousand Solidarity supporters and anti-government, anticommunist, and anti-Soviet Poles had flooded the area.

A lone church bell tolled, and the crowd broke into a banned Polish song as the motorcade neared.

The Vice President's limousine stopped on its mark at the front of the church—precisely where the Secret Service site advance agent was standing with his upstretched right arm high in the air.

The Secret Service assumed their assigned positions as the limousine sat idling. Once everyone was set, the right rear passenger-side door was opened by the Secret Service Special Agent in Charge (SAIC), or detail leader of the Vice-Presidential Protective Division, Hubert Bell.

Walesa exited the limousine first, followed immediately by Vice President Bush. Both men waved. The courtyard reverberated with shouts made louder by the echo chamber created by the concrete and masonry facades of buildings bordering the church square. The crowd broke into repeated chants.

The people on the street nearest the limousine erupted into a full-throated cheer as they recognized Walesa. The cheer quickly turned to a roar as the entire crowd finally realized Walesa was standing publicly with the Vice President of the United States.

The crowd broke into three-syllable chants: "Long Live Bush!" "Long Live Lech!"

At 9:00 a.m., the two men approached the grave site and stood silently behind five kneeling members of Father Popieluszko's family.

A heavy, thick metal link chain connecting a ring of large stone boulders that very much resembled a set of stone rosary beads bordered the expansive grave site. Beyond the ring was a ten-foot-high iron picket fence. Suspended from the fence, displayed on either side of the grave site, were dozens of red-and-white pro-Solidarity banners and signs. The production and display of many of these placards had been orchestrated by the advance team.

Walesa lifted his own circular red-and-white flower arrangement and together he and the Vice President stepped over the chain link and boulder border and followed two US Marines in their "dress blues" uniforms as they carried a large wreath bedecked with violet and white flowers. They positioned the wreath at the foot of the thick, oversized, polished, stone cross with rough-hewed edges that rested on the ground and capped the priest's grave.

The Vice President and Walesa stepped forward and stood on either side of the wreath and unfurled an attached long, white cloth ribbon bearing a heartfelt message for Father Popieluszko and all freedom-loving Poles: "TO AN HONORED VICTIM OF THE CONTINUING FIGHT FOR THE LIBERTY OF ALL POLES—FROM THE AMERICAN PEOPLE."

Vice President Bush next reached into his right-side front pants pocket and produced a piece of white material given to him by Keller earlier that morning. As he unfolded the cloth, the bright red letters of Solidarity were evident. He spread the free trade union rectangular banner across the upper half of the wreath for the crowd to see and stepped back. Walesa, with hands clasped together at his waist, looked on and nodded approvingly. It was another highly visible, very public demonstration of America's support for a free Poland and, in particular, Solidarity.

The Vice President walked to a small microphone stand and offered solemn words honoring the slain priest and asked the crowd to pledge to pursue Father Popieluszko's "quest to overcome evil with good." When Interpreter Litwinski finished translating, the crowd interrupted the Vice President's next sentence with a spontaneous chant of "We Pledge, We Pledge, We Do!"

As the emotional ceremony ended, the Vice President turned and faced the Popieluszko family. He embraced the tearful mother and anguished father, who thanked him for visiting their son. The group, including Walesa and Davis, was ushered inside the church to the sanctuary where they were met by Father Zdzislaw Krol, who escorted them through a private room filled with numerous objects memorializing the life of Father Popieluszko.

"This way, sir," a Secret Service agent said softly as Vice President Bush thanked Father Krol and turned to depart. The agent shifted to his left, intending to lead the entourage to the waiting limousine repositioned in the street outside the church's main entrance.

Because of a briefing earlier that morning by Keller and Fuller, the Vice President knew to turn right and look for his personal aide, Tim McBride. McBride caught the Vice President's eye and motioned toward Athey, who was standing a short distance away in front of a doorway with his hand upright high in the air—the advance team's universal signal to "follow me."

The Vice President, Walesa, and church ministers followed Athey out of the sanctuary and into the nave. Security agents from both sides scrambled to adjust to the surprise route.[3]

The group quickly proceeded down the center aisle of the nave, flanked by annoyed US and Polish security, to a set of balcony stairs located in the vestibule. The pews on both sides of the nave were filled with worshippers, all of whom applauded and smiled broadly as the group traversed the prayer hall. Many of the Poles flashed the "V" sign, the Solidarity symbol.

Keller and Grubbe were already waiting topside on the open-air balcony as Vice President Bush and Walesa climbed the narrow, stone stairway. There they readied the two microphones that previously were secreted on the perch in the early morning hours.

Fendler positioned himself at the bottom of the balcony steps and tried to redirect staff and guests away from the entrance.

---

3 According to Craig Fuller, he had informed the head of the Vice President's Secret Service detail that if everything was in place, a surprise address from the balcony was the plan.

"Clean up the shot, please," Fendler said, referencing the photo op that was planned for the balcony.

At the same time, Zanca repositioned the press pool on the ground level to capture the Vice President and Walesa when they appeared at the balcony railing and greeted the thousands of Polish faces swarming around the church property. The larger group of media were also staged so they could view the balcony.

Vice President Bush and Walesa appeared at the top of the church stairs, walked out on the balcony, and waved as the throngs in the street cheered their approval when they saw the two leaders side by side.

Keller and Grubbe were waiting with two microphones. As Vice President Bush and Walesa approached the railing and gazed out on the teeming crowd, Keller proceeded to duckwalk toward the railing. The Vice President glanced down at his side and looked quizzically at his director of advance as Keller extended his arm upward and placed a mic into his hand and urged him to speak to the Poles in the street.

The Vice President, in his brief remarks, told the crowd how proud he was to be standing next to Walesa, a man so well-respected in the United States of America. With that the crowd began to chant repeatedly:

"Long Live Bush!" "Long Live Walesa!" "Long Live Solidarity!"

As Bush waved one last time, Keller, who was crouched low behind the leaders, inched forward and in a stage whisper reminded the Vice President to salute the crowd. The fingers on his right hand morphed from a full-hand wave to form a "V," the symbol for Solidarity. When the crowd recognized this salute, in complete disregard for any retribution from the communist authorities, they cheered wildly and chanted:

"We Thank Reagan, We Thank Reagan, We Thank Reagan!"

In 2017, remembering the 1987 visit of Vice President Bush and how it affected the future of Poland, then former President Walesa said: "That visit spread around a very important conviction: Who could be against us, if such major players *are for us?*"[4]

Editor's note from Tom: *I was part of the traveling staff on this trip and was deeply moved by the events described here. The crowd was the largest we had ever seen in the sixty-five countries the Vice President had visited. We all had a sense we were witnessing history in the making, and the advance team had a central role in helping Vice President Bush convey messages that expedited Poland's march to freedom.*

We'll stay in Poland for one more story, this time about a somber trip made by Vice President Dick Cheney.

Longtime advance man Judd Swift's essay is adapted from his book, My Presidential Life: The Showdown at Putin's Dacha and Other Misadventures on the Diplomatic Road.

JUDD SWIFT,
advancing Vice President Cheney:

The agreement when I signed up for the job was unspoken but clearly understood: Advance staff were meant to perform their duties and stay out of the way. We were never to get involved in the debate. We were process, not diplomacy. We were expected to add neither emotion nor opinion.

By the time I found myself in Krakow, Poland, in January 2005,

---

4   Note from Fendler and Keller: Tadeusz "Ted" Lipien, former Voice of America Polish Service director, covered the 1987 visit and in 2017 was instrumental in obtaining former President Lech Walesa's responses to important questions about the trip.

for a solemn ceremony to commemorate the sixtieth anniversary of the liberation of the infamous Auschwitz-Birkenau death camp, I had traveled the globe with American presidents for more than a decade.

That five-day trip to Poland would for me become a dark moment. I loved my work and would continue doing it enthusiastically for another four years, but the Poland trip gave me pause.

My job was to assure that things ran smoothly when the American delegation, led by Vice President Dick Cheney, arrived at the Auschwitz-Birkenau Memorial and Museum.

Every day, the drive between my hotel and the concentration camp became a little tougher.

Instead of concentrating on the details ahead that I needed to corral, I was filled with foreboding, struggling to control a visceral resistance to spending any time in a place of such unspeakable evil. Every evening, my fourteen-hour days would end with me standing atop a set of stairs between what had been two crematoriums on the memorial site. I would stare down at the steps where so many innocent human beings had walked to their deaths. I was drawn there, unable to digest the horror.

I was not prepared.

The memorial service would be attended by more than a thousand survivors and leaders from some forty countries, including delegations from Poland, Israel, Russia, France, and Germany.

My own dark tour of the two camps covering more than forty acres was a stark reminder of how easily evil can insert itself into daily life. I walked slowly through rooms filled with the shorn hair of victims, towering piles of eyeglasses, and luggage so efficiently taken from the 1.5 million men, women, and children who died there. It was numbing.

Auschwitz-Birkenau remains a stark reminder to me of the sometimes impotence of diplomacy, the very thing I had spent so many years helping to promote. The memorial is a paralyzing demonstration of the folly of world leaders, self-interest, and war itself. More than anything it speaks loudly to the very human tendency to avert one's eyes from things too dark to understand.

Despite my struggles, I did my job well. Everything went according to schedule, our leaders were protected and safe, and the entire advance team was efficient and accommodating. I had no complaints from anyone. From a purely operational perspective, it was a good trip.

But I will never place the word "good" anywhere near that haunting memorial. Thinking about it now, I wonder how I managed.

The world's press attended and wrote movingly about the ceremony. But there was a small subset who chose instead to focus on Vice President Dick Cheney's attire at the solemn remembrance.

I might have had a hand in what the Vice President chose to wear that day.

My job called for managing the site—arranging seating and hotel accommodations and coordinating security, transportation, schedules, and the individual demands of a group among whom egos were always oversized. By then I had grown used to juggling the avalanche of minutia. That was my job.

But on that trip, the details I thrived on arranging seemed trivial beyond my comprehension. In the presence of such darkness, how was I supposed to robotically assure a VIP that their limousine would be roomy and comfortable, their hotel room large, and their flights on time?

It was the only time in my twenty-year career I felt trivial.

The elephant in the room was that Vice President Cheney was not a healthy man. By the time he attended the memorial service, he had suffered four heart attacks.

The weather for the ceremony was expected to be atrocious, the ceremony long, and the accommodations for attendees spartan.

Cheney's health was behind a memo I wrote to the lead advance, Bob Athey, and to Ken Fairfax, the deputy chief of mission in our embassy in Warsaw, warning them of the extreme cold temperatures and the longevity of the outdoor ceremony, and the distance the Vice President would have to walk over rough terrain. I recommended the Vice President dress accordingly.

And he did.

Cheney's attire at the ceremony—an olive-green US Air Force parka with a fur-trimmed hood and hiking boots—prompted ridicule from a fashion columnist at *The Washington Post*. The column was picked up by the wire services and television networks and took on a life of its own.

I dealt with the press frequently and respected them, even admired their doggedness. Respecting the press and ingratiating myself to them was prudent in my line of work. It was a way to encourage favorable coverage.

But *The Washington Post* column on Cheney's wardrobe, calling it "the kind of attire one typically wears to operate a snow blower," irritated the hell out of me.

I felt it was a cheap shot, inappropriate, and entirely devoid of useful commentary, given Cheney's fragile health and the purpose of the ceremony.

I must admit Cheney had done himself no favors. The week before, in a snowy Washington, Cheney had sat outside in the chilled air to attend the second inauguration of George W. Bush and his own swearing-in as Vice President, dressed in only a formal overcoat—sans parka or woolen ski cap for protection. After the Auschwitz ceremony, pundits were quick to point that out.

Even more irritating, the Vice President had given a very moving speech to a forum of world leaders in Krakow before the ceremony. It essentially went unnoticed in the coverage of his fashion misstep.

He stressed the importance of confronting evil before it takes hold:

"The story of the camps remind us that evil is real and must be called by its name and must be confronted. We are reminded that anti-Semitism may begin with words but rarely stops with words, and the message of intolerance and hatred must be opposed before it turns into acts of horror," he told the small group.

The ceremony itself was moving. It lifted my sagging spirits and injected, if only momentarily, a sense of optimism.

But at day's end, I was spent, emotionally exhausted. Then, as I always did, I returned to Washington to await my next assignment.

In the life of presidents and vice presidents, there are the big, bold moments that change history. And then moments that are . . . well, just memorable, such as these three stories from Doug Brook.

DOUG BROOK,

advancing Vice President and Mrs. Bush:

Mrs. Bush traveled to Ghana in November 1981 with Peace Corps Director Loret Ruppe to commemorate the twentieth anniversary of the Peace Corps. (Ghana was the first country to accept Peace Corps volunteers.)

After she toured Ghanaian villages to meet with village elders and observe the Peace Corps volunteers at work, the big finish of the visit was a "durbar" festival with much colorful drumming and dancing performed in front of the honored visitors.

What could go wrong?

It was beautiful until one man from a dancing group, covered in white ash, approached the grandstand and stood in front of Mrs. Bush and Mrs. Ruppe with a live chicken under his arm. He proceeded to chew his way through the chicken's neck, squirting blood all over himself. We were told later that it was a deliberate attempt by an opposing faction to embarrass the government.

A few weeks later my wife and I hosted Mrs. Ruppe and the advance team at a party at our home to look at pictures and reminisce about the trip. The menu? Fried chicken!

Editors' note: *Mrs. Bush wrote about this incident in her memoirs. Her description of the . . . well, colorful event: "I'm not sure when it came to me that the feathered thing was a live chicken. I think it was just before this crazy man put its head in his mouth and bit it off. He then rubbed the blood all over his body. He got closer and closer to me until someone yelled at him and led him off."*

DOUG BROOK:

During a three-day visit to Israel, Vice President Bush was to give a major speech to the Knesset, Israel's parliament. Our access to the Knesset building was limited, but it was a formal government venue that routinely hosted visiting bigwigs.

What could go wrong?

On the morning of the speech, we finally were allowed in for the first time. The building was beautiful, sparkling, and ready. Except at the center was the smallest and shortest podium we had ever seen. When questioned, the Knesset staff just said that's their podium, the one they use all the time. No other was available.

The VP can't use this podium! We're going to get killed.

With time passing much too quickly, we managed to get the White House podium out of the press center, loaded into a truck, and driven to the Knesset where the members and the press were already arriving. Deciding we needed to make this look as if it were planned, we put on our suit coats, pulled up our ties, and, with dignity, carried the podium into the center of the Knesset floor as if it were a coffin lying in state.

Editors' note: *This story illustrates the point that if you dress up and act like you are doing something you are supposed to be doing you can usually get away with it—something advance folks did and do a fair amount.*

And then there is France again . . .

Advancing a trip to Paris, the French protocol office team was only mildly cooperative. But over a week or more of negotiations we managed to agree on the schedule, sites, and scenarios.

What could go wrong?

The day of the arrival, we on the advance teams got into our cars and followed our French escorts to the airport—but not to the airport site we had advanced! The French had changed the arrival site from the Dugny Air Base side of Le Bourget airport to a different location at Le Bourget without informing us. I raged at my French counterpart like a baseball manager kicking dirt on an umpire's shoes. We held the Vice President on the plane for what seemed like forever—really, just a few minutes—while we and the Secret Service got ourselves re-arranged for arrival.

Were it not for the great food in the staff holding rooms I would never do another advance in France.

Vice President and Mrs. Bush went to Africa in November 1982 for a multiple-country tour: Cape Verde, Senegal, Nigeria, the Soviet Union, Zambia, Zimbabwe, Kenya, and Zaire.

Wait, the Soviet Union?

The Vice President was three countries into the African tour when the traveling party received word of the death of Soviet President Leonid Brezhnev. President Reagan made the decision that his Vice President should represent the United States at the funeral. It would be the first of three Soviet funerals Vice President Bush would attend, the other two being Yuri Andropov's in 1984 and Konstantin Chernenko's in 1985, at which time the Vice President met with yet another new leader of the Soviet Union: Mikhail Gorbachev. The Vice President's good friend and the White House chief of staff, James A. Baker III, is credited with giving his friend the slogan: You die, I fly.

CHASE UNTERMEYER,
traveling with Vice President Bush:

After a successful visit to Senegal, Air Force Two took off over the Atlantic and headed for Nigeria, passing around the great bulge of Africa rather than fly over a prickly country or two. During the four-hour fight, the Vice President's chief of staff, Admiral Daniel Murphy, came up to me, bent down, and put his hand on my knee. "You're going to Moscow."

So after two action-packed days in Nigeria, we left on Sunday, November 14, for the six-hour fight to Rhein-Main Air Force Base in Germany. Upon landing, the United States Air Force outfitted the staff with warm parkas, long underwear, and padded socks.

On board Air Force Two was a uniformed Soviet air navigator, who guided us into Moscow. In his honor, the Secret Service kept a vigilant watch at the door of the vice-presidential cabin, although Vice President Bush did go forward and greet him at one point.

Onboard the plane was Bob Blackwell, a CIA specialist in Soviet political affairs, who gave the Vice President a highly valuable and fascinating analysis on the post-Brezhnev period. Toward the end of the flight, Admiral Murphy called all the staff into the lounge to say, "The whole purpose of this trip is to get him [Bush] to the funeral and back. The rest of us will just stand by." He instructed us not to have any contact with Soviets who might approach us, and he warned that anything we said would be overheard by someone or something.

Around 9:00 p.m. Moscow time, our plane began maneuvering jerkily on its approach to Sheremetevo Airport. We were met by a long line of cars to accommodate the Bushes, Secretary of State George Shultz, who had already arrived, and Ambassador Arthur Hartman. As we descended the ramp, Bob Blackwell held back to watch which Soviet officials greeted the Vice President, which would provide a clue to how Moscow was treating his visit.

When we arrived at the Kremlin, the staff dutifully followed instructions and remained in our cars while Vice President Bush and Secretary Shultz went inside to pay respects at Brezhnev's bier, accompanied by Ambassador Hartman and Mrs. Bush.

The next day most of the staff watched the funeral on television at the embassy. The only Americans in Red Square were George and Barbara Bush, Secretary Shultz, Ambassador Hartman, an interpreter, and Lieutenant Colonel Bill Eckert, the Vice President's military aide. As he always did, Bill tightly clutched "the football," a briefcase containing the top-secret codes required to authorize a nuclear strike. Only the creators of the classic Cold War comedy *Dr. Strangelove* could imagine a scene in which George Bush, attending a funeral in Red Square, would excuse himself from the proceedings in order to rain missiles down on his own location.

Even before our 7:00 p.m. takeoff, the Vice President called for Bob Blackwell to come to his cabin on Air Force Two. While several of us listened in fascination, the Vice President debriefed on the meeting with Andropov. During dinner, both Bushes told the staff about the past twenty-four hours, surely among the most remarkable in their lives so far. For example, they detected not one bit of sorrow from ordinary Muscovites they saw in the streets. Then the Bushes retired for the night. When we landed at Rhein-Main, we refueled and picked up our fellow travelers to resume a trip to Africa that was not even halfway over.

DAN SULLIVAN,
head of advance for Vice President Bush:

While we were refueling in Germany, we were notified by the US Embassy in Moscow to please bring flowers as there were none available in Moscow. We had little time to plan as our plane was scheduled to take off within an hour.

Someone mentioned to me that there was a German war memorial just outside the American base. We grabbed a truck and went hunting. Sure enough, there they were: Four large wreaths in West Germany's colors: black, red, and gold. There was no one around to ask so a small act of larceny occurred. We took the four wreaths back to the plane and off we went to Moscow, regularly spraying the flowers during the plane ride to keep them as fresh as possible.

When we landed in Moscow, the US Ambassador's wife was there waiting for the flowers. She, along with a small team of intrepid foreign service wives, got to work dyeing the flowers red, white, and blue. They very creatively fashioned a beautiful wreath to be placed at Brezhnev's bier. The extra flowers were given to other embassies, and I asked that West Germany especially be given whatever flowers they needed.

In case you're curious, we did reimburse West Germany for the wreaths that we "borrowed."

Back to Africa . . .

CHASE UNTERMEYER:

By far the most memorable stop was in what was then called Zaire and now is once again called the Congo. It was headed by Joseph

Mobutu, a classic third-world dictator whose signature look was a leopard-skin cap worn at a jaunty angle.

Mobutu hosted the Bushes and their delegation aboard his yacht, *Kamanyola*, on a cruise on the Congo River. True to his big-man style, he arrived by helicopter while his guests came by car. The river, seen from *Kamanyola*'s rail, evoked Joseph Conrad's *Heart of Darkness*, with rusted hulks of old river steamers, warehouses, customs houses, and masses of water hyacinth that had floated from the interior of the continent.

Upon arrival at Stanley Pool, a broad spot in the river, we were shown to the paneled dining saloon for lunch, a huge but unappetizing buffet of Zairian and continental fare. After the meal, we docked at N'sele, the site of President Mobutu's private demonstration farm (run by Israelis), where we were greeted by young dancers and singers chanting praise of the great Président-Fondateur.

Mobutu took the Vice President and Mrs. Bush to his favorite fishing hole, a spot so small and overstocked that fish practically leaped onto the hook, happy to escape. Other Zairian officials sped on to the next event, running over a child en route.

We in the official party proceeded to the People's Palace, an enormous structure built by the Chinese, for the welcoming ceremony. Many vice-presidential staff members had slipped away back to the capital to go shopping, so a group of embassy officers and I stood on the steps along with Mrs. Bush (she had left the fishing hole early), impersonating the entire US delegation. Below us swayed and sang thousands of people. We waited and waited for Mobutu and the Vice President to finish fishing. When they came at last, Mobutu suddenly plunged into the delirious crowd with the American Vice President at his side. Yes, this made the Secret Service go bananas. This was called a *bain de foule*, or crowd bath. There followed a snappy pass-in-review by the Presidential Guard, goosestepping in leopard-skin vests.

When the ceremony ended, we all dashed for cars in the motorcade with Joe Hagin, who was then the Vice President's personal aide, yelling "I've had enough!" He and I barely managed to jump in a vehicle with advance man Rick Ahearn. As our driver crawled through a mob of Zairians, Rick said, "I have never been happier to leave a site in my life!"—and he was at Ronald Reagan's side at the Washington Hilton on March 30, 1981.

KIM BRADY CUTLER,
aide to Barbara Bush:

When we landed in Zaire, the lead Secret Service agent told me that our hosts wanted Mrs. Bush to visit a local market, but he highly recommended she not go as it was a crowded and hard-to-secure place. They asked me to brief her and to make sure she kindly regretted any offers from President Mobutu.

The next day, as we were steaming up the Congo River on the presidential yacht, I was on a balcony with the agents overlooking the stern and taking in the view when we saw a helicopter coming our way. I turned to the agent beside me and asked, "Are we expecting company?" No, they were not, but after a flurry of nervous activity, calm set in as the helicopter landed and a string of waiters dressed in all white exited the chopper carrying huge silver trays on their shoulders—lunch had arrived from the palace!

Things settled down until the agents called me to come to the lunchroom ASAP. I hurried there thinking something had happened to Mrs. Bush only to find out from the agent sitting behind her at lunch that she had accepted President Mobutu's invitation to visit the market!

The next morning we arrived at the market to a beehive of activity. Our first sight was that of a huge bowl of wiggling centipedes (or the African equivalent) with the locals dipping their hands into the bowl and eating them whole! Mrs. Bush turned around and gave me a look like, "This is different." No kidding.

We proceeded deeper into the crowded market, each place showing their wares to us. Mrs. Bush acknowledged them all with a smile until we were stopped at a table that had an unconscious monkey strapped under it, with only its skull protruding through a hole in the table. They proceeded to cut open its head with a spring-loaded blade that propelled the top of his skull into the air, which they caught and ate the brains out of it. Mrs. Bush turned around, going weak in the knees, and said, "I think it is time to go!" We headed to the limo as fast as possible! On the way back to the residence, she asked what the horrible smell was in the limo, and her Secret Service supervisor informed her that it was the dead six-foot catfish in the trunk she had been given as a gift.

Another African adventure four years later.

DAVE RYDER,
advancing Vice President Bush:

In August 1986, Vice President and Mrs. Bush went to Egypt to visit President Hosni Mubarak and to attend the opening of a new water plant on the Nile River.

As we departed the meeting with Mubarak, I was a bit surprised to see a couple of red Chevy convertibles, along with five or six motorcycles, waiting alongside the Vice President's motorcade with both the Egyptian and the Secret Service security teams. Seeing two red Chevy convertibles as part of security for our motorcade was a new one for me, even after I had done many international visits for the Vice President over the years.

Thousands of curious onlookers lined the motorcade route, but things were going very smoothly until we came to a narrow bridge overpass. As the motorcade approached the bridge, I noticed the Egyptian security team in one of the red convertibles was attempting to pull ahead of one of our Secret Service vehicles, which was right behind the Vice President's limousine. The agent driving the security vehicle tried to avoid a collision with the convertible, but the car insisted on getting in front, which it did. At the same time one of the motorcycle drivers was also trying to get past everyone. Unfortunately, the narrow overpass proved to be too small for all these vehicles at the same time, and the motorcycle and convertible collided, forcing the motorcycle over the side of the bridge. At the same time, the driver of the convertible had to slam on his brakes in order to avoid ramming his car into the back end of the Vice President's limo, causing a rear-end collision between the Secret Service vehicle and the convertible. The two vehicles locked bumpers and came to a dead stop in the middle of the bridge with no room for the other cars in the motorcade to pass.

Immediately, a very stout Secret Service agent jumped out of his car, with his Uzi in hand, and started jumping up and down on the two bumpers to free the vehicles from each other.

While this scene was unfolding, the Vice President's limousine continued on its way to the event site. It took less than a minute to release the two bumpers, thanks to the Secret Service, but once separated, we realized that the four-lane road the motorcade was to proceed down was being overtaken by pedestrians and local traffic, causing a slight distance between the Vice President's limousine and the rest of the motorcade.

Then it got worse. The vehicle I was riding in just behind the security vehicle began having engine problems. The accelerator pedal became stuck wide open and the car began accelerating very quickly. I got on my knees as best as I could to go under the dashboard, to see if I could operate the gas pedal by hand, which I was able to do. But the gas pedal kept getting stuck. The agent driving the car began yelling instructions to me of when to accelerate and when to back off. We caught up with the Vice President's limo, as did the rest of the motorcade, just as we were arriving at the water plant event site.

An agent was just opening the door to the Vice President's limousine so he could head up the stairs and into the building as our car was pulling up into position. The agent driving our car tried to turn off the car's engine but to no avail. The car simply would not shut down. As the car's engine continued to roar, dust from the dirty parking lot was billowing out from under the car, and then very unexpectedly, the car began to backfire with loud booms. It sounded very much like a gun going off. This startled everyone, especially the agents leading the Vice President into the building. He was surrounded by his security detail, who provided cover and protection while pushing him into the building to safety.

It was the first time that I thought I was going to be in the line of gunfire, not by the Secret Service, but by the Egyptian Security team who seemed a bit rattled by what was going on.

CRAIG FULLER,
chief of staff to Vice President Bush:

The invitation was a speech at the University of Minnesota on April 28, 1987.

We had no reason to be in Minnesota in April 1987. And, with the Iran-Contra issue brewing,[5] we really had no reason to be on a

---

5 The Iran-Contra scandal centered on arms trafficking to Iran between 1981 to 1986, carried out by several members of the Reagan administration. Iran was under an arms embargo at the time, which would have made sales to Iran illegal. It was discovered there were a few individuals who found a way to use the proceeds of the arms sale to fund the Contras, an anti-Sandinista rebel group in Nicaragua. Although several members of the administration were indicted, President Reagan and Vice President Bush were cleared of any illegal activity by a special counsel.

college campus with the Vice President speaking to students in an audience we had no way to control.

So why did the Vice President go? Because the invitation came from a family friend, George Pillsbury.

It was trouble from the beginning.

When the advance team hit the ground, there were concerns registered immediately. The campus had a strong anti-Bush contingent. We could not control access to the large hall where the speech was planned. Everyone urged reconsideration. The Vice President said he had been assured it would be fine and he would be giving the speech.

We flew into St. Louis aboard Air Force Two for a fundraising event on April 27. It was an evening event and it had been a long day when we quit for the night, still worried about how the next day would go. We had no idea what we were in for.

The next morning the staff, press, guests, and others went to the airport ahead of the Vice President and boarded Air Force Two. Vice President Bush, his sister, and a few others of us arrived and got on board. As was the procedure, once the Vice President was on board, the doors were closed and a taxi out would commence. But it didn't.

The door remained open and the stairs remained at the aircraft. Our head of advance, John Keller, came back with the words that set our most unusual day in motion: "The captain would like to see you."

As a pilot for a good part of my life, I knew there was nothing good I was going to learn. It was explained that, in a final check, a hydraulic fluid leak had been discovered and the issue needed to be resolved before the aircraft could depart. I certainly had no argument. It was one of those "do not fly" kinds of problems. Unfortunately, there was a part needed that was nowhere near St. Louis.

As John Keller, senior staff member Tom Collamore, and I stood on the stairs discussing the situation, someone told me the Vice President wanted me immediately. I found him sitting in his stateroom perturbed that we were not moving. I explained the problem.

With little sympathy, he simply looked at me and said, "I am giving that speech this afternoon." To which the only acceptable answer was, "Yes, sir."

Back on the steps to the aircraft, we were joined by the lead Secret Service agent. As we spoke about how no other military aircraft was available and anything flown out from Washington couldn't get us into Minneapolis in time, I noticed that a private business jet was parked next to us with its red tail beacon light on, powered up, and waiting for us to depart.

I asked the agent to write down the tail number, contact the Federal Aviation Administration, and ask if there was any reason why the Vice President should not fly on that aircraft. Then I walked over to the pilot of the business jet and presented him with a unique opportunity: "Leave your client here and fly the Vice President of the United States to Minneapolis today." He agreed, as long as I spoke to his client and got his agreement.

The client was a banker heading to a meeting in Michigan. I suggested I could give him a story he could tell for the rest of his life if he let us commandeer his aircraft. He laughed and said he'd probably missed his meetings anyway and readily agreed.

The Vice President was thrilled with the idea. So we boarded a small but comfortable private jet for the one-hour flight, leaving most of the traveling staff and guests behind.

Upon arrival, the staff advance lead kept radioing his team that we were taxiing up to the arrival point and the greeters. The puzzled staff kept radioing back that they could not see Air Force Two. The one promise we had made to the Secret Service was that no one would know what we'd done until we got on the ground. I am thinking the people on the ground were a little surprised when the Vice President stepped off a business jet.

As for the speech, it was cut short by student protests. The Vice President stepped backstage after making a sincere effort to deliver his message. He looked at me with an expression that said, "Do not say a word."[6]

BRIAN MONTGOMERY,
advancing Vice President Bush:[7]

It was 1986, and Vice President Bush was home in Houston when he decided to accept the offer of the Houston Astros owner, John McMullen, to attend a game the next day. After a quick conversation with the Secret Service and a heads-up to the Astros front office to keep things quiet, we decided to make the visit a surprise. The Vice President also accepted McMullen's offer to throw out the first pitch.

A couple of hours before the game, a few Secret Service agents and I arrived at the Astrodome. We met briefly with the front office staff, including the Astros' PR representative. She was thrilled to have the Vice President throwing out the first pitch, but then she issued a directive: "You need to let the person who was originally scheduled to throw it out know they're no longer doing it. They'll get to do it another time."

At first, I wondered why I had to be the one to break the news, but I figured it wasn't worth arguing about. I asked, "Who was it?"

"Smokey Bear," she replied, adding with a hint of importance, "And by the way, don't say Smokey *the* Bear—it's just Smokey Bear."

---

6 This paragraph was in the minutes of the next meeting of the University of Minnesota Board of Regents: "[The University President] further reported on the disturbing events associated with the visit by Vice President George Bush to the Twin Cities Campus noting that there was continuous disruption during the Vice President's speech at Northrop Auditorium on April 28. He stated that he had sent Vice President Bush a letter apologizing for the disruption."
7 This story is adapted from Brian's book, *White House Blue Pass*. Publication date is pending.

I could tell she'd been corrected on this point before.

Great, I thought, and made my way down to the field, figuring it wouldn't be too difficult to find a guy in a bear costume. Sure enough, Smokey Bear was standing near the first base line, next to a USDA Forest Service representative.[8] (For the record, Smokey Bear is part of the USDA Forest Service, not the National Park Service.)

I approached them, ready to explain the situation, but before I could even finish my sentence, the Forest Service guy cut me off.

"Hey—we're in public, so don't talk to the Bear. Talk to me," he said, with a tone that made it sound like I was dealing with some kind of VIP, not a guy in a fuzzy costume with blue overalls. He acted like I'd just barged into a meeting with the Queen.

I was rightfully thinking, "I'm pretty sure there's a person inside that bear suit," but I didn't let it show. I nodded and addressed the Forest Service agent directly: "All right, well, tell Smokey Bear he's not throwing out the pitch anymore," I said, turning to walk away.

As I took a few steps, I heard a muffled voice from inside the bear costume ask: "What did he say?"

The absurdity of it hit me. I couldn't help but chuckle.

Before moving on to another vice president, we have one more Soviet funeral story to tell.

ROGER WHYTE,
advancing Vice President Bush:

I was asked to go to Moscow to do the advance lead for Vice President Bush when he attended the funeral of Soviet President Yuri Andropov, who died February 9, 1984. The funeral was to take place on a very

---

8   United States Department of Agriculture.

cold February day in Red Square, with the daytime temperature a mild ten degrees below zero.

So my first important job was to make sure the Vice President did not get frostbite.

The Vice President was going to be located with other foreign leaders in a reserved section right next to Lenin's tomb, standing for more than an hour on the very cold cobblestones in Red Square. In preparation for the Vice President's arrival, my embassy contact was tasked to locate a pair of size ten and a half Ski-Doo boots and a very warm parka.[9]

The morning of the funeral I met the Deputy Chief of Mission at Spaso House, the ambassador's residence where the Vice President was staying. He presented me with the boots and the parka, and I proceeded up to the Vice President's suite.

Ready and waiting for departure, he asked me what I was carrying. I explained to him that the outside temperature was fifteen degrees below zero and that he was going to be standing on very cold cobblestones for more than an hour, so he needed to wear these Ski-Doo boots to prevent frostbite.

I was quickly advised that his wife had packed his favorite rubber boots and that he was going to be just fine. Realizing that I was about to send the Vice President of the United States out in below zero temperatures in Johnston & Murphy rubber boots, I had to pull out my best argument to get him to put on these boots.

"Mr. Vice President, I will have hell to pay if I return you home to Washington with frostbitten toes, so I am going to speak to you as your mother would address you, 'George, put on your boots.'"

The Vice President stared at me for a few moments, then sat down and put on the boots. As we were getting ready to leave, I handed him the parka, and he said back, "This parka is not very good looking,

---

9   Ski-Doo boots are made in Canada and are worn by winter sports enthusiasts.

but I guess it would be what she [his mother] would want?" I told him yes.

The funeral was long and very cold and concluded about an hour and a half later. As we were walking out of Red Square, I was about ten steps in front of the Vice President when he said, "Hey, Roger, my mother would be very proud of you. Thanks!"

KIKI MCLEAN,
advancing Vice President Gore:

There is a myth that serving on the vice-presidential nominee staff is not fun and was even easier. Nothing could be further from the truth, especially if you worked for Al Gore.

Advance staff learned to keep up with his adventurous side as well as being ready with the level of detail he demanded. Consider the staffers who watched him surf down the aisle of the 1992 campaign plane on a plastic cafeteria tray. Or the first trip director, who while on a Texas bus tour was asked by the boss what town we were driving into. He confidently replied with the incorrect name while then Senator Gore read the correct name off the highway sign as we drove by.

His staff learned quickly that we needed to have the level of discipline the presidential nominee expected.

We will end this chapter with how it began: A story about how vice presidents often take on important and significant assignments that make a difference and even save lives.

In October 2019, Turkey launched a long-threatened military incursion against a US-backed, Kurdish-led militia alliance in northeastern Syria. Two members of the Trump administration tell the story of Vice President Mike Pence's emergency trip to Turkey.

ED MIYAGISHIMA,
advancing Vice President Pence:

On a Sunday in October 2019, I received a call from Aaron Chang, Vice President Pence's director of advance, saying that the Vice President and his chief of staff, Marc Short, had just come out of an Oval Office meeting with the President.

"The Vice President is going to Turkey," Aaron said, which meant pack a bag. About twenty-four hours later I found myself on one of two C-17s headed for Ankara, Turkey. The planes were filled with Secret Service agents, members of the White House Military Office (WHMO), WHCA, and the advance staff. We had twenty-two hours to organize a trip that normally would take ten to fourteen days.

I had visited Ankara once before in 2008 with then Vice President Dick Cheney. From my experience with that trip I knew what to expect from our counterparts.

We needed to negotiate two meetings: a smaller executive bilateral meeting with a few principals and a second meeting with more staff.

The Turkish team pushed for a tête-à-tête—a one-on-one meeting with only two people. They were fine with the larger meeting. We negotiated for a few hours, but I knew from my last visit to Turkey what was going to happen: The Turks would "roll" us, meaning they would go with what they wanted no matter what.

Home court advantage.

As the lead advance person, I reported back to Washington, who okayed a meeting with just the principals plus an interpreter on both sides.

About forty-five minutes prior to the Vice President's arrival, we were told that President Recep Tayyip Erdoğan's interpreter was going to be his National Security Advisor who spoke English. That now meant the principal meeting would be their President and a top advisor with just our Vice President and an interpreter.

We quickly came up with the suggestion that Ambassador Jim Jeffrey join the Vice President instead of the interpreter. So there we were on the tarmac of the Ankara airport calling Aaron Chang, who was traveling with the Vice President and Marc Short. We were given the go-ahead to let our Turkish counterparts know that is what we were going to do.

What was supposed to be a ten-minute meeting became an hour and a half. The Vice President was then joined by Secretary of State Mike Pompeo, National Security Advisor Robert O'Brien, Marc Short, and some other staff. The marathon meeting ended in a cease-fire agreement between the Syrians and the Turks.

Aaron and I often talk about this trip where everyone on our team—from the Secret Service to the State Department, WHMO, WHCA, and staff—worked together to make this trip happen.

And because of everyone's hard work we were able to save lives.

MARC SHORT,
chief of staff to Vice President Pence:

We will probably never know the extent of the violence Erdoğan's government inflicted on the Kurds, but he had clearly crossed the line. President Trump called Pence down to the Oval Office and they called Erdoğan to discuss the situation. During the call Trump put the speaker on mute and asked Pence if he would go to Turkey. He then informed Erdoğan he was sending Pence to iron things out. We had very little time to prepare, and the Secret Service in particular wasn't happy. Advance was minimal and it was clear we wouldn't be able to stay the night. That's a long way to go for a meeting and immediate turnaround flight home, even on Air Force Two.

Less than forty-eight hours after Pence's Oval Office meeting and phone call we were in the air, along with Secretary of State Mike Pompeo.

Ed Miyagishima is right: The one-on-one meeting between Pence and Erdoğan went unusually long and it was strange not to have eyes on Pence to gauge how it was going. Pompeo finally had enough and informed the Turks that he was going to join the meeting unless they adjourned to the larger expanded meeting originally planned and agreed to. Pence later told me on the flight home that he believed Erdoğan was trying to wear him down and get his agreement that their incursion was okay and they could keep the territory they had claimed. Pence held the line that it was not acceptable and there would be sanctions unless they retreated. That position eventually prevailed, and a press conference was hastily put together at the embassy before our departure back to Washington.

Erdoğan had clearly miscalculated, as he didn't think Trump would elevate the issue and was clearly surprised Pence had stood firm. Erdoğan made a lot of noise and wasn't happy with us, saying this was no way to treat a NATO ally. But the Kurds were also our friends, and President Trump and Vice President Pence were determined to have their back.

CHAPTER SEVEN

WHEN THE PRESIDENT IS NOW A "FORMER" AND THE "TEAM" IS "YOU"

*C*ertainly *when the president and First Lady leave the White House for good, their life literally turns upside down.*

Gone is a devoted White House staff, available to them 24/7. Gone, too, is the residential staff, who tries to anticipate your every need and move, not to mention makes your bed and cooks your meals.

Barbara Bush loved telling the story of how one day shortly after they moved back to Houston, she was attempting to make a vegetarian smoothie for then nine-year-old granddaughter Lauren when the top came off the blender and suddenly carrots and tomatoes were dripping from the kitchen ceiling. Somehow that very same day, she managed to knock over a large jar of spaghetti sauce that President Bush 41 had bought on his first of many visits to Sam's Club.

They ordered pizza.

Although the transition from the White House to a more normal life is not as traumatic for the staff, there are some similarities. The team shrinks from an entire administration of folks to just a handful.

That would include the world of advance. There is no team. You will likely travel with a Secret Service agent, but they have their own issues to resolve. If you are overseas, you might have embassy support. Or not. You often are a lone wolf.

And sometimes there is no advance at all, and it falls to the personal aides traveling with the boss to figure it all out on their own.

JON DAVIDSON,
chief of staff to President Clinton:

President Clinton had a roommate during his Rhodes Scholar days at Oxford named David Edwards. What began in college became a lifelong friendship.

Later in life, David's health took a turn. He called 42 and laid out his final wishes with impressive specificity:[1] He wanted his ashes divided into five urns and scattered in five different places, each by someone he trusted. President Clinton was one of the chosen stewards. His mission: Return to their old, shared house in Oxford and quietly lay a portion of David to rest in the backyard.

Fast-forward to 2013, more than forty years after his Oxford days. We're headed to England for a speech, and 42 turns to me and says, "We need to bring David with us."

I've helped coordinate everything from summits to surprise birthday parties, but I had no playbook for a semiclandestine ash-scattering operation in suburban England.

I call our advance man, Connor, and we go over the usual checklist: venue logistics, drive times, Oxford's photo requests, RON,[2] greeters, the moderator—every box ticked. Then I add:

1 President Clinton was the forty-second president of the United States. The first time 41 called President Clinton "42," he simply said: "I have arrived."
2 RON is White House lingo for "remain overnight."

"Connor, one small OTR. We need to bury human remains in the backyard of Clinton's old college house."

Silence.

I continue: "Back when the President was at Oxford, he lived on Leckford Road. We need to find that house and see if someone lives there. It may be a museum for all I know. Or a gas station. Anyway, we need to very politely ask if we can inter some ashes in their yard. The catch is . . . we can't say too much in case they're not Clinton fans."

"What do I say?" Connor asks.

"Maybe just knock on the door, and if they answer, say something like 'Hi, my name is Connor and I think Bill Clinton used to live here,' and see how they react."

I *assumed* they'd know a former US president once lived in their house, but then again, thinking back to my own college days, I'm not sure I'd have noticed or cared, let alone grasped the significance.

I continue to Connor, "If they act nonchalant or open to talking, make the pitch. Offer them a photo with Clinton if they help you. But if they react negatively toward hearing his name, we'll need to come up with a Plan B."

Connor, who's already juggling the entire visit, now has to pivot from planning dignitary greetings to staging a covert backyard burial. Not something covered in Advance 101.

He scouts the house the day before we land. No one answers the door, but there's laundry flapping on the line—proof of life. The backyard gate is padlocked.

I tell him to go to a hardware store and pick up three items: a bolt cutter, a new padlock, and a trowel. Connor goes back the next day. Same story: no answer. So after the Oxford speech, I give the green light.

We roll up in the motorcade eight cars deep, police motorcycles and all. Connor snips the lock when we're two minutes away. We roll up slowly, sneak into the yard, dig a small hole, bury David's ashes, snap a few quiet photos for his widow, and slip out. We hang the new lock with its keys on the fence, a little thank-you for the unknowing homeowners.

To this day, we don't know if they ever noticed. Maybe they came home, saw a shiny new lock where the old one had been, and chalked it up to neighborhood kids or a blackout memory. Maybe they will read this story and learn they've had a quiet houseguest in the garden all along. Either way, mission accomplished.

Thanks to a very talented and nimble advance man, David Edwards found his way home, and the President kept his promise.

JIM DAHLEM,
advancing President Reagan:

President Reagan famously traveled to the Brandenburg Gate at the Berlin Wall in 1987 to challenge the Soviet president: "Mr. Gorbachev, tear down this Wall."

After splitting the city of Berlin in half for twenty-six years, the Wall finally came down on November 9, 1989, a year after President Reagan had left office.

The German government was so appreciative for his role in helping to end the Cold War, President Reagan was invited back to Germany for a week of meetings and award presentations. I had the distinct honor of being asked to be one of the lead advance people for the trip.

We were almost done with our week of planning before the Reagans were due to arrive, so the rest of the team and I—Joanne Drake, who was President Reagan's chief of staff; and Stefanie Davis, a longtime Reagan advance person—decided to have dinner and a couple of good German beers. We finished the evening and returned to our rooms, feeling pretty good about where we stood.

I had just turned the lights off to go to sleep when the telephone rang. It was Joanne. She told me she needed to see me and Stefanie in her room now.

The breaking news: The President and Mrs. Reagan were now going to fly from Berlin to Bonn, Germany—then the capital of West Germany—for a meeting in the middle of their week in Berlin. That changed everything. We worked all night changing meeting days and times and juggling who would be the lead advance of which site. I was wishing I had passed on the beer at dinner!

President Reagan would be flying into what had been Tempelhof Air Force Base (now a commercial airport) late at night aboard Malcolm Forbes's jet. Forbes's plane was named *Capitalist Tool*, and the name was emblazoned on the tail of the aircraft. Okay, we won, the communists lost the Cold War. But we decided to take the diplomatic high road and not intentionally rub their noses in the fact that they had lost. We instructed the US Air Force that the airplane should stop with the nose of the aircraft facing the press so the tail of the aircraft would not be visible for the press to see.

We thought everyone understood this, but apparently everyone received this message except for the Air Force crew member with the batons guiding the aircraft. As the plane came in, the crew member guided the aircraft straight ahead, as we had asked, and just when we thought he was going to cross the batons to stop the airplane, he motioned left, the airplane turned broadside, and *Capitalist Tool* was in our face.

We all reacted as one would expect, together saying the exact same word at the same time: "Sh*t"!

One of the sites for which I was the lead advance was the newly constructed parliamentary building, the Reichstag, which had been burned by the Nazis in February 1933. With the newly constructed building, Berlin would soon become the capital once again.[3]

---

3 Berlin would become the capital of reunified Germany in October 1990.

The next stop would be walking from the Reichstag to the Brandenburg Gate. It was a relatively short walk, so we all felt good about not using cars.

During President Reagan's tour of the Reichstag, a Secret Service agent walked up to me and whispered that they were going to need help with crowd control when we walked outside. I asked what he meant, and he motioned for me to come to one of the windows facing the Brandenburg Gate. I was stunned at the size of the crowd that was there to greet President Reagan.

As we made the walk to the gate, we needed to gently push back the crowd in a nice but forceful way to get President Reagan safely where he needed to be. Thankfully, we succeeded.

The Reagans left for Bonn, and I got a much-needed day off. I met them on their return to Berlin, and everyone hustled to the motorcade for the ride to the hotel. Before I got in my vehicle, I was handed a box and was told to make sure the box got on the plane when they departed for the trip home.

Once we had arrived at the hotel and the Reagans retired to their room, the staff decided to go out to dinner. I took the box to my room, laid it on my bed, and met everyone for the night out. At the dinner there was much discussion about the trip to Bonn and how exciting it was that he had unsuspectingly received this award, which I was told was absolutely going to be on display at the Presidential Library. When I inquired about this further, the Bonn traveling team told me it was the Grand Cross of the Order of Merit, the highest award that could be given to any non-German citizen. They said, "You know, the box we gave to you when we got off the airplane."

There I sat with the vision of this great award sitting in the open on my bed. I could not wait for dinner to end and to get back to my room to ensure it was still there. I was elated to see it was where I had left it. Now I had to secure it until the date of departure. There were no safes in our rooms but then I had a thought: I had been in Berlin for ten days and

I had accumulated quite the pile of laundry. What the hell, I thought, I'll stuff it in my dirty clothes and if someone ransacks my room and has the desire to go through my dirty laundry, they can have it!

For the record, the medal now safely resides at the Reagan Presidential Library Center.

BUNNY MURDOCK,
advancing President Bush 41:

In April 1993 President and Mrs. Bush were invited by His Highness the Emir of Kuwait to visit so that the Kuwaiti people could show their gratitude to President Bush for getting Saddam Hussein out of their country.

At that time I was working for Sheikh Saud Nasir Al-Sabah, the Kuwaiti ambassador during the Gulf War and now Kuwait's Minister of Information. I was his person in Washington. He put me in charge of arranging the Bushes' departure from Houston and accompanying them to Kuwait.

Easy enough, right?

We boarded a special Royal Kuwait 747 jet at Ellington Field.[4] Mrs. Bush marveled at the presidential suite with the gold bathroom fixtures but also asked me, when moving to the bedroom, "How do they think George will lie down in that short bed"?

Within just a few minutes of takeoff there was a loud bang or thump. Kuwaiti security came flying from the back of the cabin and up the stairs to the cockpit, followed by the Secret Service and a slightly hysterical me.

---

4   A former Air Force base, Ellington Field in Houston now serves as a base for the Texas Air National Guard. It also is where Air Force One lands when the president of the United States visits the Houston area.

The plane's captain was coming to speak to President Bush, but I jumped in and asked: "What's happened?" He calmed me down first and said, "Just a little skin has come off the wing and we must land for caution," to which President Bush replied, "Oh that's no problem, that happened to me once in the war." As always, he was wonderfully calm.

President Bush left his seat upstairs and came down the aisle looking for me. "Bunny, do you want to look at the wing?" To which I replied, "No thank you." But later I did, and there was an enormous hole—almost nothing was left. You could see houses through the hole as the aircraft slowly descended to Houston International Airport (before it was renamed for President Bush). We made an emergency landing there instead of going back to Ellington in case of a terrorist plot.

Little did we know at the time that a terrorist plot *was* waiting for us in Kuwait. Saddam Hussein had bombs planted along the motorcade route coming from the airport to the palace. Our overnight delay waiting for a new aircraft gave the Kuwaitis time to find the bombs and change our entire program.

Before I got off the plane, I called my boss in Kuwait to let him know what had happened. Putting his hands on my shoulders, President Bush told me to tell Sheik Saud he would wait a day, a week, or whenever it was convenient for the Emir to reschedule the trip.

That night the plane's captain, knowing what a nervous traveler I was, called me in my hotel room and asked how I was. He said it was much more serious than he had let on. The Secret Service also told me later that the captain had done a magnificent job of descending the aircraft slowly so the wing would not fall off!

We left the next day on a new aircraft.

After the trip, President Bush sent me a handwritten letter. My favorite line: "May a thousand camels kneel and pay you homage."

QUINCY HICKS CRAWFORD,
aide to Barbara Bush:

Although I had served as an aide for several years, I hadn't been involved in much true advance work until the Bushes planned a trip to Beijing in September 1996. I was dispatched to Beijing with a team of Secret Service agents to coordinate with both the US Embassy and Chinese government officials.

One Chinese man, in particular, stood out and seemed to have close ties with the embassy. He was tall, handsome, and exceptionally polite, and it was clear he was very well connected within China. One embassy staff member even shared a story about a bicycle gone missing. This man was notified, and despite the city being overcrowded with bicycles, he somehow managed to find and return it.

We met with him and his team multiple times to go over every detail—movements, motorcades, and meetings. Every person and every minute of the day was planned.

However, when the Bushes arrived, the Chinese representatives seemed to implement what had likely been their plan all along.

Upon landing, the Bushes were supposed to be greeted solely by this Chinese man and then taken directly to the hotel to rest before continuing their meetings. However, a group of Chinese officials appeared, and they directed the motorcade to make an unscheduled stop for tea with additional people. I was furious, but I was reassured that this is just how Chinese officials operate and there was nothing that the Secret Service or I could do about it.

I should mention I made one big faux pas: Before the Bushes' arrival in Beijing, I had a phone conversation with President Bush to go over a few requests from the embassy, one of which was a meeting with the CIA's counterpart at the embassy. When I mentioned "CIA," President Bush immediately hung up. Jean Becker called me back, explaining that I should never mention "those letters" during a phone call in China.

My sons love to hear the story about me staying in my room at the China World Hotel. I had been told that every building in China has an extra floor at the top, exclusively for government listening purposes. It turned out to be true as I found out when I was trying to set the alarm clock in my room. The buttons weren't working, so I kept pressing harder until, suddenly, the whole face of the clock swung open like a hinge—and there, behind it, was a microphone!

JIM MCGRATH,
press spokesperson and speechwriter for President Bush 41:

I have been privileged both to advance and to accompany a former leader of the free world—and a former First Lady—to a myriad of far-flung places. The south of Spain for the 1997 Ryder Cup comes to mind, as do trips to the South of France, Hong Kong, and Istanbul for various speaking events.

Still, for me, the most memorable advance work actually centered on the driveway of George and Barbara Bush's private residence in Houston.

That's because, right after he left Washington, it became routine for many of the world leaders with whom George Bush had previously worked with as President to make a point of visiting him in Houston whenever their travels brought them to the United States. President Bush had rather famously placed a high premium on personal relationships in the conduct of US foreign affairs, and these visits showed that his fellow world statesmen clearly valued his friendship and counsel as well.

Most often these informal state visits would occur following the various leaders' annual pilgrimage to New York for the opening of the United Nations General Assembly, or while here for other official business. Such was the case when Argentina President Carlos

Menem made a point of adding Houston to his travel schedule in October 1995.

While in office, President Bush both knew and genuinely enjoyed Menem from their official meetings both at Camp David and in Buenos Aires, where the two had also enjoyed *very* competitive tennis and golf matches. In fact, when Menem visited Camp David during Mr. Bush's presidency, he brought his own tennis pro all the way from Argentina to try and tip the odds of the match in his favor.

George Bush always admired the pure, unadulterated gamesmanship of that particular maneuver.

As 41's post–White House spokesman and chief media wrangler, I had the responsibility during visits such as President Menem's to alert the regional Texas media corps—which included reporters and photographers from local, national, and international media outlets—and let them know the logistical details that would facilitate their coverage.

On October 25, 1995, awaiting Menem's motorcade arrival with President Bush in his driveway, with fifteen or so assembled media members with us, I noticed the President was holding a golf club in his hand. When I asked why, the ever competitive forty-first president replied, "Carlos may have held his own in tennis, but I got him in golf!"

PLO leader Yasser Arafat also came calling at the Bushes' home in March 1997 while in Houston to speak at the Baker Institute at Rice University.[5] Though the security and the traveling entourages for this visit were much more intense, at one point I found myself standing right next to this controversial global figure in the entryway of the Bushes' home.

At five eight, I rarely experience the sensation of "towering" over anyone, but I was immediately struck by what a diminutive figure

---

5 PLO is the Palestine Liberation Organization.

the five two Arafat cut. In that instant, he stopped being the demi-celebrity I had seen so often on TV and became instead a source of intense wonder about how such a small man could cause so much chaos in our world.

GIAN-CARLO PERESSUTTI,
aide to President Bush 41:

One of the newer additions to the Bahamian landscape in 1998 was the Atlantis Hotel on Paradise Island. Situated prominently on the grounds of the hotel was a waterslide built within a Mayan-temple-looking structure. It's quite stunning to see in person and the slide certainly caught President Bush's eye as his motorcade approached the hotel.

Bush 41 was giving a paid speech later that evening (to whom, I can't honestly recall) and was in his usual jocular mood. He turned to me in the back of the limo and said something to the effect of, "Look at that thing. Do people actually go down it?!" I laughed and confirmed that, in fact, they do. "What time's my speech?" President Bush asked. That's when I knew we were in trouble.

I cleared my throat, and said, with trepidation, "Not until around dinnertime." Please leave it alone, I thought. Please leave it alone.

"So we have some time to kill," he said. I should have known better. "Yes, sir," came my wary reply.

"Do you think I should try the waterslide?" Boom. There it was. It didn't take a side-eye from President Bush's Secret Service detail leader, Jim Pollard, for me to click into damage control. "Uh. Really?" was all I could muster.

"Yeah. I should," he said. This was familiar territory to anyone working in the office of George Bush. We used to joke that the four most feared words in the English language were, "I have an idea."

"Ohhhkaay," I managed.

Once the motorcade pulled up to the hotel and President Bush got out, I saw Jim coming toward me. "Please tell me he wasn't serious," said Agent Pollard.

"Jim, we both know he was, and I don't think we're getting out of this with the excuse that, 'they-don't-have-a-Speedo-in-your-size, sir.'"

Fast-forward thirty minutes or so. I'm handing President Bush a garish-looking bathing suit with the tags still on it. "Did you tell the agents?" he asked.

"I did, sir." I didn't add that they all wanted to kill me.

Ten minutes later the forty-first President of the United States was walking through the Atlantis Hotel lobby in a bright yellow bathing suit surrounded by a bunch of men in suits and a sweaty, defeated aide leading the way to the waterslide.

Word must have gotten out. When we arrived, the area around the slide was mobbed. There was an agent stationed at the top of the slide and one around the "arrival pool" at the bottom.

Much like when President Bush jumped out of a plane in 1997, the security calculation here was, what happens between the beginning and the end of the journey is something in which only God can intervene.

The agent at the top was accompanied by (you can't make this up) a squad of cheerleaders from the University of Arkansas. They had timed their slip 'n slide right that day. To say these young women were excited was an understatement. They greeted 41's ascent with a rousing cheer, and any trepidation he may have had was vanquished.

Down he went. A few seconds later, the soaked former leader of the free world emerged at the other end of his descent to the cheers and whoops of amazed, flabbergasted, and likely impressed vacationers.

Somehow, we did manage to get President Bush out of the pool, into a towel, and back to his room without further incident. I can only imagine the vacation photographs shared around the world by his fellow visitors.

ANDY MANER,
advancing President Bush 41:

Our story begins on the back loading dock of a nondescript Chicago hotel in 1998.

President Bush was now a former president, carrying out the role of a Republican Party fundraiser. He was in town to do an event for an Illinois politician, which, yes, carries a not-perfect sound to it since so many Illinois politicians have gone to jail. I am certain his friend Governor Jim Edgar asked him to do the event, and President Bush could not say no. (And this candidate is *not* in jail!)

President Bush had a genuine and unforced habit of always meeting the hotel manager and usually a few hotel staff on arrival. And trust me, as we walked through the kitchen area to the big, old service elevator, President Bush shook the hand of every worker he encountered. That is who he was—probably more comfortable here than in the opulent lobby just a mere door away.

At this point, I had been working for President Bush for more than five years and knew him well. I worked for him in the White House press office and also moved with him to Houston after his election loss to continue to work on press and political affairs. By this time I had left his office and was now a new Chicago resident, grateful that the former President's staff reached out to me to advance his trips to Chicago and other nearby cities.

Still present for me was the awe and admiration of being with him and the anxiousness of wanting everything to work perfectly.

This day was proceeding nearly perfectly—for a pre-9/11 former president, the entourage was smaller and more relaxed. We entered the elevator—the President and me with two Secret Service agents. Inside there was a shorter gentleman who was there to operate the slightly larger elevator with big vertically closing doors. While his key chain showed us that he was likely adept with a lot of tasks and equipment, his nervous smile showed all of us he likely hadn't done this before. As we began the journey President Bush and I chatted about topics of the day, including, of course, Chicago politics.

Then our elevator suddenly lurched to a stop.

There are few incidents that the Secret Service hasn't thought of and likely rehearsed, but this one would take a few minutes to diagnose and solve, stuck somewhere around the thirtieth floor of a Chicago high rise. In the corner of the elevator, the poor elevator operator was busy trying to use his key to do something while calling other colleagues from the elevator phone. Nothing was working.

Perhaps reaching the end of his checklist and emergency procedures, and while the agents were radioing their colleagues outside the elevator, the operator seemed to curl up a bit and put his head down against the elevator control panel. He possibly was weeping while trying to gather himself.

"What is your name, sir?" George Bush calmly asked the operator. While I don't remember the name, I recognized it as being of Polish origin.

"Don't be upset," President Bush counseled him. "Happens all the time." (I am fairly certain that was not true.)

The man began to explain that he had been looking forward to this role for many days and that it was the "highest honor of his life" to transport President Bush up and down this day. He went on to explain that when he left for work that morning, his wife chided him several times, "Don't mess up the ride with the President!" Sweat began to appear on his brow, and he began to fidget nervously as he realized our predicament was serious and that he would later have to report to his wife the failure of the ride!

"Oh no, we can't have her think that—you are doing a great job. Let's call her."

He asked me for my cell phone and instructed the operator to dial his number. I know I wasn't the only one excited that his wife answered. I know the agents and I were all smiling because while President Bush's compassion and sense of humor weren't new to us—this particular one was a first.

"Hello, dear, this is George Bush and I am here in an elevator with your husband and no matter what you hear, he is doing a great job and is a great guy. You are a lucky lady." The call ended with her saying, "Thank you, thank you, sir."

The Secret Service then informed us that we were between floors, and they likely would be lifting us out after they pried open the doors. On queue the doors slowly opened and we had only a roughly three-foot opening and about four feet above us to pull the President out, which they did. (Yes, they pulled me out, too.)

We'll end with a scary tale from former Secret Service Agent Andy Almblad, who describes how difficult the agents' jobs become when they no longer have the full support of a White House team.

ANDY ALMBLAD,
advancing former President Bush 41:

Doing foreign advances for a former president presents unique challenges, much different than for a sitting president. Our resources are limited, which means we have to rely on the host country's resources, which means we have to play by their rules. This often means doing things differently than we would like.

In 1996 I was the lead advance agent for President Bush's visit to Damascus, Syria. He was scheduled to meet with President Assad (the elder), specifically to thank him for Syria's support during Desert Storm. We then would travel to Beirut by helicopter for one night, returning to Damascus the next day. There were no commercial or private aircraft flying out of Beirut at the time, and there were also no cell phones available in Syria.

There were numerous security concerns about this trip. Several times I received late-night calls from the marines at the US Embassy that I had secure calls coming in. With no WHCA support—meaning no secure phones in our rooms—this meant getting dressed and finding a taxi at midnight in Damascus to take me to the embassy. Not an easy feat.

After President Bush arrived, it was decided that for various reasons it would not be feasible to fly,[6] so President Bush would motorcade the approximately two hours from Damascus to Beirut. There is only one main road between the two cities, and it goes right through the Bekaa Valley, also known as the home of Hezbollah and the location of their terrorist training bases.

My Syrian security contact was a high-ranking commander in the National Police, who was in charge of the motorcades and police support around Damascus. He was not impressed with the plan, to say the least, and I was not at liberty to discuss the reasoning for the change in plans.

There was talk of possibly canceling the Beirut stop (that had my vote), but even after being briefed on the situation, President Bush wouldn't hear of it. He did not want to disappoint Lebanese Prime Minister Rafic Hariri, as a visit by a former American president would be historic. He liked Hariri a great deal, and felt he deserved a show of support from the United States.

So, we planned the motorcade.

While President Bush was visiting with Assad at one of his

---

6 I am not at liberty to disclose those reasons.

palaces, we were readying the motorcade vehicles. When 41 came out of his meeting, he said that President Assad had guaranteed his safety and had ordered his presidential security to take us to the Lebanese border. At the border, we would change motorcades, and a motorcade from the US Embassy in Beirut would take him the rest of the way to Beirut.

So without any time to plan seating or communications arrangements, the presidential security brought their vehicles around and we loaded up. Everyone just tried to find an empty seat. The National Police Commander and his vehicles were unceremoniously pushed aside.

It soon became evident that the Syrians' electronic countermeasures were jamming our radios, an issue that with more planning could have been avoided. Since we also had no cell phones, we had no way to communicate between vehicles or to the motorcade from Beirut, led by my good friend and fellow agent Andy Pohutsky, who was coming to meet us.

When we arrived at the border, the Lebanese motorcade thankfully was waiting for us. It looked like a military convoy, with mounted machine guns on the vehicles. I had informed everyone to race from their Syrian car to the Lebanese car; we needed to be quick about this.

But President Bush had other ideas. He agreed to take pictures with the Syrian security, and then of course the Lebanese security guys wanted to get in on the action. So here he is standing in the middle of the Bekaa Valley taking pictures with the security officers from two large motorcades.

I was standing off to the side with the general in charge of Assad's security detail whom I had met briefly at the palace. For some reason he insisted that my last name was Syrian, which to him meant that we shared a common bond. That was strange enough, but then he grabbed my hand, and we stood there holding hands (which I understand is an Arab custom) watching the picture taking as if it was the most normal thing in the world. Truly one of the most bizarre moments of my life.

After the photo op ended, 41 headed to Beirut and we headed back to Damascus. The bad news is that we had to do it in reverse the next day. The good news is we lived to talk about it.

CHAPTER EIGHT

THE DAY I THOUGHT I WOULD BE FIRED

You've already read a number of stories where a nervous advance person thought as they watched their event go off the rails: "Well, this is it for me. I'll be flipping burgers this time tomorrow."

The Queen's purple hat story comes to mind.

We wanted to give a few other advance folks a chance to tell some of their "oops" stories. That would include Michael Smerconish, advancing Vice President George H. W. Bush:

MICHAEL SMERCONISH:

For a semester I interned in the advance office of the Vice President located in the Old Executive Office Building just down the hall from Vice President Bush himself. I was playing the role of planning the logistics of a vice-presidential visit and seeking out volunteers in different communities who might be willing to assist with the trip.

But when my internship was over, I continued to advance when

I could. The Vice President's trip to Belgium in February 1983 stands out.

The purpose was to meet with our allies at NATO Headquarters so that the Vice President could sell them on deployment of Pershing and Cruise missiles, part of President Reagan's strong defense policy. One thing I recall is leaving my passport and driver's license in my hotel and nevertheless gaining admission to the inner sanctum of NATO. Talk about a pre-9/11 world.

And then there was the night I stumbled into a Brussels brothel.

The lead advance guy on the trip was Ronald Eberhardt. If he reads this story, he will be hearing what I have to tell you for the first time. Ron was a talented fellow and very compulsive about planning. And that compliment comes from a person with many anal-retentive traits! We worked long hours prior to the Vice President's arrival, and I remember feeling a little stir-crazy because although I was in a foreign city, most days were spent going from the hotel to the US Embassy and then back to the hotel late at night. We were staying at the Hyatt Regency Brussels. Each night when we would return, I would notice that across the street from our hotel there was a very formal doorman in front of an unmarked building. Finally one night I asked our hotel doorman what was across the street. He told me it was a casino. Back home I lived in a fraternity and often we made road trips to Atlantic City. The idea of playing a few hands of blackjack was appealing, so I asked the doorman if it was open to the public. He said I should just tell them where I was staying and I'd be fine. He smiled—and I went on my way.

Armed with a few traveler's checks (remember them?), I went to play cards. The casino doorman greeted me, opened the door, and escorted me into a foyer. Then he pulled back a curtain revealing a staircase leading to a second floor, which did indeed have a casino. A very small casino. Maybe a half-dozen tables of blackjack. So I took a seat and started to play and had a drink, too. I caught a good "shoe" and was enjoying the entire experience. Here I was, a college student, traveling with the Vice President of the United States, in Europe playing some blackjack while sipping a White Russian. Yep, a White Russian, the only mixed drink I knew at the time. That cracks me up now just to think about it. Anyway, I was soon making conversation with the dealer, and I asked him what was downstairs given that I was so quickly shown the staircase. "A champagne bar," was his reply. "You should visit." That sounded pretty nice. Sure, why not a glass of champagne to finish a nice evening, I thought.

So I cashed in my chips and headed for the downstairs area. The same doorman downstairs now pulled back another curtain, this time to reveal the champagne bar. I remember that it took me a few seconds for my eyes to adjust because the place was very dark. And when I could see, I recognized that I was the lone male in a room of about twenty women. And based on their demeanor and attire, there was no doubt as to their employment. Oh, the guys at Zeta Psi were never going to believe this! Wait a minute. Was prostitution even legal in Brussels? (Yes, was the answer.)

But before I got comfortable, I saw my work for George Bush flash before my eyes. And now that I knew where I was, there was no way I was walking out the front door lest anyone from our team over at the Hyatt would see me and ask where I'd been. So I left by a rear exit and the last thing about that night that I recall was jogging down some cobblestone alley behind the brothel feeling like I was in a James Bond movie.

DAVID HARRIS,
advancing President Reagan:

I had the great privilege of being on President Reagan's advance team for many years. One of the most difficult assignments I had was being the lead advance for the President's infamous visit to a Nazi cemetery in Bitburg, Germany, in 1985.

First, a little history: West German Chancellor Kohl convinced President Reagan that a wonderful way to show how strong the alliance was between the two former World War II enemies would be for President Reagan to visit a German military cemetery. The President agreed, later saying he felt he owed Kohl, who despite considerable public and political opposition, supported him on the deployment of Pershing II missiles in West Germany.

There are innumerable on-the-ground stories I could tell about that difficult visit, beginning with how the site-selection team—led by then deputy White House Chief of Staff Michael Deaver—visited Kolmeshöhe Cemetery during a snowstorm when thirty-two rows of tombstones were covered with snow.

So what they did not see was that forty-nine of the two thousand German soldiers buried there had been members of the Waffen-SS, the military arm of Nazi Germany's Schutzstaffel (SS). The entire unit was judged to be a criminal organization at the Nuremberg trials.

When the news eventually came out about who was buried in the cemetery, all hell broke loose. The decision was made at levels way over my head that to embarrass Kohl would be a bigger mistake than to cancel the visit. While another possible cemetery site for a visit was located, the President held firm to his commitment to Chancellor Kohl.

By the time my team arrived, there was not much we could do. One element of the stop at Bitburg was a visit and speech to the F-15 Air Base at Bitburg and the US military personnel there. No problem with that part.

There were some small but important elements that the advance team could accomplish for the cemetery visit. First was to make sure the visit was short. The President was on site for only eight minutes. Another was to control the music. The Germans had arranged for a band to be on-site to play the German soldiers' funeral song, "Der gute Kamerad." I insisted with the band leader that the music be played sotto voce—sung quietly, under the breath—to minimize as much as possible the element of German wartime activities.

An interesting reminder of that visit now hangs on my office wall. It is a signed editorial cartoon from famed political cartoonist Jeff MacNelly showing the President laying a wreath at a tomb. The title of the cartoon is "Reagan Lays a Wreath at the Tomb of the Unknown Advanceman."

As director of advance for President Reagan, Jim Hooley was part of the site advance team led by Mike Deaver. He shares some of his memories of the ill-fated Bitburg cemetery visit.

JIM HOOLEY:

Yes, we failed, unforgivably, to see the Waffen-SS markers on some of the graves. We took the word of an US Embassy official and the Mayor that there were no Nazi soldiers or Gestapo buried there. I recall our own embassy guy being disdainful of Deaver asking about just that: "What, are you worried that Josef Mengele is buried here?"[1] To which Deaver responded, "*Yes*, that's exactly what I'm worried about."

As for the Mayor, he reassured us and promised to provide a cemetery registration, which was never provided.

A CBS crew, for whatever reason, made a survey of the site before the President's visit—and the graves were not covered in snow. They broadcast a video and that's when all hell broke loose.

We looked for alternative sites, but Chancellor Kohl repeatedly

---

1 Mengele was a doctor who became known as the Angel of Death; he performed deadly experiments on the prisoners at Auschwitz.

rejected President Reagan's personal appeals to change the site from Bitburg, saying his government would fall if we canceled Bitburg, which was in his parliamentary district.

I never saw President Reagan so visibly upset as he was at the reaction of news media, Jewish groups, and a public rebuke from Elie Wiesel, the Holocaust survivor and chronicler of life in the death camps.

We added a visit to the Bergen-Belsen death camp (Anne Frank is interred there in a mass grave along with thousands of others) to try to counter the reaction, and speechwriter Ken Khachigian wrote what is among the best speeches President Reagan ever gave, although sadly it was somewhat ignored by the media in all the frenzy about Bitburg.

ALIXE GLEN MATTINGLY,
deputy White House press secretary to President Bush 41:

During President Bush's administration, the "war on drugs" was among the top issues for almost every Cabinet agency and every Andean nation ally.[2] President Bush was marshaling all efforts to interdict the flow of drugs out of Colombia and put down the cartels.

Almost every day the media clamored for specific details about what we were providing, doing, thinking of doing, not doing, confirming, or denying.

We spokespeople always said, "all options are on the table," but for obvious reasons, much of that was classified. The Drug Czar's office was developing a comprehensive plan to be announced in late January 1990, but there wasn't much we could say until then. There were many speculative stories that the United States was planning to

---

2 The Andean Pact includes Colombia, Bolivia, Ecuador, and Peru.

send our military to "invade" Colombia. We said there were no plans to do that.

On a cold, rainy Saturday in early January, I was the press duty officer for the weekend, which meant all press calls to the White House went to me. It should have been a quiet weekend, so I decided to go to a matinee movie.

Moments into my popcorn, my beeper goes off. I go to a pay phone outside (think pouring rain) and call the White House switchboard.

I am told that Rita Beamish from the Associated Press needed to talk to me.

Rita tells me she is hearing from sources that a naval blockade is headed to the coast of Colombia. (Rita was also on weekend duty, alone in the press room, and I could tell was looking for something.) No, I tell her, nothing new since this week's briefings where we said repeatedly that there were no plans to send warships to Colombia. Period. Review what Marlin said.[3] That's all I got.

I return to the movie. Minutes later, the beeper goes off again. It's Rita again, insisting that her AP colleagues in Bogotá, Colombia, and at the Pentagon say something is happening with naval ships. No, I tell her. Those ships are on routine training exercises. Same as we said all last week. Use that guidance. Nothing is new. I hung up and returned to the movie. (Weekend duty officers are trained to say nothing and make no news.)

Minutes later the beeper goes off again and the White House operator says, "I have Brent Scowcroft, Jim Baker, and Dick Cheney all insisting to speak with you. Would you like to take them in any order?"

They would be the National Security Advisor, the Secretary of State, and the Secretary of Defense. I had an ominous feeling.

Rita had moved a story headlined: "US Warships are steaming

---

3 White House Press Secretary Marlin Fitzwater.

to Colombia's borders and a naval blockade is being attempted." She inserted a lame quote from me, and several quotes from unnamed sources, just so her story had someone to quote, making it look like I had confirmed something.

Colombia's President Virgilio Barco Vargas was furious and had called our senior officials to decry this story.

I raced to the West Wing to blow my stack at Rita for totally misrepresenting me. I then met with General Scowcroft to figure out what to do. This was a huge diplomatic and strategic disaster that took all weekend to unwind. Rita did send out a correction, but it was too late. I spent the remainder of the weekend at the White House dealing with every reporter wanting to follow up on her story.

Now it was Monday. All the staff knew what had happened. And knew that I had a big black cloud over my head. Fingers were being pointed and I was being blamed for a major screw-up. Marlin said to me, "Maybe you should say you have the flu and go home?" Other staffers would pop into my office with "that look" of empathy.

Was I going to be fired?

About 11:00 a.m. the phone rang. It was Mrs. Bush, wanting to know if I was free for lunch. Yikes. Was I getting fired by the First Lady? My heart sank. I of course said yes and asked if I should come to the residence.

"No," she said, "let's meet in the White House Mess."

I thought, What?! Mrs. Bush never goes to the Mess. Ouch, this is really bad.

During our lunch at the middle table in the Mess, for all to see, there was no mention of warships or Colombia. She was clearly the symbolic emissary to show the West Wing staff, and me, that I was fine, and that the Bushes had total confidence in my loyalty and job performance.

Message received.

By the way, I have no idea what movie I was trying to watch.

Editor's note from Jean: *I will tuck in here a story of how a former president kept a young advance man from getting fired.*

Vice President Biden was coming to Houston to visit MD Anderson Cancer Center to discuss the Obama administration's "Cancer Moonshot" initiative, founded in honor of the Vice President's son Beau, who had died of brain cancer.

His office had called to ask if he could pay a courtesy call on the former president and his friend, George H. W. Bush. President Bush said of course he would love to see the Vice President.

Working with the young advance man in charge (I feel badly I don't remember his name), we decided it would be best for President Bush 41 to visit the Vice President in his hotel suite, which was a short ten-minute drive from the Bushes' house.

The day Vice President Biden was to arrive in Houston, the panicked advance man showed up in my office. The Vice President had read his schedule on the way to Andrews and was mortified that the former President was calling on him. The Vice President felt strongly that out of respect, he should call on President Bush, either at his house or his office. I took the young man into President Bush's office, so he could explain the situation. President Bush would have none of it. He pointed out that unlike the Vice President of the United States, he had a two-car motorcade.

This is the conversation as I remember it:

"Joe's motorcade can't even fit on my street," President Bush told the advance man. "I will go to Joe."

The advance man said he might be fired if he didn't get this changed.

Then President Bush said to him, "Let me show you how this works."

He summoned the head of his Secret Service detail into the office and explained what was going on. "Marlon [Harris], I need for you to declare that out of security precautions, the Secret Service has asked me to go to the Vice President's hotel rather than him come here or to the house."

"Yes, sir, so declared," said Marlon, who admitted it made more sense anyway.

"See, this is how you do it," President Bush said. "You throw the Secret Service under the bus but always tell them you are doing it. They will understand."

President Bush went to Vice President Biden's hotel room; the young advance man was not fired.

CHAPTER NINE

THE DAY I KNEW I WAS BLESSED

Despite the long flights and even longer hours, despite often working under conditions that are uncomfortable and sometimes even scary, despite the constant fear that if you make one wrong move you might start World War III, most advance men and women know they have the best job in the world.

They are, after all, the proverbial fly on the wall to history.

They witnessed the handshake that ended the Cold War, the speech that helped inspire a revolution, the smile that replaced mistrust with trust.

Yet, when they talk or write about the stories they remember the most, it's often the smaller moments they will never forget, the moments that touched their hearts the most.

LLOYD HAND,
chief of protocol, President Johnson:

Throughout my long and exciting run with Lyndon Baines Johnson, I was a part of so many special and historic moments. But hanging out with the Pope has to be among my favorites.

In October 1965, Pope Paul VI visited New York City, the first trip made by a pope to the United States. His plan included speaking before the United Nations General Assembly, leading mass at Yankee Stadium, blessing Cardinal Francis Spellman at St. Patrick's Cathedral, and visiting the Vatican pavilion from the 1964 World's Fair. He also wanted to visit with President Johnson, and I was dispatched to advance that encounter.

The challenge for us was that in 1965 the United States and the Vatican did not have a formal diplomatic relationship.[1] As a result, LBJ couldn't treat Pope Paul as a visiting head of state. We couldn't hold a state dinner for him or pull any of the pomp levers usually available for such a visit.

That wasn't going to stop LBJ!

We scheduled a meeting at the Waldorf Astoria, the hotel where LBJ and his White House entourage (which included me) were staying. While there were hundreds of thousands of people lining the streets of New York City to see the Pope, LBJ forbade anyone from lining the hallways of the hotel as the Pope made his way to their meeting room.

He then sent me on an incredible mission: Take Lady Bird's limousine to Cardinal Spellman's home, pick up the Pope, and bring him back to the hotel. What a thrill! Back at the Waldorf, my wife, Ann, and our friend Mary Margaret Valenti (wife of Jack) loitered outside our suite in hopes of seeing the Pope when we passed by on our way to the meeting with LBJ. Their act of defiance was rewarded when Pope Paul graciously stopped to greet them. The moment was all the sweeter because the President did not witness their act of treason.

---

1 According to Wikipedia, diplomatic relations with the Vatican were cut off in 1867 when several Catholics were accused of conspiring in the death of President Lincoln, and due to rising anti-Catholic sentiment in the country. President Reagan and Pope John Paul II reinstated diplomatic relations in 1984.

The Pope then disappeared into his private meeting with the President, which lasted roughly fifty minutes and focused on the subject of his United Nations General Assembly address: peace. The event set an important precedent for papal visits with future presidents that exists to this day.

Later, LBJ invited my wife, the Valentis, and other staff to be officially presented to the Pope. In an act of heavenly benevolence, neither the Pope, Ann, nor Mary Margaret let on they had already met!

STEVE BULL,
aide to President Nixon:

On May 25, 1973, President Nixon hosted a spectacular dinner on the White House lawn honoring the recently released Vietnam POWs.

Despite the presence and participation of numerous Hollywood luminaries, including Bob Hope, Sammy Davis Jr., Jimmy Stewart, and John Wayne, the most memorable and moving moment was when the elderly Irving Berlin, the composer of "God Bless America," sang his song in tribute to the men he characterized as "my boys."

But it might not have happened had there not been a lead-up two years earlier when President Nixon invited Mr. Berlin to be honored at a formal East Room function where some of his well-known compositions would be presented by the Marine Corps Band, culminating with Mr. Berlin receiving the Presidential Medal of Freedom.

It initially fell to me to contact Mr. Berlin and extend the invitation while advising him that the President would call him personally at a later date. Through the creativity and ingenuity of the White House operators, they tracked down a man who represented Mr.

Berlin and put me in touch with him. When I explained the plan, he was most enthusiastic and gave me a phone number where I could reach the famous composer.

When I called Mr. Berlin, he politely declined. So after the conversation ended, I called back his representative who assured me that Mr. Berlin was just being modest and said he would talk to him and would certainly obtain his consent.

A few days later I received a call from a tearful and distressed Irving Berlin asking why I wouldn't respect the wishes he expressed to me during our first conversation and why did I go behind his back to persuade him to change his mind. He wanted no White House honors, he wanted no Medal of Freedom, and just wanted me to leave him alone.

After offering a sincere apology and feeling about two feet tall, I concluded our call. It was only after some time that I learned that he had been suffering emotional problems that probably contributed to his decision.

Rewind to where we began: the POW dinner at the White House.

When the POWs were released from Hanoi, Vietnam, on February 12, 1973, the first stop of one of the three planes carrying them home was at Clark Air Force Base in the Philippines. A brief, informal ceremony was planned where President Nixon, through an amplified telephone call, would welcome them back on behalf of the American people. The first man deplaning was the most senior officer, who descended the stairs and declared "God bless America." After delivering his welcome, President Nixon invited them all to what would be a gala event in their honor at the White House sometime in the spring.

The dinner was held in a beautiful tent on the South Lawn with chandeliers suspended from the top, dozens of lights strung from the top to the sides of the tent, and tables with white tablecloths and large pillar candles, all ready and waiting for the arrival of nearly six hundred American POWs and their guests.

It was all set to be a perfect evening.

Then, as it often does in May in Washington, it started pouring rain.

The women in elegant gowns, and the soldiers, sailors, airmen, and marines decked out in their finest formal military attire entered the tent, which was already beginning to develop puddles. But the weather failed to dampen anyone's festive spirits. The evening proceeded as planned with the entertainers, all of whom had previously entertained US troops in Vietnam at one time or another during the years-long conflict, providing uplifting and memorable performances.

And that takes us back to Irving Berlin's reluctance to be honored himself two years earlier.

The day before the dinner I received a call from Mr. Berlin himself saying that he wanted to come to the POW dinner to sing his song to "my boys." His offer was accepted immediately with extreme gratitude and excitement.

On the evening of the dinner, as the entertainment portion was coming to an end and the tent had quieted with only the sound of rain on the roof, an elderly Irving Berlin walked haltingly out on the stage, and without introduction or musical accompaniment, sang the first verse of "God Bless America." When he finished, he waited a moment before he began singing the same song again, but this time accompanied by the Marine Corps orchestra. At its conclusion, with the rain coming down and all present visibly moved with faces dampened by tears, everyone stood up and together—the composer, the orchestra, and more than one thousand proud Americans happy to be home at last—sang "God Bless America" for the third time in an incredibly moving exclamation of faith, patriotism, and gratitude.

With nothing said or done further, Irving Berlin exited the stage.

GREG WILLARD,
advance man and attorney to President Ford:

You could call it my final advance.

For every person entrusted with the solemn responsibility of planning a presidential state funeral, the process is enormously complex and intense. And the sad conclusion of the process is, by definition, inevitable.

A private moment with President Ford vividly illustrated both the raw emotions of planning his state funeral and a special part of his character.

On January 11, 2006, while I was meeting with him in his living room to review the updated plan, President Ford suddenly became very quiet. Tears welled up in his eyes. He said softly, "Greg, I need you to do something that's very personal."

"Of course, Mr. President," I said. "Whatever you need—consider it done."

With tears glistening on his cheeks, he leaned forward: "Promise me that on the Air Force One flight taking me home to Michigan you'll make certain that Jimmy and Rosalynn Carter are with Betty."

I was gobsmacked. Here was the thirty-eighth president emotionally asking for assurance that the man who narrowly defeated him for the presidency would be at Betty Ford's side at the saddest moment of her life.

I replied, "Sir, I promise to the depths of my soul I will make it happen."

And so it was. On January 2, 2007, Betty Ford watched as President Ford's flag-draped casket was carried across the Andrews tarmac to Air Force One while a military band played "Goin' Home." And close by her side at every moment of her beloved husband's final journey home were Jimmy and Rosalynn Carter.

PHIL WISE,
White House staff, President Carter:

On August 22, 1978, President and Mrs. Carter pushed off for a three-day float trip down the middle fork of the Salmon River in Idaho, guests of their good friend Cecil Andrus, the former governor of Idaho and now secretary of the interior.

While I spent three days on the raft dodging numerous fly-fishing casts gone off course, the Carters enjoyed a breathtaking trip through some of the most gorgeous wilderness areas of our country.

Once the trip was over, the Carters headed to Yellowstone Park for a few more days of solitude. I flew back to Washington, DC, to assist in the logistical planning for the Camp David summit involving Prime Minister Menachem Begin of Israel; President Anwar Sadat of Egypt; and President Carter.

Camp David is very serene and private, providing a comfortable, well-maintained, and secure environment, but it was not designed to host a major foreign policy negotiation with three heads of state. And no one thought the summit would last thirteen days. Among the challenges: providing meals for the large number of folks in the three delegations with two of the groups having strict dietary rules.

After many ups and downs and sessions that tried everyone's patience and endurance, the talks led to the Camp David Accords that brought peace between Israel and Egypt.

On Sunday evening, September 18, the three principals boarded Marine One for a helicopter ride to the White House for the announcement of the Accords. I was onboard also. We left Camp David in twilight, and as we traveled across the Catoctin Mountains, the state of Maryland, and the bright glow of Washington, DC, at night, I reflected on the many adventures with President and Mrs. Carter that led to this important accomplishment in their lives and mine.

From a float trip to a historic peace agreement, this point in time was truly a blessing.

JOANNE DRAKE,
traveling with President Reagan:

I am often asked if, in my almost forty years of service to Ronald Reagan, I have one or two favorite days. One that always stands out is June 10, 1987, while President Reagan was in Venice, Italy, for the annual G-7 summit.

It was my birthday, and my advance office colleague (and dear friend) had asked me what I wanted to do to celebrate. Without much hesitation, I told her I'd like to sit out on the patio of the Hotel Cipriani and have a cappuccino and some fresh air before we had to go start compiling all the information for the President's trip to Berlin, for his now famous "Tear Down This Wall" speech. We agreed that we would wait until the President's boatcade (similar to a motorcade but in a boat driven by US Navy personnel) had departed for his morning meetings with the other heads of state.

And so around 8:30 a.m. the next day we found ourselves sitting at a round table, overlooking the Grand Canal of Venice, sipping our Italian-born coffee and enjoying some sort of decadent chocolate pastry. All of a sudden, I heard over my shoulder the familiar tune, "Happy Birthday," sung by a rather familiar voice.

Here was the President of the United States, singing to me, and I was seated in a chair. The photos that were taken that day show an increasingly reddened face. When the President finished, and I was able to wriggle out from my chair to stand, I said something brilliant like, "What are you doing here, Mr. President?"

I knew his schedule, and I knew he wasn't supposed to be here!

His answer, as humble and gracious as ever, but with a twinkle in his eye: "Well, I was told it was your birthday, and I wanted to come wish you a happy one. And besides, we are waiting for that man."

The truth is, he was caught in an international protocol debacle and "that man" was none other than François Mitterrand. As the senior member of the G7 leaders, President Reagan was entitled to arrive last at a meeting and depart first.

In a sign of disrespect, as the week had gone on, the French delegation had boorishly been arriving to events last and leaving them first. By June 10, the American security and advance teams were weary of the bad behavior and held back the boats carrying President Reagan that morning until they knew the French had arrived at the meetings. I guess I have the French to thank for my birthday present that year.

DAVE RYDER,
director of advance for Vice President Bush:

In February 1986 we were headed to Boise, Idaho, for an event with Senators Steve Symms and Jim McClure. As Boise was my hometown, I asked Craig Fuller, the Vice President's chief of staff, if I could invite my father to fly with us to the next stop, which was San Diego. I mentioned to Craig that my father was a former naval aviator who later made flying a career, logging more than 24,400 hours of flight time in thirty years.

The Vice President said that he would enjoy having Dad fly on the plane and gave the go-ahead. I made sure that I paid the airfare, which at the time was the cost of a first-class flight plus $1 between Boise and San Diego.

As we were about to depart Boise, I took Dad to the cockpit and introduced him to the crew. I had briefed the chief pilot ahead of time, who invited Dad to sit in the jump seat behind him and handed him headphones to listen to the crew as they prepared for departure. Dad was finally in a place he was most comfortable in, the cockpit. As Air Force Two prepared to depart Boise, the pilot informed the Boise control tower that Bill Ryder was on board to fly with them to San Diego. All the staff in the tower knew Dad well, as he flew out of Boise his entire career.

About thirty minutes into the flight, the Vice President's voice came over the plane's PA system, telling everyone that he heard there was another World War II Navy pilot on board. He asked Dad to join him in his personal cabin. I went up to the cockpit, tapped him on the shoulder, and said, "The Vice President would like you to join him."

They spent the entire time talking about the war and their own flying careers. The Vice President talked about being shot down in the Pacific and how much he enjoyed flying the Avenger aircraft. My father, normally a very quiet person who never talked much about his military days, told him about his time in the Navy and the planes he flew, the Grumman Hellcat and the Grumman F7F Tigercat. They talked as if they were old friends who had not seen each other for a long time.

My father, being extremely nervous at first, ended up having an incredible day, telling me it was the trip of his life.

Mine, too.

JAY ALLISON,
traveling with President Bush 41:

In December 1989, after much prayer and deliberation, President Bush committed US troops to overthrow Manuel Noriega of Panama. After the brief conflict had concluded, he traveled to San Antonio to meet with wounded soldiers and their families. After leaving the room of a nineteen-year-old army ranger who had lost an arm and a leg in the conflict, the President was peppered with questions by a small group of reporters known as the travel pool. They were asking about the significance of the American flag in the pocket of his blazer. After dodging the question multiple times, he finally answered. He relayed the fact that the young army ranger told him that he knew the Panama invasion was unpopular, but that he supported the President and even had he known he would lose two limbs, he still would have answered the call. His request was for President Bush to always remember that and to keep the flag he gave him close by.

That flag was placed in the President's pencil cup in the Oval Office and remained there throughout his administration. It now sits on a replica of his desk in the George Bush Library and Museum.

STEPHANIE STREETT,
White House staff, President Clinton:

On August 12, 1993, President and Mrs. Clinton, their daughter, Chelsea, and every Catholic in the Clinton Cabinet and on the White House staff that could squeeze onto Air Force One headed to Denver, Colorado, to welcome His Holiness Pope John Paul II to the United States. The Pope was coming to celebrate World Youth Day with young people from across the globe.

President Clinton graciously included as many of his Catholic staff as he could fit on the plane to accompany him for this important occasion.

The days leading up to this trip were intense for the staff on my team in the White House scheduling office and in the office of advance. Along with our colleagues from the protocol office, we had been through tough negotiations with the Vatican on every possible detail for the visit. The Vatican advance and protocol staff were legendary for their formidable negotiating skills and in adhering to the precise itinerary that had been painstakingly agreed on.

In short, they weren't going to be very flexible on game day.

The chatter on the plane that morning was if anyone besides the First Family and a few high-ranking officials would get to meet the Pope. I had been lowering everyone's expectations all week since the Vatican team representatives were quite explicit on the very small number of senior officials who would have this once in a lifetime opportunity.

As we were about to deplane, I told President Clinton how grateful I was to be accompanying him, as were two of my siblings who were on the advance team. And I shared that my very devout Catholic mother was ecstatic and would be glued to the TV for the entire day. He responded with a big smile and said something like, "That's great. Now you make sure all the Catholics with me today get to have their picture made with the Pope, OK?"

I was stunned.

The timing and logistics for the meeting were scripted down to the minute. The first few moments were designated for the US and Vatican press pools to "spray" the meeting. Once they were ushered out, the private meeting with President Clinton and the Pope took place followed by an expanded meeting including US Ambassador Ray Flynn, NSC Deputy Director Sandy Berger, Vatican Secretary of State Cardinal Sodano, and the Apostolic Pro-Nuncio to US Archbishop Agostino Cacciavillan.

Then the First Lady and Chelsea joined the group for tea and coffee and the exchange of gifts.

During the meetings, a few of us—including the unflappable Alexis Herman, one of the key White House advisors involved in the months of planning for this trip—huddled outside the meeting rooms trying to figure out how on earth we were going to follow through on President Clinton's directive. We discussed going to the Vatican team and relaying the President's request for staff photos, but if they said no, which they most likely would have, then we would really be out of luck.

We had hoped to enlist Ambassador Flynn, the former mayor of Boston who was beloved by everyone and was an experienced negotiator and seasoned political leader. We figured if anyone had the juice to make this happen, it was him. Unfortunately, he was behind closed doors in the meetings with President Clinton and precious time was slipping away for our plan to be hatched.

The next thing we knew, the doors flew open and out came President Clinton and the Pope. The plan was for the two leaders to proceed across the courtyard directly to their lecterns for brief departure statements. But President Clinton immediately assumed the role of lead advance and instructed everyone to form a line for photos. The Pope seemed quite happy—jovial actually—to go along with this radical change in plan.

The word got around immediately and every Catholic in our delegation, including the Secret Service, military, Air Force One personnel, and advance staff got their picture made with President Clinton and Pope John Paul II. And our friends from the Vatican advance and protocol teams along with their delegation also got to participate in this extraordinary experience.

When it came my turn to approach the Pope, I was in complete awe and lost my words. President Clinton thoughtfully came to my rescue, introduced me to the Pope, and told him about my very large and devout Catholic family in Arkansas.

That iconic image of me, standing between President Clinton and Pope John Paul II, still hangs today as the focal point of my mother's "wall of fame."

RALPH BASHAM,
former director of the United States Secret Service:

When Pope John Paul II came to the United States for World Youth Day, I was in charge of his security.

Having been with the Secret Service for more than twenty years and having worked many, many presidential trips, I found it rather interesting to sit across the table from the White House advance team.

As they typically did, the team walked into the room, taking charge immediately—or at least that's what they thought—and began to lay out what the President's schedule was going to be for the meeting and his events with the Pope.

Pope John Paul II's team was led by the Reverend Roberto Tucci, who at that point in his career was in charge of organizing the Pope's foreign trips. (He would become a cardinal in 2001.) A close friend of the Pope, he was known for being a tough negotiator. He listened patiently as the White House advance team laid out the President's agenda and movements for that day.

When they finished, Father Tucci thanked them for their input and then told them Pope John Paul II's schedule. "If the President wishes to join him that will be fine, and if not, that will be fine too," he said.

The look on their faces was one of astonishment. That anyone would dare to challenge the White House in such a direct and dismissive way was unheard of. After all, they were talking about "The President." But fortunately, and perhaps wisely, they decided not to challenge Father Tucci's position.

After it was made clear in everyone's mind who would be running the show, we all settled into the extensive planning and details that are required to manage a meeting between two of the most powerful leaders in the world.

And as usual, to the credit of all involved, the events came off without a hitch.

I guess the moral of the story is: The White House team realized that there is a higher authority that exists than the President of the United States!

Well, sometimes. Only the President himself could "roll" the Vatican staff to get the photos he wanted for his team.

By the way, during the entire visit Pope John Paul II referred to me as his "guardian angel," a reference I am sure I could never live up to!

RICK JASCULCA,
advancing the opening of the Clinton Presidential Library:

Sometimes it's the little things you see and the moments you witness that make you realize advance people have the best job in the world.

In 2004, at the opening of the William J. Clinton Presidential Library and Museum in Little Rock, Arkansas, all the presidents and First Ladies—the Carters, the Bush 41s, the Clintons, of course, and the President of the United States, George W. Bush, and Laura Bush—attended a VIP/donor's breakfast immediately before the ceremony.

At the conclusion of the breakfast, the guests were escorted from the second floor of the library to their outdoor seats, leaving only the four presidents and First Ladies, plus the White House advance lead, Joe Ellis, and me.

Barbara Bush had brought along her small, 35mm camera, and Joe told me that she loved taking photos on special occasions such as these. She wanted Joe to take a photo of all four presidential couples together. But the President was busy looking around, possibly getting ideas for his own library. Barbara at first waited patiently for her son to return to the group. But as the clock ticked closer to the moment when they would need to head down to the stage, she stared in his direction as he blissfully kept exploring. Then she both stared and started tapping her foot. Joe and I looked nervously at each other. Should we say something?

Finally, like moms everywhere, Barbara had enough and sternly said, "George, you get over here right now. Can't you see I want to take this photo?"

And the forty-third president of the United States pivoted like a roadrunner, and as he started walking back over, turned to Joe and me with a big grin and said, "Boys, I always listen to my mama."

Priceless moment!

BRIAN JONES,
advancing President Bush 43:

There's a great moment in the 1993 film *Philadelphia* when Tom Hanks's character is asked why he loves the law. He responds, "It's that every now and again—not often, but occasionally—you get to be a part of justice being done. That really is quite a thrill when that happens."

"Every now and then" occurred for me on June 8, 2006, at the J. W. Marriott hotel in Washington, DC.

The event was the National Hispanic Prayer Breakfast, an early-morning engagement on President George W. Bush's schedule. The run-of-show was routine—arrival, photos, remarks, rope-line greetings, and departure.

Ahead of the President's arrival, I positioned about twenty members of the military, injured in the line of duty, on the front row of the rope line so he could acknowledge them during his speech.

After his remarks, I led the President down the stage steps and into a partitioned-off pen mobbed by guests hoping to shake his hand. He graciously greeted every supporter, took every photo, and signed every autograph.

President Bush finished the rope line by spending extended amounts of time with the assembled service members. As he did so, I noticed that the large entourage that usually shadows the President when he moves was reduced to his Secret Service protection lead and me. All other staff members had already departed the room en route to the motorcade.

As I did the same, I noticed the President talking at length with one young man in particular. His name was Noe "Lito" Santos Dilone—a soldier inspired to serve in the military after 9/11. On his first deployment in Iraq, and only nine months before the prayer breakfast, an attack on Santos Dilone's vehicle took his left leg and the lives of two members of his team. His injuries required over two years of recovery at Walter Reed.

Watching their interaction, it was clear that Santos Dilone was asking the President for something more than a photo and the President was listening. Because as he did, and because I was the only nonsecurity person around, he motioned for me to come to him.

"Where's [Deputy Chief of Staff] Joe Hagin?" he asked.

"He headed to the motorcade, Mr. President," I responded.

"Go get him!" he instructed.

With that, I sprinted through the hotel hoping, more praying, that Joe Hagin would appear before me. After turning a few corners, I caught his silhouette off in the distance and yelled, "Joe! The President needs you!"

Hagin started toward me, and together we ran back to the ballroom. By the time we made it there, though, the President had already begun exiting. I also noticed that he had a business card in his hand, and he was not pleased. Once we met up, I listened to the cause of the President's frustration.

Santos Dilone had just chronicled his difficulty achieving US citizenship despite an executive order President Bush had issued in 2002 that expedited the process for "noncitizens who have been serving in the US military since the September 11 terror attacks." As one senior administration official described at the time, it was "a reward for their service at a time of war." Santos Dilone had not benefited from this expedited process. He had not received his reward or the justice it represented, and he wanted the President to know.

He said, "Joe, I want this fixed. Today. And don't think I'm going to forget."

Just six weeks later, the President attended Santos Dilone's naturalization ceremony at Walter Reed.

President Bush made sure justice was done, and just as Tom Hanks had suggested, it was quite a thrill to witness.

ANITA MCBRIDE,
chief of staff to First Lady Laura Bush:

In 2008 we were nearing the end of the Bush 43 administration when we planned a trip that would fulfill a promise Laura Bush had made to herself:

To visit all fifty states.

Last but not least: North Dakota.

She wanted to go to Medora, located in the Badlands, the rugged landscape that shaped Teddy Roosevelt and the course of his life. But there already was too much snow, making the trip nearly impossible.

So we ultimately planned a trip focused on a civic education project she helped lead with the National Endowment for the Humanities called "Picturing America," which showcased iconic works of art for students to study and learn about American history.

We touched down in Bismarck, North Dakota, on a really cold day. But that didn't stop the most adorable group of first and second graders from Riverside Elementary School from standing without coats at the foot of the plane dressed in the cutest handmade red, white, and blue costumes and caps to greet the First Lady. I think they recited the Pledge of Allegiance or sang a patriotic song to welcome her.

It was a sweet start to a memorable day of visiting the heartland and seeing the best of America. Always the teacher, she went to the school to participate in a Picturing America lesson with students studying the painting *Washington Crossing the Delaware*.

But maybe the best moment of the day was a potluck supper in a nearby town, held in a simple church hall with folding tables and plastic tablecloths and attended by people from the congregation and the community.

Toward the end of the meal, an elderly gentleman stood up and spontaneously began singing "God Bless America." Soon everyone joined in. The good people of small-town America were so proud to be her host. I saw the emotion in Mrs. Bush's eyes, and in our staff's. It was a moment in which we knew we were blessed and privileged to work for the President and First Lady.

We couldn't have planned a more fitting trip to her fiftieth state.

PETER NEWELL,
advancing President Obama:

There's no such thing as a true "presidential vacation," a lesson I learned quickly as director of the White House Travel Office in President Obama's first term.

My job was to wrangle hotel rooms and logistics for the immense traveling party, from Secret Service to the press corps. For a president who often described himself as an "island boy," these vacations naturally gravitated toward places like Martha's Vineyard and Oahu. What that meant for me was an endless scramble for rooms in already-booked high seasons and improvising press briefing centers in school cafeterias.

When the Obamas headed to Hawai'i for their first Christmas, as a single thirty-year-old who didn't need to stay home for the holidays, I took on my first White House advance lead, envisioning calm weeks of OTRs and golf. I should have known better, especially when his arrival was delayed until Christmas Eve because of health-care negotiations in DC.

Christmas morning, at 3:30 a.m., I was awake, my body still on DC time, adrenaline pumping for my first full day. Arriving at the President's rental house at 5:00 a.m., thinking we needed to get the cars organized for his early workout (yes, even on Christmas), I found National Security staff already in motion. Word spread quickly: A terrorist had attempted to bomb a flight landing in Detroit.

President Obama, clearly unhappy, spent his first Christmas Day on secure conference calls, his vacation shattered.

My mind raced to the logistical nightmare. We hadn't planned for a formal press conference on the North Shore of Oahu. Bringing the President to Waikiki for an emergency briefing was infeasible. We scrambled, packing what we could, racing to the nearby marine base to find a room we could convert into an emergency press conference space.

Despite the chaos, one "pinch me" moment stands out above all. President Obama had planned to go snorkeling at Hanauma Bay, a beloved spot from his youth, hoping to share it with his daughters. But the day of snorkeling was also the day he needed to deliver a televised statement to the American public about the attempted bombing. His family went ahead, while he went to the marine base.

By the time he arrived at the bay, his family had finished snorkeling, and he was clearly annoyed, both by the missed family time and the national security crisis weighing on him.

"Screw it," he seemed to say, "I'm still going snorkeling if anyone else wants to." I didn't need to be asked twice. Flipper-footed, I followed him over the rocks and into the ocean, joining a small group of staff and Secret Service.

Under the water, the world fell silent. The reality of being with the forty-fourth President vanished; we were just a bunch of guys pointing at turtles and fish. Out of the corner of my eye, two figures in scuba gear patrolled below us—Secret Service agents, one a former Navy SEAL, presumably with their own contingency plans for sharks or emergencies. For forty-five minutes, submerged in that breathtaking silence, I was in total shock at the surreal situation. While future basketball games and golf outings with him would bring their own memories, that moment in the ocean was truly something almost no one would ever experience. I was so blessed to be there.

We will end this chapter with a list from David Anderson of all that he learned from watching the men and women he was privileged to get to meet during his many White House advances. Our guess is that it could have been written by everyone in this book about their respective boss.

DAVID ANDERSON,
advancing President Bushes 41 and 43:

As you will have read many times in this book, there is no shortage of stories in the advance world! They are countless and, in some cases, may have grown a bit over the years. (Think of the size-of-the-fish-caught story.)

Instead of telling yet another story, I would like to focus more on the "things learned" during my years as an advance person.

Unfortunately, when I started on this advance journey, I was not smart enough to fully understand the unbelievable, unique, and life-changing opportunities that had been presented to me. As my career has taken me on an entrepreneurial adventure as a founder, CEO, and board member, the leadership skills I learned have remained with me to this day. I observed these leadership and people skills not only by the President but also by the amazing leaders that these presidents surrounded themselves with.

My top ten life lessons learned while doing advance:

1. **Surround yourself with the best people.**
   Not only smart people but ones who will challenge you. You don't need a bunch of "yes people" around you.

2. **Don't worry about what history will say; do what is right.**
   Obviously, presidents will be analyzed and examined for decades. While the view of our world and work is much smaller, the premise is the same—do what you believe is right regardless of what others will say and think.

3. **Stand for something. Have a vision.**
   In this day of wishy-washy politics, we need leaders who will have values and a vision to guide them—not which way the wind is blowing or what the latest polls are saying. This is a foundation for being a successful leader in any profession.

4. **Never let them see you sweat.**
   There is no greater example than how 43 handled being told, "Mr. President, America is under attack," by Secretary Andy Card on 9/11. Leaders must maintain calm even if others lose it during difficult situations.

5. **Make difficult decisions.**
   Decisions that get all the way to a president's desk usually mean there is no easy answer. Same for many in leadership positions, the task and timeliness of decision-making is difficult but must be done.

6. **Faith matters.**
   For some reason, many people frown on discussing their

faith openly. Both 41 and 43 were shining examples of people who wore their faith on their sleeves and openly discussed how it led them in their daily lives. I am personally still growing in this area.

7. **Give back, show compassion, and make a difference.**
   Points of Light, Compassionate Conservatism, and PEPFAR.[2] No need to say anymore.

8. **Personal relationships matter.**
   Bush 41 was a master at this. His personal relationships allowed for the greatest coalition against an aggressive dictator that history has ever seen. He also was from the days when politicians worked together for the good of the UNITED States of America, based on relationships built over the years. In our new era of digital communications, building personal relationships, at all levels of our lives, is still important.

9. **Communication matters.**
   The Bush presidents maybe communicated differently than Presidents Bill Clinton and Barack Obama, but they all knew the importance of what and how you communicated made a difference. Their communications focused on strong reasoning and a vision.

10. **Gotta get away.**
    I learned from both of the Bushes the importance of getting away—to 43's ranch in Crawford, Texas; to 41's beloved Kennebunkport, Maine; and of course on most weekends, a short helicopter ride to Camp David. You need time to recharge, think, and bring clarity to the many things thrown at you.

---

2 Points of Light was founded by President George H. W. Bush, to encourage volunteerism among all Americans. Compassionate Conservatism was an oft-used term by President George W. Bush. PEPFAR (President's Emergency Plan for AIDS Relief) was his AIDS program in Africa.

Finally, and probably most importantly:

Respect the position and the people who came before and after you.

It is easy to blame others or put down their efforts. A focus on "divisional leadership" is not leadership at all. While we may disagree, we must find ways to forge a path forward together. Both 41 and 43 did this. We, as leaders in our professional and personal lives, have to do the same thing all the time.

Having the best job in America has helped me throughout my lifetime to help others find "their best job."

EPILOGUE

A president cannot be successful without a talented and professional advance team. It's that simple. Throughout my career I have seen firsthand how advance people play an indispensable role in providing the president the opportunity to convey his message to important audiences at home and abroad.

All too frequently advance people work insanely long hours, under often trying conditions, with no expectation of receiving any recognition for their accomplishments. It's always been this way, and so I am glad this book sheds some light on what goes on behind the scenes when the president travels to your hometown or represents the United States around the world.

There's an unwritten code among advance veterans that "what happens on the road stays on the road." This code comes from the correct idea that advance is all about doing everything possible to make the principal (parlance for the boss—the president, vice president, or candidate) look good and to keep the light shining on them, not the staff. Sorry to disappoint, but the code wasn't broken with this book, yet I'm hopeful it has enlightened the reader while bringing some well-deserved credit to those hard-working folks behind the scenes.

I firmly believe advance people are unsung heroes. As you've read here, they work under enormous pressure, have to be flexible and react to last-minute changes and instructions, and serve as part diplomat and negotiator while navigating the various personalities and agendas of their local hosts. They can't afford to be risk averse, and they often tackle the tough tasks others avoid. Their work can make a president happy or angry. Yes, it's not a job for the faint of heart.

They must balance pressure from countless sources, including the Secret Service, military, speechwriters, press staff and members of the press, members of Congress and local VIPs, foreign dignitaries, hotel managers—the list goes on and on. And rarely do these groups of people want the same thing.

And yes, they do sometimes make mistakes. A shout out to Jon Meacham for pointing out one of mine!

Apparently, juggling all these demands while delivering on the mission is great training for life. You've heard from some who did advance and went on to jobs later in their careers where they had advance people taking care of them. Secretary Bob Gates and Senator Rob Portman are just two examples.

I'd like to share a story of my own. In the 1988 election I worked for George H. W. Bush in New Hampshire. We had an idea for an event on New Year's Eve that we thought was perfect for connecting then Vice President Bush with key voters in the capital city of Concord. We talked a local furniture store owner into letting us rent his place and turn it into George and Barbara Bush's living room, where folks would be invited for New Year's Eve for apple cider and doughnuts.

Well, the Vice President was reluctant, Mrs. Bush was reluctant, and the campaign and White House staffs were dubious. Truth is, the Bushes would have preferred to spend a quiet evening at home rather than fly north on a cold night and return home in the wee hours of the morning. And that was true for the traveling staff and the advance team, too, who would have preferred to be anywhere else.

But the decision was made to move forward, and the advance team, along with our local volunteers, worked their tails off.

They hit a home run.

It wasn't easy to turn out a big crowd on New Year's Eve when most people already had plans, but the advance team put their crowd-raising skills to work, and the line that night to get in to meet the Vice President and Mrs. Bush was around the block. The Bushes heard about that event everywhere they went in New Hampshire until Election Day a couple of months later. I believe to this day the hard work of the advance team that night was a determining factor in the Vice President's victory in the primary.

Fast-forward thirteen years when, as White House chief of staff for President George W. Bush, I relied on the advance team to represent the president with dignity and class since they were often the external face of the White House. Our approach was to give the team enough rope to get the job done and hope they didn't hang themselves. (Occasionally they did . . .)

By now you can tell that I am a great admirer of the men and women who choose to do advance work, and I am proud to call many of them my friends. I hope you've enjoyed this peek behind the curtain.

Secretary Andrew H. Card Jr.
White House Chief of Staff, 2001–2006
Secretary of Transportation, 1992–1993

ACKNOWLEDGMENTS

We begin by thanking our editor, Sean Desmond. This is Jean's third book working with Sean, and Tom's first book—ever. It's hard to imagine a better partner. He's been nothing but supportive and encouraging all along the journey, even when he's had to politely and sometimes firmly remind us about deadlines and decreasing the word count.

Others on the HarperCollins team we want to thank: Jackie Quaranto, who was patient answering our many, many questions; publicist Kate D'Esmond; marketing director Sam Lubash; production editor Crissie Molina; and production supervisor Michael Siebert.

Both Jon Meacham, who wrote the foreword, and Andy Card, who wrote the epilogue, encouraged us to do this book. Jon's historical perspective and Andy's experience in the campaign and White House trenches led them both to believe more needed to be told about the importance of advance men and women and the work they do. We're grateful to them for their insight and support.

Nearly one hundred contributors took time from their hectic lives to share their stories. Most are experienced advance professionals, but many others were senior staffers or folks who played a critical role in the complex work that goes into supporting a traveling president, vice president, national candidate, or First Lady. We are forever grateful to them all, and we will be picking up bar tabs at the Old Ebbitt Grill in Washington, DC, or equivalent establishments around the country for the rest of our days in an attempt to thank them all.

One of our primary goals with this book was to give a voice to the unsung heroes of advance work. They are trained to stay in the shadows and do hard work that often results in public praise for others. Our sense is our contributors enjoyed writing their stories, and we hope they are pleased with the final result as we worked to weave them into a narrative that was both fun and informative for the reader.

Almost every author ended their stories talking about the love, respect, and admiration they had for their president or First Lady. To keep this from being a five-hundred-page book, we had to remove their passionate words. We hope you felt the love as you read their stories.

You likely noticed that the two of us have no shortage of friends and contacts who worked for both Presidents Bush. (Oddly, there are forty-one stories about President Bush 41 in this book. It wasn't planned, we swear.) But we were committed to telling these stories in a bipartisan fashion, and to do so we reached out to friends and veterans of every presidency from LBJ to Obama. We are grateful to Mark Updegrove and Hannah Green at the Johnson Library Foundation; Phil Wise with President Carter; Joanne Drake and Jim Hooley, who connected us to the Reagan network; Alyssa Mastromonaco, who hosted a Zoom call with team Obama; and Stephanie Streett, with the help of Rebecca Tennille, who made sure we heard from key folks from the Clinton years.

The book is better, and far more accurate, because of the efforts of our volunteer proofreaders: Governor Jeb Bush; Jean's sisters, Millie Aulbur and JoAnn Heppermann; former White House staffers Ambassador Chase Untermeyer, Tim McBride, Brian Jones, and Jim Hooley; and Nancy Lisenby, who worked in President Bush 41's postpresidency office in Houston. And to Jean's brother, the Reverend

Ed Becker, who volunteered to proofread the galley, sparing our other proofreaders from reading the book yet again.

A big thank-you to Doug Campbell, supervisory archivist at the George H. W. Bush Presidential Library, who was a tireless fact-checker for us. And to Mckenzie Morse, head A/V archivist at the Bush Library, who not only tracked down 41 photos but who helped us find her counterparts at other presidential libraries.

Speaking of which—a big thanks to everyone who helped us with photos: Chris Banks and Jay Goodwin at the LBJ Library, Jason Schwartz at the Nixon Library, Amy Williams and Lauren Gay at the Carter Library, Steve Branch at the Reagan Library, John Keller at the Clinton Library, and Sarah Barca at Bush 43 Library. Others who came to our rescue: David Kennerly, who donated one of his photos from the day Sara Jane Moore tried to kill President Ford; Dennis Brack, who donated his wonderful photo of Senator Dole with his Hollywood "friends"; and Pete Souza, who helped us navigate finding photos of President Obama.

Ours is not the first book written on this topic, and we certainly hope it won't be the last. We were educated and inspired by Jerry Bruno and Jeff Greenfield's 1971 classic, *The Advance Man*; Anne Collins Walker's *China Calls*; Ken Khachigian's *Behind Closed Doors*; Josh King's *Off Script*; Terry Baxter's *November's Gladiators*; and Judd Swift's *My Presidential Life*.

We hope this book will play a small role in inspiring young people to jump in and volunteer to advance on a campaign. Our political system and our country need a new generation of committed and tireless folks to get in the game with passion and make a contribution to perpetuating our democracy.

GLOSSARY OF CONTRIBUTORS

Below are brief biographies of the people who contributed a story for the book. We're so grateful to each and every one of them. They represent the very best of their profession, and each was completely dedicated to the office seeker or officeholder they worked for.

Abell, Tyler: Served as United States Chief of Protocol under President Lyndon B. Johnson. Before that, he was President Johnson's first presidential appointment as Assistant Postmaster General for Facilities. After retiring from the practice of law in Washington, DC, he focused on developing and preserving Merry-Go-Round Farm in Potomac, MD. Additionally, he has edited several books. Tyler was married to the late Bess Clements Abell, and they have two sons, four grandchildren, and four great-grandchildren.

Aiken, Robbie: Vice President of Federal Affairs for Phoenix-based Pinnacle West Capital Corp since 1986. Robbie did advance for the 1980 Reagan campaign and held senior congressional affairs positions at the Departments of Energy and the Interior, and at the Small Business Administration in the Reagan administration. He's been a senior advance representative for five US presidents (40, 41, 43, 45, and 47) and three vice presidents (Bush, Quayle, and Cheney) as well as three presidential nominees (Romney, McCain, and Dole). Robbie is the proud father of two children, Gillian and William.

Allison, Jay: A public affairs executive specializing in the oil and gas and automotive industries. Jay started his career as a lead advance representative with Vice President George H. W. Bush and transitioned to assistant press secretary and part-time travel aide for President Bush 41 in the White House. Midway through the administration he moved to the State Department as director of the Office of White House Liaison. He and his wife, Missy, a fellow Bush alum, live in Bastrop, Texas, and have two grown daughters.

Almblad, Andy: Andy served twenty-four years as an agent with the US Secret Service. He spent eleven years on former President George H. W. Bush's protective detail. He retired in 2007 as special agent in charge.

Anderson, David: Served as a lead advance representative during both 41's and 43's terms and their reelection campaigns. He also served as a senior staff member for the President's Commission on Base Closure and the President's Commission on the Assignment of Women in the Armed Forces. David is an entrepreneur who has started and grown several companies. Today, he spends his time as a business coach, speaking, sitting on boards, and traveling. David and his wife, Debbie, live in Arizona and have two grown sons.

Austin, Ben: White House Office of Political Affairs staff member who coordinated politics for the President and Mrs. Clinton in western states, and part of the Office of Presidential Advance where he traveled internationally to coordinate events from 1993 to 1999. He is currently the founding director of Education Civil Rights Now, a national nonprofit with the mission of establishing a constitutional right to a high-quality public education for children in multiple states across the nation.

Barnum, Laura Melillo: A seasoned communications strategist and brand builder with a career spanning corporate, nonprofit, and public service sectors. She spent over two decades at Yum! Brands in senior leadership roles and began her career in broadcast television. Laura served in the Bush 41 White House press office as special assistant to the president and deputy press secretary, after serving as an assistant press secretary in the Reagan White House.

Basham, Ralph: A law enforcement official who served as director of the United States Secret Service, commissioner of US Customs and Border Protection, director of the Federal Law Enforcement Training Centers, and the first chief of staff of the Transportation Security Administration.

Bates, David: President George H. W. Bush's personal aide from 1978 to 1981, David served Vice President Bush as deputy to the chief of staff, and during the presidency as assistant to the president and secretary to the cabinet. From 1994 to 2009, he was managing director and then senior advisor for Public Strategies Inc. He now is CEO of his own consulting company. He and his wife, Anne, live in San Antonio.

Blakeman, Brad: Deputy assistant to the president for appointments and scheduling for George W. Bush from 2001 to 2004. Advance staff for Presidents Ronald Reagan and George H. W. Bush. Regular contributor on various television networks and news outlets. Current president and CEO of Kent Strategies LLC. Award-winning professor of public policy, politics, and international affairs at Georgetown University and a senior faculty member at Georgetown University's Global Education Institute.

Brady, Phil: During President Bush 41's administration, Phil served as general counsel in the Department of Transportation and then as assistant to the president and staff secretary in the White House. Later positions included president of the National Automobile Dealers Association and senior vice president of government affairs for Phillips 66. He and his wife, Katie, live in Alexandria, Virginia, and have three sons and five grandchildren.

Brook, Doug: Doug did volunteer advance for Bush 41 from 1980 to 1989. In the Bush 41 administration he served as an assistant secretary of the Army and acting director of the Office of Personnel Management. In the Bush 43 administration he was an assistant secretary of the Navy and acting undersecretary of defense (comptroller). He is a visiting professor of public policy at Duke University. He and his wife, Mariana, live in Elon, North Carolina.

Bull, Stephen: An advance man for Richard Nixon's 1968 campaign, Steve was a staff assistant to the president from 1969 to 1973. He became special assistant to the president and appointments secretary in 1973 and continued to work with Nixon after he left the presidency.

Bumgardner, Randy: Served in the Office of the Chief of Protocol at the Department of State from 1984 until 2017. In 1993 he was appointed assistant manager of Blair House, the president's guesthouse, and in 2001 was appointed general manager of Blair House and assistant chief of protocol. He retired in 2017 and lives in East Tennessee.

Burch, Thèrése: Has spent her career in politics, government, and the private sector. She worked as director of special events for the City of New York and has worked for the last four Republican presidents in leadership positions at the White House. She and her husband, Jim, are both retired and live in Leesburg, Virginia.

Cancilla, Russ: An army combat veteran whose military career culminated at the White House as the military aide to President Bush 41. After retiring from the military, he was principal deputy assistant secretary of the US and Foreign Commercial Service at the Commerce Department. After government, Russ had a twenty-one-year corporate career at two different firms. He managed a large real estate and general services portfolio, followed by executive responsibility for Enterprise Security, Business Resiliency, Cyber Security, Health, Safety, Environmental Affairs, and Corporate Social Responsibility programs. He retired as a vice president at Baker Hughes. He is currently the chairman and president of Wounded Veterans Relief Fund, a nonprofit that provides emergency dental care and financial support to Florida's wounded veterans. Russ and his wife, Loretta, have two sons and six grandchildren.

Card, Andrew H.: Andy was deputy White House chief of staff under President Bush 41 before being named secretary of transportation in 1992. He was White House chief of staff under President George W.

Bush from 2001 to 2006. He got his start in politics serving in the Massachusetts House of Representatives from 1975 to 1983. His post–White House career has included serving as acting dean of the Bush School of Government and Public Service, president of Franklin Pierce University in Rindge, New Hampshire, and CEO of the George and Barbara Bush Foundation. He and his wife, Kathleene, live in Bryan, Texas, and have three children and six grandchildren.

Cicconi, Jim: Policy assistant to James Baker when he was chief of staff to President Reagan, Jim was deputy to the chief of staff for President Bush 41 and served as a senior issues advisor to his presidential campaigns. Jim was a partner at Akin Gump Strauss Hauer & Feld, and then general counsel and senior executive vice president for AT&T for eighteen years. Now retired, he and his wife, Trisha, have three daughters and nine grandchildren, all close to them in northern Virginia.

Costello, Paul: Served as a press spokesman for First Lady Rosalynn Carter, Ohio Governor Dick Celeste, and Kitty Dukakis during the 1988 general election. Paul is adjunct faculty at the Stanford School of Medicine and a Faculty Fellow at the Stanford Center for Innovation in Global Health. He served as chief communications officer for eighteen years at the Stanford School of Medicine. In the private sector, he has held senior communications positions at Ogilvy Mather, Home Box Office, Weber Shandwick, and Marshall Field. Prior to joining Stanford, Costello was a vice president at the University of Hawai'i System in Honolulu. He is married to journalist Rita Beamish.

Crawford, Quincy Hicks: Starting as a receptionist in the office of George Bush, Quincy served as Barbara Bush's personal aide from 1994 to 1998. She was director of scheduling and advance to First Lady Laura Bush from 2001 to 2002. She is currently an executive recruiter for Tangent West. She and her husband, J.T., live in New Orleans with their two sons.

Cutler, Kim Brady: Starting as a volunteer for George Bush for President in 1979, Kim worked for Vice President Bush in his scheduling and advance offices before serving as personal aide to Barbara Bush from 1981 to 1985. She served in a variety of roles for the Bushes over the years, including as director of advance for the First Lady from

1989 to 1991. Now a full-time volunteer, Kim and her husband, Nick, live in Wenham, Massachusetts, and have two children.

Dahlem, Jim: Jim worked in the advance office for President Ronald Reagan. He then worked in the presidential transition office of President George H. W. Bush before taking a position with Senator Mitch McConnell. Jim currently works in the field of commercial real estate. He resides in Louisville, Kentucky, with his wife, Cathy, and has two adult children.

Davidson, Jon: Chief of staff to President Bill Clinton since 2019, Jon has served on Clinton's staff since 2008. He works closely with President Clinton to advance the mission of the Clinton Foundation with focus on areas of global health, climate change, and economic development.

Demarest, David: Currently a lecturer at Stanford University School of Business, David served as communications director of President Bush 41's 1988 presidential campaign, then was White House communications director during his presidency. He is married to the former Dianne Burch, enduring the joy of six daughters in their blended family, and living in Sausalito, California.

Dooley, Peggy: A researcher in the speechwriting office of George H. W. Bush, Peggy went on to various writing and editing positions in politics, media, and business. She was associate producer of the 2014 documentary *41 on 41* featuring forty-one storytellers on our forty-first president. She lives in Whitefish Bay, Wisconsin.

Drake, Joanne: Served in the presidential advance office at the White House from 1985 to 1989. In 1989, she returned to California with President and Mrs. Reagan and eventually served as their chief of staff and spokesperson for the last ten years of their lives. She is currently the chief administrative officer of the Ronald Reagan Presidential Foundation and Institute. She lives with her husband, Bill, in Thousand Oaks, California, and they are the proud parents of Caitlin and Danielle.

Fendler, Gary E.: Currently executive director of a family mental health nonprofit focused on student athletes (Morgan's Message Inc.) and a consultant for a communications and relationship firm in Washington, DC. He served in the Reagan-Bush and Bush-Quayle administrations as deputy director of presidential advance for press, director of communications for the US Securities and Exchange Commission, and associate commissioner for public affairs at the Food and Drug Administration. Gary lives with his wife, Michele, in Pawleys Island, South Carolina, and raised a son, Patrick Cashman Renstrom, who now lives in New York City with his fiancé, Chase Willman.

Fink, Wendy Weber: Served as deputy press secretary to First Lady Nancy Reagan from 1983 to 1989. She also served briefly as communications director for the speaker of the California state assembly. After state and federal politics, she became a public relations and marketing consultant in her native Southern California for many local business and government organizations. She also served as communications director for Western Growers Association. She is retired and lives in Costa Mesa, California.

Friendly, Andrew: President Clinton's personal aide at the start of his first term and then his trip director through his reelection. He is now an executive with a California-based software company. He and his wife, Kelly, met on the 1992 campaign and both worked in the Oval Office. They live outside of Boston with their two daughters.

Fuller, Craig: Craig arrived in Washington at the start of the Reagan administration serving as assistant to the president for cabinet affairs, a post he held throughout the first term. Named chief of staff to Vice President Bush in early 1985, he traveled to more than sixty countries and every state in the nation with the Vice President. Following the successful 1988 election, he served as co-chairman of the president-elect Bush transition team. He remained in the Washington, DC, area leading business and associations as president and CEO. He and his wife, Diane, now reside with their three dogs on the Eastern Shore of Maryland.

Fuller, Kim: Began her advance career in 1986 working for Vice President Bush and later served as a lead advance representative for President Bush 41. Kim was tour director for the 1996 Dole campaign.

In 2020 she did advance for the Biden-Harris campaign, and in 2024 worked for vice presidential nominee Tim Walz.

Gannon, Kelley L.: A seasoned communications executive, Kelley served in both President Bush White Houses—the only female full-time press lead (41) and as director of press advance (43). She also worked in the Reagan and Trump administrations. In the private sector Kelley worked as the chief communicator at US Steel, M&M Mars, and Academi, among others. She lives in Alexandria, Virginia, with her husband, Mike, and their black Lab, Bella.

Gates, Robert M.: Served Presidents Bush 43 and Obama as the nation's twenty-second secretary of defense from 2006 to 2011. He is the only secretary of defense in US history to be asked to remain in that office by a newly elected president. Gates previously served as interim dean of the Bush School of Government and Public Service and later as president of Texas A&M University. He served President Bush 41 as deputy national security advisor and as director of Central Intelligence. The author of numerous books, he and his wife, Becky, live in Washington state and have two children.

Gibbons, Gene: Former chief White House correspondent for Reuters news agency, Gene covered Presidents Carter through Clinton and was a panelist in one of the presidential debates during the 1992 campaign. Now retired and an avid photographer, Gene and his wife, Becky, have seven children and fourteen grandchildren between them and live in Alexandria, Virginia.

Goodin, Stephen: Executive director, strategic engagement at NextEra Energy Resources. Stephen was President Clinton's personal aide, managing the president's daily schedule on visits to more than 150 American cities and over thirty foreign countries. He worked on Capitol Hill and held leadership positions with the 1992 Clinton-Gore presidential campaign and at the Democratic National Committee.

Goodwin, Bob: In 1974 Bob joined President Ford's advance office, having done volunteer advance the last year of the Nixon presidency for Nixon and Vice President Ford. He met George Bush in China in 1975 when he was the lead advance for Ford's visit. He helped the

1979–80 Bush campaign and later did advance for Vice President Bush. In 1988 he was the Bush campaign's debate manager. Bob served as a commissioner on the International Joint Commission and was also US ambassador to New Zealand. In 2001 he was deputy director of the Bush 43 Inauguration, and he was the director of official proceedings for the 2005 Inaugural. He was executive director of the 2004 G-8 summit hosted in Sea Island, Georgia. Bob and his wife, Sydney, live in Bethesda, Maryland, and they have three grown children.

Hagin, Joe: Joe served as White House deputy chief of staff from January 2001 to July 2008 for President George W. Bush and held the same position from January 2017 to August 2018 for President Trump. For President George H. W. Bush his jobs included deputy assistant to the president from 1989 to 1991; assistant to the vice president for legislative affairs from 1983 to 1985; and personal aide from 1981 to 1983. Joe lives in Cincinnati, Ohio.

Hand, Lloyd: Staff assistant to US Senate Majority Leader Lyndon B. Johnson. Later named chief of protocol of the United States by President Johnson, who called him a "trusted and respected friend and associate." Joined the presidential campaign of former Vice President Hubert Humphrey in 1972 as senior traveling advisor; then returned to the practice of law, providing counsel to Fortune 500 companies, foreign governments, and institutional clients.

Harris, David: David served on President Reagan's advance team going back to the snows of New Hampshire in 1976. A career public servant in Illinois, he served eighteen years in the state legislature while also maintaining his military service. He was selected as the adjutant general of Illinois, and he retired as a major general. He was later appointed the director of the Illinois Department of Revenue. He and his wife, Michelle, have two sons.

Hooley, James: In a public service career spanning more than fifty years, Jim served two presidents, a vice president, and a Republican presidential nominee. He was Ronald Reagan's chief advance man, serving as director of presidential advance and assistant to the president. He was director of foreign liaison for the 1990 Economic Summit in Houston, Texas, and designed and ran President Bush 41's three multistate train trips in 1992. In 1995 he became director of national campaign operations for Senator Bob Dole's presidential race. From 1997 until 2018, Jim served as a private sector executive for Bank of America Securities and later Siebel Systems, and ran the Washington operation of T. Boone Pickens and Clean Energy Fuels corporation. He retired in 2019 and lives on the North Fork of the Shenandoah Valley in Virginia.

Jablonka, Curtis: Served on the George W. Bush 2000 campaign plane, worked as a director in the White House Travel Office, and was director of travel on the 2004 Bush-Cheney reelection campaign. He has started multiple private jet companies and currently runs a small private equity/investment company. Curtis lives with his daughter Evelyn in Philadelphia.

James, Gordon: Gordon joined President George H. W. Bush's staff at the White House in 1989, serving as lead advance representative for the President and as director of invitations and ticketing for the 51st Presidential Inaugural Committee. In 2004, Gordon spent more than five months in Baghdad serving as the advance director for the Coalition Provisional Authority and director of the Presidential Palace Studio. He was inducted into the Arizona Veterans Hall of Fame in 2015. Gordon and his wife, Lisa, live in Scottsdale, Arizona, and have eight children.

Jasculca, Rick: Cofounder of a Chicago-based public affairs firm, Rick was an advance lead for President Jimmy Carter, First Lady Rosalynn Carter, President Bill Clinton, First Lady Hillary Clinton, and Vice Presidents Walter Mondale, Al Gore, and Joe Biden. His advance career extended over forty-five years and included two US visits by Pope John Paul II, as well as international summits and peace talks.

Jenkins, Greg: Served George W. Bush as deputy assistant to the president and director of presidential advance. After 9/11, he was dispatched to Afghanistan to organize the coalition's communications effort there. He later served as executive director of the President's second inauguration. A former Washington-based journalist, he has worked in the private sector since 2005.

Jones, Brian: Speechwriter and later senior advance lead for President George W. Bush. Prior to the White House, Brian worked on Capitol Hill in a variety of capacities including policy aide, speechwriter, and committee counsel, in both the House and the Senate. He began his career in politics working in the Majority Leader's Office of Senator Robert J. Dole. An Emmy-nominated filmmaker and currently a government relations attorney and University of Virginia Center for Politics Scholar, he lives in McLean, Virginia.

Kennerly, David Hume: Kennerly won the Pulitzer Prize in Journalism for Feature Photography for his photos of the Vietnam War. He was President Gerald R. Ford's chief White House photographer. The author of six books, he has been photographing history for more than sixty years.

Kilberg, Bobbie: Served as deputy assistant to the president for public liaison and as deputy assistant to the president and director of the Office of Intergovernmental Affairs in the George H. W. Bush White House. After twenty-two years, Bobbie retired as president and CEO of the Northern Virginia Technology Council. She and her husband, Bill—both former White House fellows—have five children and seventeen grandchildren, and live in McLean, Virginia.

King, Josh: Served in the White House from 1993 to 1997 as director of production for presidential events, accompanying President Bill Clinton to key moments of his administration both domestically and overseas. King's 2015 book, *Off Script: An Advance Man's Guide to White House Stagecraft, Campaign Spectacle, and Political Suicide,* documents the major mishaps in presidential campaigns from 1998 to 2012. Currently the head of corporate affairs for Citadel, King lives in New York City with his wife, Amy Theobald. They have two children.

Lake, Mike: Mike began his political career as a member of the travel staff on President Reagan's 1980 campaign. Mike worked on Capitol Hill as assistant press secretary to California Senator Pete Wilson before joining the 1984 Reagan-Bush campaign as a full-time advance man. Following the election, he joined the Reagan White House advance office. Mike worked on three additional presidential campaigns for Bush and Dole. In the private sector, Mike led the public affairs practice at global public relations firm Burson-Marsteller and has been an executive practitioner in public affairs and communications at BSMG (now Weber Shandwick), Purple Strategies, Teneo, People Results, and his own firm, HudsonLake.

Lamb, Lucy: Shortly after graduation from the University of Richmond, Lucy joined President Bush 41's administration in the White House advance office, serving first as a trip coordinator and then as executive assistant to the director of press advance. She finished the term as executive secretary to the US ambassador to Iceland. She currently works for Fairfax County Public Schools. She and her husband, Faron, live in Alexandria, Virginia, and have five daughters and three grandchildren.

Littlefair, Andrew: Worked in the Reagan White House from 1983 to 1987 in the presidential advance office, traveling the country and the world on behalf of President Reagan. After his time in Washington, Andrew worked in the alternative fuels business including as president and CEO of Clean Energy Fuels Corp., a company he cofounded with T. Boone Pickens in 1997. He has served on the board of directors of the Ronald Reagan Presidential Library since 2012. He and his wife, Karen, have two sons.

Maner, Andy: Andy is the executive chairman of NewSpring Federal. He was chief financial officer of the Department of Homeland Security and chief of staff of US Customs and Border Protection in the Bush 43 administration. He served in President Bush 41's White House press office and accompanied the President as his aide into private life following the 1992 election. Andy was the special assistant to the 1993 United Nations Envoy to Somalia in Mogadishu. Since 2009, Andy has served on the Board of No Greater Sacrifice, a veterans charity focused on education for children of the fallen and severely wounded.

Marshall, Capricia: A partner at FGS Global, where she advises clients on geopolitics, foreign affairs and diplomacy, national security, and strategy. From 2009 to 2013, Capricia was chief of protocol of the United States. From 1997 to 2001, she was deputy assistant to the president and White House social secretary. From 1993 to 1997, she was special assistant to First Lady Hillary Rodham Clinton.

Mattingly, Alixe Glen: Alixe was a longtime spokesperson for the Bush family. She began in the 1980 Bush for President campaign as a traveling press aide, was assistant press secretary to Vice President Bush from 1981 to 1986, a press secretary for the 1988 campaign, and special assistant to the president and White House deputy press secretary for President Bush 41, from 1989 to 1992.

McBride, Anita: Executive in residence at American University's School of Public Affairs, Center for Congressional and Presidential Studies. She served in three presidential administrations, including as chief of staff to First Lady Laura Bush from 2005 to 2009. Anita is the coauthor of three books on First Ladies: *U.S. First Ladies: Making History and Leaving Legacies*; *Remember the First Ladies: The Legacies of America's History-Making Women*; and a children's book, *First Ladies Make History*. She and her husband, Tim McBride, former personal aide to Vice President and President George H. W. Bush, reside in Washington, DC, and have two children, Andrew and Giovanna.

McGrath, Jim: George H. W. Bush's post–White House spokesman and speechwriter. Jim lives in Houston with his wife, Paulina, and their three mostly wonderful children.

McLean, Kiki: A strategic communications and public affairs expert who began her career as a campaign scheduler and advance person. Kiki is a veteran of six presidential campaigns, including the 1992 Clinton-Gore campaign. She served two tours of duty on the vice-presidential nominee travel staff. Kiki is a native Texan who lives with her family in Washington, DC.

Meacham, Jon: A presidential historian and professor at Vanderbilt University, Jon is the author of *Destiny and Power: The American Odyssey of George Herbert Walker Bush*. In 2009, he won the Pulitzer Prize for *American Lion: Andrew Jackson in the White House*. He and his wife, Keith, live in Nashville, Tennessee, with their three children.

Miller, Jim: Served in several federal posts, leading to President Reagan's cabinet as director of the Office of Management and Budget. Jim was a director of several corporations and financial institutions. Holder of a PhD, he taught economics at the University of Georgia, University of Virginia, Georgia State, Texas A&M, George Washington University, and George Mason University. Author of nine books and more than one hundred articles in professional journals. He and his wife, Demaris, reside in Rappahannock County, Virginia.

Miyagishima, Ed: Advance professional for three presidents and five vice presidents. Ed has traveled the globe, representing the United States and promoting its policies through a myriad of assignments, most recently for the second Trump administration. Ed hails from his adopted home state of Florida.

Mohr, Lawrence: Dr. Mohr was a White House physician to Presidents Reagan and Bush. After his White House service, he joined the faculty of the Medical University of South Carolina where he is a distinguished university professor. He and his wife, Linda, live in Charleston, South Carolina, and have one daughter.

Montgomery, Brian: Served in the George W. Bush White House as deputy assistant to the president, first as director of presidential advance from 2001 to 2003, then as secretary to the cabinet from 2003 to 2005. Brian also served in the White House under George H. W. Bush from 1990 to 1993. Brian was commissioner of the Federal Housing Administration twice and in three separate administrations: George W. Bush, Barack Obama, and Donald Trump. He was deputy secretary of HUD from 2019 to 2021. He is a partner at mortgage advisory firm Gate House Strategies and resides in Alexandria, Virginia, with his two children.

Murdock, Bunny: Served in the Reagan administration and for Mrs. Barbara Bush at the 1990 Economic Summit before working for the state of Kuwait. Earlier, she was Tiffany's diamond buyer and in investment banking. She serves on the board of the Blair House Foundation.

Newell, Peter: A former Illinois state government staffer and Obama advance operative, Peter served as President Obama's first White

House Travel Office director and served in leadership roles on the 2012 Obama-Biden campaign. In 2015 he launched Advanced Aviation Team, a private jet service with his counterpart from the Bush administration, Gregg Brunson-Pitts. He lives in the Chicago suburbs with his wife, Katelyn, and their three children.

Palmese, Kimberley: Worked for President George W. Bush from 1999 to 2009 at the US Departments of State, Homeland Security, and Education, and the White House. Previously Kim worked on the Global Events team at BlackBerry and prior to that she used her international skills at Fairfax 2015 World Police and Fire Games.

Parmer, Jay: Served George H. W. Bush as special assistant to the president and director of presidential advance from 1991 to 1992, deputy director of presidential advance 1989–90, and in Bush's vice presidential advance office. Jay joined the Reagan administration in 1985 as program director at the US Agency for International Development. He is a veteran of numerous presidential campaigns and was campaign tour director for Vice President Richard Cheney.

Peressutti, Gian-Carlo: Aide to President Bush 41 from 1996 to 2000, he left in 2001 to join the White House staff of George W. Bush as associate director of the Office of Public Liaison. He currently is executive director of public affairs at IFM Investors and serves on the advisory board of the George Bush School of Government and Public Service. He lives in Ridgefield, Connecticut, with his wife, Amanda, and two daughters.

Portman, Rob: Rob served two terms as US Senator from Ohio, was a congressman for twelve years, and held two cabinet-level jobs in the Bush 43 administration. He got his start in public service working as a volunteer advance person and campaign coordinator in Ohio for Vice President Bush, then as associate counsel and deputy assistant and director of the Office of Legislative Affairs for President Bush 41. Now retired, he and his wife, Jane, live in Cincinnati, Ohio, and are the parents of three children.

Prosperi, David: Served as assistant White House press secretary from 1981 to 1982 after serving as a traveling press aide to Governor

Reagan from 1979 to 1980. David worked as the senior communications leader for Secretary Don Hodel at the Departments of Energy and Interior between 1985 and 1988 before becoming the spokesman for Senator Dan Quayle during the 1988 campaign. After working in senior roles in financial services in Chicago for more than thirty years, David "unretired" in 2022 to lead the KemperLesnik public relations agency before selling it in 2024. He and his wife, Nadine, live in Northbrook, Illinois, and are the proud parents of three children.

Ray, Topper: Founder of Muirfield Court Partners, a public affairs strategy firm operating at the intersection of media, messaging, and advocacy. He began his career as an advance man for President Bush 41, who encouraged Topper to keep his nickname, because he liked it. Topper and his wife, Carrie, have three daughters and split time between suburban Philadelphia and Wellington, Florida.

Riggs, Barbara: A thirty-one-year veteran with the United States Secret Service. At the time of her retirement on January 31, 2006, she held the position of deputy director. She served six US presidents— Gerald Ford, Jimmy Carter, Ronald Reagan, George H. W. Bush, Bill Clinton, and George W. Bush. She currently resides on a farm in Middleburg, Virginia, where she pursues her equestrian interests and volunteers for local charities.

Ruemmler, Michael: Michael joined the Obama campaign in March 2007 and then was an advance lead at the White House for nearly two years. He worked on Rahm Emanuel's first campaign for Chicago Mayor, then at city hall, and managed Emanuel's reelection campaign in 2015. He lives near Chicago with his wife, two kids, and their dog.

Ryder, Dave: Served as the thirty-fourth and thirty-ninth director of the United States Mint under President George H. W. Bush and President Donald J. Trump, respectively. Prior to returning to the Mint in 2018, Dave was global business development manager and managing director of currency for Honeywell's Authentication Technologies. Previously, he was CEO of Secure Products Corporation, which developed highly advanced anticounterfeiting technologies for the protection of global currencies. Other government service included being deputy treasurer of the United States, deputy chief of staff to Vice President Dan Quayle, and deputy assistant and director of advance to Vice President Bush.

Saikin, Greg: A former assistant United States attorney, Greg is a partner with BakerHostetler and maintains a national practice representing clients across industries in high-stakes white collar criminal defense and internal investigation matters. Greg and his wife, Lauren, live in Houston, Texas, with their two children.

Scully, Tom: General partner at Welsh Carson Anderson & Stowe (WCAS), a New York City private equity firm, since 2004. Tom was the administrator of the Centers for Medicare & Medicaid Services (CMS), from 2001 to 2004. He served as president and CEO of the Federation of American Hospitals from 1994 to 2001; deputy assistant to President George H. W. Bush from 1992 to 1993; and associate director of OMB from 1989 to 1992. Tom worked on the Bush for President campaign in 1988. He practiced law for twenty-plus years with Akin Gump, Patton Boggs, and Alston and Bird. He and his wife, Ann, live in Alexandria, Virginia, and Easton, Maryland. They have three daughters and three grandsons.

Short, Marc T.: American political advisor. Marc was chief of staff to Vice President Mike Pence.

Smerconish, Michael: SiriusXM and CNN host, attorney, author, and onetime advance man for Vice President George H. W. Bush. Smerconish served in the Bush 41 administration as a regional administrator in the Department of Housing and Urban Development. He resides in the Philadelphia suburbs where he and his wife have raised four children.

Streett, Stephanie S.: Executive director of the Clinton Foundation since 2001. She oversees the operations of the Clinton Presidential Center, which offers diverse cultural and educational programming focused on civic engagement and leadership development. Stephanie served President Clinton as assistant to the president and director of scheduling. Previously, she worked on Capitol Hill as a staff member for the Senate Committee on the Budget. Stephanie and her husband, Don Erbach, reside in Arkansas and are the proud parents of three daughters.

Studdert, Stephen M.: Served as assistant to President Bush 41, executive director of the Bush-Quayle Inaugural Committee, a member of the President's Export Council, and chaired a Federal Home Loan Bank board. Stephen has directed postconflict reconstruction efforts in Iraq and Kurdistan. He and his wife, Bonnie, have six children and reside in rural Utah.

Sullivan, Dan: A lifelong public servant and world traveler who visited all seven continents and 160 countries, many of them with Vice President Bush for whom he was assistant to the vice president for scheduling and advance. He served six presidents in different roles, retiring as director of International Enforcement at the Department of Homeland Security in 2009. Dan and his wife, Emma, lived in Alexandria, Virginia, and have a daughter, Emma. Dan died in October 2024.

Swift, Judd: Former deputy assistant secretary for international affairs, US Department of Energy; advance man for three presidents; founder and CEO of Swift Global Results, an international energy consulting group; and a proud veteran of the United States Army.

Temple, Larry: Served as special counsel to President Lyndon B. Johnson in the White House from 1967 to 1969. Before that he served as legal assistant and then chief of staff for Texas Governor John Connally and as a law clerk to United States Supreme Court Justice Tom Clark. He has practiced law in Austin, Texas, for more than fifty years and is chairman of the Lyndon B. Johnson Foundation. He and his wife, Louann, live in Austin, Texas, and have two children.

Untermeyer, Chase: Chase worked for the Bush for Congress campaign in Houston in 1966. Afterward he was a Texas state representative, executive assistant to Vice President Bush, and an assistant secretary of the Navy. During the first Bush administration, he was director of presidential personnel and director of the Voice of America. President Bush 43 appointed him US ambassador to Qatar. He and his wife, Diana, who met in the West Wing of the White House, have one daughter, Elly, and live in Houston.

Varghese, Maju: Served as deputy director of advance and director management and administration under President Obama. Maju was the COO and senior advisor for President Biden's 2020 campaign and later served Biden as the executive director of the Inaugural committee and director of the White House Military Office.

Walker, Anne Collins: She was not only one-half of a strong, dedicated political couple, she served in Ronald Reagan's White House and in his Commerce Department as deputy director of public affairs for Secretary Malcolm Baldrige. Anne authored *China Calls: Paving the Way for Nixon's Historic Journey to China*, which tells the story of the advance team sent to China to prepare for President Nixon's visit.

Wallace, Charity: Founder and president of Wallace Global Impact, advising clients on foreign policy, global development, impact investing, and women's economic empowerment. Charity is a speaker, author, board member, and media contributor. She served President George W. Bush and First Lady Laura Bush for more than sixteen years, notably at the White House as director of advance for First Lady Laura Bush, and as chief of staff and senior advisor to Mrs. Bush and founding vice president of the Global Women's Initiatives at the Bush Institute in Dallas, Texas.

White, Peggy Swift: Aide to Barbara Bush from 1989 to 1993, Peggy now dedicates her time as a civic volunteer after a career in public relations, corporate communications, and project management. She lives with her husband, Brian, and their Norfolk terrier, Shecky, in Chicago and Charleston, South Carolina.

Whyte, Roger: Served the Reagan administration as special assistant to the Secretary of Labor for International Affairs and Deputy Under Secretary of Commerce. Was involved in the "You Die—We Fly" advance team for Vice President Bush, advancing Bush's trips for many heads of state who passed away.

Willard, Greg: Greg and his wife, Annie, served on President Gerald Ford's White House staff. They have three sons and six grandchildren. He is an attorney and professor at St. Louis University, where he teaches a constitutional law course on presidential power. Greg was responsible for the overall planning and conduct of President Ford's state funeral.

Wise, Phil: A native Georgian, he was involved in every political campaign of President Carter and served as his appointments secretary in the White House. He also served as vice president of operations and development at the Carter Center until retiring two years ago. He resides in Atlanta with his wife, Allison, and daughter, Rainey.

Zanca, Bruce: Bruce was a longtime press aide to Vice President and President Bush 41. Later in life he had a very successful career as a C-suite corporate business executive. He and his wife, Michele, split their time between Bluffton, South Carolina, and Ludlow, Vermont.

INDEX

ABOUT THE AUTHORS

Jean Becker served as chief of staff for President George H. W. Bush for nearly twenty-five years. She is the editor of *Pearls of Wisdom* (with Barbara Bush) and the author of the *New York Times* bestseller *The Man I Knew: The Amazing Story of George H. W. Bush's Post-Presidency* and *Character Matters: And Other Life Lessons from George H. W. Bush*. She also served as deputy press secretary to First Lady Barbara Bush and was a newspaper reporter for ten years, including four years at *USA Today*.

Tom Collamore first met President George H. W. Bush in 1978 as his driver and became part of his inner circle of staffers. Tom served in various senior roles throughout the twelve years of President Ronald Reagan's and President George H. W. Bush's administrations and has been an advisor to the George and Barbara Bush Foundation for over thirty years. After government Tom enjoyed a long career as a senior corporate executive and trade association leader. He's the founder of Collamore Consulting Group, which provides strategic counsel to the CEOs of companies, associations, and nonprofits. He lives in Maryland with his wife, Jacqueline, and they are the proud parents of four grown children.